THE KEYS to the
DOORS OF PERCEPTION

A Portrait of the Artist IN THE MIND OF MAN

WILLIAM AUSTIN MOORE M.D.

BALBOA.
PRESS

A DIVISION OF HAY HOUSE

Balboa Press books may be ordered through booksellers or by contacting:

Balboa Press
A Division of Hay House
1663 Liberty Drive
Bloomington, IN 47403
www.balboapress.com
1 (877) 407-4847

Because of the dynamic nature of the Internet, any web addresses or
links contained in this book may have changed since publication and
may no longer be valid. The views expressed in this work are solely those
of the author and do not necessarily reflect the views of the publisher,
and the publisher hereby disclaims any responsibility for them.

The author of this book does not dispense medical advice or prescribe the use
of any technique as a form of treatment for physical, emotional, or medical
problems without the advice of a physician, either directly or indirectly. The
intent of the author is only to offer information of a general nature to help you
in your quest for emotional and spiritual well-being. In the event you use any
of the information in this book for yourself, which is your constitutional right,
the author and the publisher assume no responsibility for your actions.

Any people depicted in stock imagery provided by Thinkstock are
models, and such images are being used for illustrative purposes only.
Certain stock imagery © Thinkstock.

Print information available on the last page.

ISBN: 978-1-5043-4018-2 (sc)
ISBN: 978-1-5043-4020-5 (hc)
ISBN: 978-1-5043-4019-9 (e)

Library of Congress Control Number: 2015914525

Balboa Press rev. date: 10/20/2015

CONTENTS

AUTHOR PROFILE

Doctor W.A. Moore is a medical graduate of University College Dublin, Ireland. He interned at Saint Mary's Hospital, Rochester New York, USA. During his undergraduate training he spent a short period of time working at the Appalachian Regional Hospital in Harlan, Kentucky, and subsequently with the Dept. of Indian Affairs at a Cree Indian reservation in Northern Manitoba, Canada.

Doctor Moore completed his postgraduate training in Family Practice at the Methodist Medical Centre and the University of Illinois, in Peoria Ill. USA. Upon completion of his State Boards he entered partnership practice with Doctor F.Z. White, past President of the American Medical Association, while continuing in his post as Clinical Tutor at the University of Illinois in Peoria.

He currently resides in County Wicklow, Ireland.

In Loving Memory of Jacqueline Gagnon-Moore

DEDICATED TO MY CHILDREN

Jack, Jennifer, and Tara,
Aubrey- Epiphany, Taylor, and Dean.

PROLOGUE

Authors note and Acknowledgement.

Without a copy of these Keys,
You may find yourself locked out,
Forever deprived of a true vision
Of your purpose, and your destiny.

If you are seeking Peace of mind,
Open these ancient Doors,
And follow the Ancestral path
As now set out before you.

Just how well, and how accurately, do you perceive yourself as an individual within society? How valid is the intellectual discernment as it has been applied in relation to yourself, others, and towards the world in general? There are Four Keys that can open the door onto a vision of an authentic reality and a true paradigm of our lives upon this earth. Should you look, and listen, carefully with an open mind you may discover these hidden keys within the content of this book. Reflect and ponder prudently for that which the human eye may fail to see. Perform this task within the silence and the solitude of an impartial and receptive mind. Place it within the context of your own life, and those of your own attitudes, values, and beliefs. A whole New World may then unfold before you.

I feel obliged to forewarn you given the financial outlay that you have invested in this book. Should you confine your deliberations solely to pride in the power of your gifted intellect, you will probably fail in your attempts to locate the keys to which the title of this book refers. On the other hand, (moving more towards the right), should you girth yourself in the mantel of humility and trust in the wisdom of your human intuition; you may well find that which we all intuitively seek! So, choose wisely. "It's your call my friend-it's your dime". I must apologize for the steep rise in the rate of global inflation since that Americanism was first introduced some? fifty or sixty, years ago. This is a book of symbols and metaphors, as it is a writing, albeit one in celebration of the Word. The essence and the source of all that is conveyed within this book share a common origin. The prose, poetry, and graphic imagery are derived from a shared hierarchy of analogy and symbolism. Some are expressed more explicitly, while others are more of the implicit variety. Yet, one should not seek to separate, or categorize, them in this manner. Our efforts are directed towards striving to create a synergy of concept that is simply conveyed within two different linguistic styles. We are seeking to become adept within a bilingual mode, or at the very least to perform some essential bridging work so as to achieve cognitive fluidity within our conceptual dialogue. The task has necessitated an element of "architectural restructuring" to enable greater ease of transit, and to do so with greater clarity of vision. As you progress through the sequence of chapters you will understand the meaning of these statements far more clearly. Hopefully you will come to know honor, and respect, the metaphorical hierarchy within the conceptual structure of this holy order.

"Self-respect", "honor" and "dignity"; "honesty" and "integrity"; "loyalty" and "commitment"; "empathy", "charity", and "compassion"; "reconciliation" and "forgiveness". These are among the words that may ring loud in the ears of many. Hope, and trust, is all that remain to help nurture the multitudes who hunger for the truth. It is all that exists to help sustain those who yearn for peace, justice, and equality in society. Yet, for others these words may ring empty, and hollow. They may appear to be of little relevance to self-survival, and self-enhancement, within a materialistic and competitive society. Do these words, and what they represent, not count for anything within the hallowed domain of our human intellect? Have they lost their relevance and value as virtues worthy of our consideration and of our safekeeping? And what of love, you might well ask. Surely no one would ever contemplate it being sacrificed to the self-appointed master within the venerated temple of the intellect! What matter the substance of words as they apply to anything? What matter which terms we use, and in what context they are applied in reference to ourselves, others, and within the man-made paradigm of our Shared reality?

Within this book you will discover the sacred ancestry and heritage that is applicable to all words as they expressively symbolize the concepts which they represent. We will trace their origin within the historical unfolding of humanity, and within an ancient lineage of allegory, whose roots, and essence, extend to eternity. This missive will explain the reason why we should all be well informed in this regard. We should exercise great caution, and respect, in the manner in which we use and apply our words. Someone may be listening, someone may be watching, and someone may take heed.

Having read, and reflected, upon the content of this work you may have good cause to reappraise your previous concepts, and your understandings in regard to yourself as an individual. You may reconsider your insights and your judgments in respect of others, of creation, evolution, life, and the nature of our humanity. You may find abundant reason to re-evaluate the fundamentals in regard to your spiritual or religious beliefs, (if any had pre-existed), and particularly as they may be highly relevant to those of the Christian faith.

You may discover that what is essential is only clearly visible to one's human Intuition. In order to engage in any meaningful manner with our human intuition we must first learn how to listen carefully and appropriately. Then it may be possible to appreciate the nature, and the substance, of its core content.

This listening process requires that we focus our attention, surrender, and commit ourselves to the task of discerning what is enfolded within the essence of our intuition, and within the nature of its source. In many respects this is analogous to music appreciation. As the contemporary

American composer, Aaron Copeland once remarked "If you want to understand music better, you can do nothing more important than listen to it." To do so effectively we must choose an appropriate listening environment. We need to become aware of the basic elements of its language format. It is also necessary that we can ascertain the fundamental form that shapes, and gives direction to the logistics of its progress. Yet the most important factor of all, as it applies to our intuition, is that we have the ability to place it within the authentic primacy of its context. So, relax, and enjoy the music with an intuitive ear. Let your insight do the listening, and the all-important reflective work. Then, you may find every good reason to rejoice, and may your heart be truly glad.

So, I must leave this dense and splendid woodland,
These forests that I roam and thread,
Where ancestral voices whisper,
Through the darkness in my head.

I must step across the threshold
Out onto the open plain,
Search through all the meadows
For the sheaves of golden grain.
This food, it will sustain me
Through my nights and darkest days.

The answers that you seek
Are not so far away.
They enter through the hidden gate
That you open when you pray.
They float in on the wings of silence.
Where they alight, they will always stay.

From "On the Wings of
Silence" by the author.

ACKNOWLEDGEMENTS

I am deeply indebted to the authors listed in the bibliography whose published works have served as a major source of reference in regard to the content of this book. These are listed within a related order of priority within the bibliography.

I am eternally grateful to my brothers David (M.Sc.) and Maurice (Graphic Design), and my professional friends and associates James Mc Cabe (B. Eng. M.Sc.), Ann Geary (M. Psychol.), and my dedicated comrades, Kim Kamberos and Sandra Ramosevac (Computer imaging & I.T. consultants) without whose skill, and astute observations, I could not have completed my delegated task. Fr. Kevin Lyon, Archdeacon of Glendalough, continues in his constant role as my indispensable spiritual guide, and mentor.

Finally, I wish to acknowledge that the fundamental motivation that inspired my literary endeavors was instigated by my six wonderful children. For each of them, I share the deepest of love, and parental concern, in relation to their individual wellbeing within the mystery of life's purpose, and the realization of its ultimate objective.

I Remain, Always,
True to Word, and true to my Christian name. Well, you know what I mean!
But that's another story, within another chapter, of this epic tale. In due course you will hear this "sceal eile".(i.e. other story).

William Austin Moore.
County Wicklow. Ireland. 15/9/14.

Le Belle de Lumiere

FOREWORD

We are living in a Time capsule,
A Life capsule that's running out,
Running out and folding down,
Folding down, and falling out of space.

From "In Time-Out of
Time" by the author.

In the aftermath of the loss of perfection, and the dislocation of man from within the milieu of his original life form and spiritual context, man was to be granted a divine reprieve. All that had formerly existed within the context of the first creation was to undergo a process of "de-contextualization". It would be newly reconstituted within the construct of a material context, and a physical domain. Love, mercy, and compassion would prevail on our behalf, despite our Fall from Grace.

The potential content of the entire universe, of every created thing, be it animal, vegetable, or mineral, thus constrained within an infinitesimal singularity explosively burst through a portal from within the eternal domain. The substrate of all that was to materialize as matter within the universe was contained within this minuscule point. This enigmatic source of energy was encrypted with a meticulously conceived programme that would progressively unfold from the first instance of its existence.

An inexhaustible stream of consciousness would be poured out as the Wisdom of the Spirit throughout all ages. In time it would animate all living things in due measure, and in accordance with the Word.

Over the next 13.8 billion years the awesome majesty, beauty, and complexity concealed within the core of this singularity, would be progressively unveiled. Subsequently, the realization and disclosure of this conceptual mystery would continue onwards until its purpose was fulfilled at the very end of time. The power and the glory of its creative genius would be ultimately revealed. In the interim, the Spirit of Truth would be declared to all within the world on whose behalf and benefit this creative event was planned and instigated.

> The Word had spoken,
> The Spirit speaks:
> The Devine Will be done on earth,
> According to The Word

This is the essence of the story that I have to tell, the story of our humanity. It is told from the historical perspective of the creation of man, and the subsequent evolution, and emergence, of the phenomenon of our humankind In effect then, this could be described as a history book, albeit one that extends beyond the traditional boundaries of time and space.

We will revert to a more detailed consideration of the "Big Bang Theory" and the nature of the singularity in a subsequent chapter.(Chap.5 "Creation in the Second Genesis.") We are well aware that historians do not simply reconstruct the past. Rather, they produce, or contribute to, knowledge regarding the past. Nevertheless, we also acknowledge the British historian, E.H. Carr's observation that history is a continuous process of interaction between the historian and his facts within an unending dialogue between past and present.

The importance of history, as with both memory and concepts, is that what happens now, and in the past, and what will also happen in the future, is very much governed by what has already happened in the past. You will note that the past has been referred to as events that appear to reside within two distinct timeframes or historical domains. Firstly, they may be recalled as they had been initially experienced, witnessed, and observed within the historical hour of their unfolding. We may think of this as the immediate, or "original", past. Subsequently, these same events may be recollected from a more distant point in time, and with the added advantage of hindsight. This secondary form of observation is likely to be more objective than may have been possible in the former instance. This is because it can now be viewed undistorted by the interpretative intrusion of the existent and participating ego, and because the events can now be placed within a far broader context than was possible in that original past. Neither vantage point can claim exclusive rights to the reality, or the truth, as it pertains to past events.

Besides all that, you can also appreciate that at any future moment, the present instant will reside within the past. Now I will quit while I am ahead since these time frames shifts are likely to induce a state of mental vertigo in all of us. In terms of the overall relevance of any specific experience to the course of our lives, we can appreciate that there is a constant bilateral operative dynamic that exists between past, present, and future. While we cannot alter the events of the past, we can manipulate the extent to which the relevance of past events may impact upon our lives within any present moment in time. Likewise what we do today will have a related relevance, and impact, upon the shape and quality of our future life's experience. As a consequence, knowledge and awareness of the past, as it pertains to our ability to manage and control the course and progression of our life's experience, is of critical importance to all of us at any given moment. We will refer to these types of memories, and their relevance to the lived experience in a later chapter. We can now better appreciate, that without knowledge of the past, as it pertains to history, memory, and concept, we are lost on an endless sea of time. We are disoriented and forsaken, without self-identity, nor any source of reference, and meaningful context, within which it may be guided, directed, or expressed.

Our current paradigm, and the manner in which it will unfold, is dependent upon the validity, quality, and accuracy of the knowledge that we have gleaned from the past and the manner in which it is applied within the current content of our lives. One could not use a snapshot of a bird in flight as a means of concluding that the bird was capable of flying in the absence of any prior knowledge concerning a bird's ability to execute such a feat. Likewise, we cannot determine man's potential destiny without studying his past. Consequently, knowledge concerning our evolutionary history, and the manner in which we seek to apply such knowledge in the determination of our human destiny, is of great importance to all of us.

Having said all that, all types of knowledge, as intellectual concepts, are only as meaningful and valid as the accuracy, and authenticity, of the language that is applied to their expression. The reverse of this statement is also true. Language is only as meaningful and valid as are the primary concepts upon which its linguistic content, as knowledge, is conveyed. These fundamental facts have emerged as a major issue that is of central, and of critical, relevance to us within the entire context of this work. It has become clearly evident that it is the loss of this linguistic, (and hence of conceptual), specificity and authenticity, that has resulted in the conveyance of misinformation, spurious concepts and theories, and half- truths. The progressive transmutation of language, from the implicit to the explicit, and the severance of the word and its meaning from within the context of its primacy, have seriously distorted and corrupted the global configuration of our paradigm.

So it will come as no surprise to you that a great deal of this book deals with the issue of knowledge, (epistemology), its nature, source, and validity; its acquisition, context, and linguistic expression. We are especially concerned with knowledge, as known and applied, with respect to our nature, and the purpose of our existence. Also, of major concern to us is the precise means by which we may access an intuitive form of knowledge, and the manner in which we may acquire "factual" knowledge, through the application of our human intellect. However, in the final analysis we fully accept that it is the manner and the means by which this collective knowledge is expressed, and applied, within the world that is of universal relevance to all of us.

As with any reliable, and responsible, piece of investigative journalism the essential and most critical question that demands an answer is in respect of the "why", rather than the how, when, or where, of the issue. In our instance the "why" refers to the reason and the purpose of our existence. The answer, in a single word, is simply "quest". The entire human race is on a quest in search of knowledge with regard to the enduring truth. This is a fundamental knowledge concerning self, and self within the context of (an/all) other. This quest for knowledge is not simply for the sake of its acquisition. Our ultimate objective is to unpack its contents so that it may be applied to, and within, the context of our humanity and the world in which we live. We are motivated to realize the fruits of this knowledge so that we may experience a sense of happiness, self- fulfilment, and meaning, in its actualization.

For any quest, or voyage of discovery, there is always a need to plan and prepare in advance. There is a basic requirement to ensure that the necessary resources have been provided in order to address the task and fulfil the mission's primary objective. Evolution is the historical record, the log book and the diary that describes this preparatory phase of our human journey. This is a voyage into the unknown and the unchartered domain of the unfolding future. Mankind is the only candidate entrusted with the undertaking of this great quest.

We will first address the means and resources with which mankind was equipped so that he could embark upon this mission. These will be considered from a physical, mental, intellectual, and spiritual perspective. We will begin at a familiar juncture within which we can all relate and identify. This pertains to our current acquisitions, (inclusive of the biological, and metaphysical), the manner in which they accrued, and mode by which they function and interact as an integrated human individual. However, as a prelude to this modern era of humanity we will briefly revert to the ultimate beginning as referred to in the book of Genesis. This will accommodate those who relate to, and identify with, this creative, and spiritually grounded, beginning. It will also serve as a point of reference, or essential baseline, to which they may wish to refer in chronological sequence.

We will then address the evolutionary sequence of events as they unfurl within a historical timeframe. Most of us are already quite familiar with the basics of acknowledged scientific theory concerning our biological evolution. Far less people are able to envisage, or reconcile, our biological evolution with, and within, a concurrent and collaborative spiritual evolutionary process. The term "evolution" is derived from the Latin word "evolvere", meaning "to unfold". It is within this precise context that we will consider the progressive development of that original, and embryonic, life form which was eternally destined to emerge within the living world as the human species. The evolutionary history of the fundamental nature of the human being is no less than a temporal account of the unfolding of his spiritual principle within an earthly domain. This process is seen as one of an emerging spiritual enlightenment, or of progressive "ensoulment", as directed and as revealed through the power of the Holy Spirit since the first beginning. A biological life form was thus transformed, and spiritually transfigured, to become a unique, distinct, and sacred species upon this earthly planet.

The very idea of a process of "spiritual evolution",(or rather of a"spiritual process of becoming human"), in time and space upon this earth may have never occurred to most individuals. It may have never even crossed the minds of many who share a deep spiritual conviction, and sincerely express it within some form of religious practice and beliefs. Most informed individuals within our contemporary society only consider evolution within the biological context as originally proposed by Darwin, and promulgated within those terms of reference ever since that time. Evolution is generally seen as the preserve of the academic palaeontologist, anthropologist and geneticist. The very word conjures up images of bones, teeth, fossils, and laboratory technicians who sort through fragments of DNA in order to establish ancestral links to the distant past. The very idea that any kind of evolutionary study, or discipline, might be applicable to the realm of the spirit, or the soul, would appear to many as bazaar. Some might even consider it as representative of a perversion or a profanity. Yet, if we are to ever attempt to comprehend our human nature, our individuality and uniqueness as a species, it is imperative that we search and strive with all due diligence and perseverance in order that both of these evolutionary strands are clearly recognizable as facets of our human nature. Then it may become realistically possible to pursue a process towards their mutual accommodation and eventual reconciliation. Much of our effort will be focused upon this precise need, and desirability, so that we may look forward to a new era of human understanding and enlightenment that will be forever enshrined within the history of our species and of our world.

Finally, we will attempt to reorient ourselves with regard to our current location and position on this universal journey of discovery. We will review our progress and re-evaluate our strategy as we plan to move forward on our human quest. Since the biological process proceeded through a critical juncture, at and from which, a distinctly human form emerged from within the subset "primate", our attention will be keenly focused upon this facet of human evolution. Homo Sapiens will be seen to be more than the sum of his evolutionary inheritance and more than the biological expression of his DNA. The importance of language, its use and meaning, and the manner in which we assume to convey the truth regarding our beliefs, ideas, and perceptions of the world in which we live is paramount to the task at hand. Of necessity it will be essential to clarify or redefine certain core words that we commonly use (or misuse) in order that a logical and coherent account of the topic can be communicated to the reader.

This then is a book concerning the history of mankind's evolution taken from the perspective of both a biological and spiritual process. It is not specifically a scientific, anthropological, philosophical, psychological, or theological discourse. All of these disciplines are dependent upon the use of a language which is derived from the intellectual formulation of concepts.

A critical element of this rationalizing process occurs within our Left cerebral hemisphere (or Left brain), and is dependent upon the retrieval of metaphorical concepts from memory. Such metaphors are described within the text as being "Secondary metaphors". These secondary metaphors have, in turn, been initially dependent upon the provision of a metaphorical /allegorical substrate which had been presented to the Left brain from that of the Right cerebral hemisphere. That substrate is referred to within the text as "Primary metaphors". It will be proposed that these types of metaphors are derived from a transcendental source which is referred to as the "Wisdom of the Soul".

The content of this missive is not intended as a means of providing intellectual, or scientific, proof with regard to the existence of God, of God as the Divine creator, nor with respect to the spiritual nature of our humanity. Rather this is an invitation to engage within the context of those "Primary" metaphors that are derived from such a spiritually specific source of origin. These are, by their very nature, both pre-conceptual and intuitive. They provide us with the ability to acquire knowledge without inference or use of intellectual deduction. We will also propose that the Wisdom of the Soul is representative of all that is, or ever will become, authentic knowledge. This unique form of preexisting knowledge, or "anamnesis", has been eternally archived within the universal and collective "unlived memory" of all mankind. Language, and linguistics, are simply used as a means by which this knowledge may, or may not, be conveyed within the content, and the context of its intended, and authentic meaning. They serve us within the role of the Emissary of the Spirit which is the "Word" of god.

Language has been applied in such a manner within the written word of Scripture so as to communicate the Word, as the "Good News" of Revelation to humanity. The written word of Scriptures, and Revelation, are Secondary Metaphorical concepts that are faithful to the content of their Primary Metaphors. These Primary Metaphors are derived from the Holy Spirit as the Word of God. Everything else that is contained within this book is a confirmation of this fact, and of the truths in regard to the nature of our humanity. In fact, there are but two critical, and fundamental, statements contained within the entire content of this missive that are paramount to our conceptual requirements as they apply to our human nature. This is one of them. We will verbalize the second of these core statements at a later time. If the only pieces of information, and insight, that you derive from your reading of this text are in regard to the content of these two statements, then be assured that your time, and effort have not been wasted, or in vain.

However, rather than our relying upon the more traditional form of Secondary metaphor that may have been appropriate in times past, we have chosen to engage with those which are of a more intellectual and contemporary type. To a very large extent the specific type of Secondary, and intellectual, conceptual metaphors which we have applied within this text are what we most commonly refer to as "Science". Specific references, ideas and concepts will be drawn from within a wide range of these intellectual disciplines in an effort to contribute towards a means of seeking to convey a rational, credible and holistic account of a most amazing and complex phenomenon within the present age – the universal mystery of mankind, and the purpose of his existence. No doubt but that some individuals may propose some alternative scientific view- points that those that are presented here. Neither is there any doubt that all of these scientific propositions will become redundant, and outdated, with the passage of time.

However, the Wisdom of the Spirit will endure, and hence it is that within which we ultimately place our implicit hope and trust. The objective and the goal has been to try and identify a familiar and comprehensible language as a means towards narrowing the gap that exists between the implicit and the explicit, the instinctive and the intuitive, the biological and the spiritual. In this manner perhaps some may discover that it is not in fact a bridge too far to cross, a task, or skill beyond our basic means. I am acutely aware, and indeed cautiously apprehensive, of the inherent risks attached to the means, and methods, that have been applied towards the effort to bridge this conceptual "gap".

Faith and religion are neither a science, some form of transpersonal psychology, nor philosophy of life. I have purposely employed an explicit and contemporary form of language and conceptual imagery as an appropriate and familiar means of communicating some aspects of that which is fundamentally spiritual in its absolute essence and in its very nature. However, I have also sought to revert, or redefine, the substrate of the concepts within a more implicit terminology whenever it became evident that this was either necessary or desirable. This revival strategy has been largely affected through the prescription of archetypical metaphor, or intuitive precept, in addition to that of resorting to the etymological clarification of a variety of key words. The common objective in each such case was to strive to relocate our mental faculties within a much closer range of the primacy of context from which that issue had originally been conceived and derived. These tactics are not employed as an artistic license to evade clarity or dispose of logic. Rather, they are adopted so as to provide us with an alternative location from which we may observe our subject matter. Such a vantage point helps us to generate a more three dimensional, or holographic, image. In this manner we may better trust the interpretation that we apply to that which we observe. The proximity of our vantage point ensures greater detail, and greater clarity of vision. Our perceptions are more likely to be more accurate, and far closer to the hidden truth.

There is always the danger that such efforts might be construed as one of attempting to intellectualize, or "scientize", beliefs of faith and the doctrines of religious beliefs. However, while it may be impossible to intellectually explain and prove most deeply held religious beliefs, both science and reason can complement many spiritual beliefs and greatly assist in our ability to clarify, and provide greater understanding and insight, into such issues. One of the principal mechanisms by which this is achievable is through the generation of allegories within the realms of scientific discoveries that are applicable to faith. For example, the revelations of biomedical science and astrophysics in particular, provide us with lucid mirror images of what transpires within the metaphysical domain. Beliefs that are formulated through the application of reason and intellect, and those that are of the faith based variety share a common source from which their primary allegorical, and conceptual, basis was derived. I am of course referring to the collective unconscious as representative of the repository of our unlived memory. (as opposed to our individually accrued depository of the living memory)

In short, it may be said that science, art, or indeed any form of inspirational endeavor, is a reflection of our spiritual principle and its primary source of origin. Throughout the content of this book I have sought to align science and beliefs within a complementary framework. I do not necessarily perceive them as being mutually contradictory. However, there are many cited instances where the linguistics are seen to be distorted, or corrupted, to the extent that it generates unnecessary conflict and contradiction within the implicit meaning and context of the terminology that is applied to the scientific accounts regarding the nature of our humanity, and the purpose of our existence.

Unless we engage, and are determined to address, these complex and emotive issues we will remain unnecessarily grounded in ignorance of the truth regarding our own human nature and the validity of our perceptual reality. Paradoxically, and indeed in spite of, this historic conceptual and cultural inertia, it is my firm belief that science will contribute towards the realization of a new era of spiritual enlightenment. Since such a vision is not the intended objective within the scientific community, I would anticipate that such an outcome would emerge unpredictably, unwittingly, and perhaps even reluctantly. I say this because the validity of all concepts is derived from the primacy of our archetypical metaphors that enfold the wisdom of the soul. And the purpose of science is to ascertain the nature of these intuitive truths.

While the intellectual and the spiritual, the explicit and implicit, present as opposites within a bipolar disposition of objectivity, they are representative of both sides of the one coin. These are what constitute the conflictive, yet complementary, facets of the nature of the human mind. Within this mind resides one master. This is the universal and eternal image of the artist within the soul of our humanity. As a first priority it is essential that we engage within a genuine, authentic, and inclusive form of dialect that incorporates both the language of the rational intellect, and that of the inspirational imagery that is conveyed within the intuitive content of our universal archetypes.

It is absolutely critical that no one who is in receipt of the content of this book should expect to find rational or scientific answers to the mystery of the human spirit, the mystery of our creator, or the mysteries of our faith. Neither should one anticipate, or expect, that they might become the recipients of a strategy towards the realization of some illusive and material goal within the experience of their living. On the contrary, if one was to adopt and apply to life the true content of what it is that was intended to be conveyed to reason, it would likely add to the burden of their life's mission. In the bearing of that burden and its weight of responsibilities, one might only hope to find, and share, a sense of genuine happiness, joy, and self- fulfilment along the route of their arduous journey. I dearly hope that all of you good people will take due heed of these guidelines and precautionary comments.

There may be some provocative ideas, or perhaps some outline forms of conceptual imagery, contained within the contents of this work that could strike a familiar cord within your mind and your memory. They might instigate and evoke a small cluster of fresh and intuitive insights that had been dormant, like echoes, now finally reverberated from the silence of a long and distant past. What is conveyed to you by such means is far more important than any rational interpretation you may seek to apply to the words that I have written. Consequently, I would suggest that you temporarily refrain from the temptation to surrender each successive thought, or idea, into the hands of your intellect for its division and dismemberment. Rather, it may prove to be far more personally fruitful should you choose to defer such analysis and judgment until a later, more opportune, and reflective point in time. Throughout that interlude you might ponder on the manner in which certain familiar, and perhaps long forgotten, notions or embryonic beliefs might now reemerge in a fresh and renewed context. You may discover that some of these may relate and speak to you in a more personal and meaningful language. Do not be easily lured, and drawn by simple force of habit, into premature conflict with the full might of your preconfigured intellectual defenses. Be patient and considerate so as to let your spirit speak to you within these silent intermissions. Your own individual consciousness and your abiding Spirit may have much to say. It is to the Spirit that you are beckoned and are called. Hopefully, you and all of us, within the context of our daily lives, will listen and take heed. You might come to see yourself, and all human life, within a different light, and in a manner that you had not quite ever seen before.

APPRENTICE TO THE MASTER TAYLOR

This is but a patchwork quilt
Of works crafted by great minds.
I am neither saint, nor scholar fine,
Just a ragman with a needle and some thread,
Not the keeper of a miraculous creed,
Nor the source of a sacred wine and bread.

I have sewn these words together
With some imagery, and some thoughts.
Some are roughly stitched in rhyme
While others are in verse;
Many are woven to a pattern
That is far more tense and terse.

I tripped over these ragged remnants
As they lay there on the ground,
Sitting by the threshold
With the label "Lost and Found".

So, I took them to my little room,
And stitched them all quite tight,
Adorned with thread and coloured loom
In the darkness of my night.

I hoped that someday very soon
They might shed a little light.
Pull back the shutters in your room,
Dispel the dark, help me make it bright.

By the author.

CHAPTER ONE: THE KEYS TO THE DOORS OF PERCEPTION

INTRODUCTION: The Double Stranded Story.

> The misperception of our lives
> Shapes our realities.
> It sets the path and purpose
> To ambition and desire.
> Neither lens nor prism
> Can correct these insanities
> Since a fault within the optics
> Never will you find.
>
> From "Blind Vision", by the author.

Yes, there is a great story to be told. It is an incredible story because it transcends logic and human comprehension. It is a universal story concerning life, you and I, and all of us. It also concerns our world, the universe, and the meaning and the purpose of creation and of human existence. Many of us still yearn for some peace of mind, for understanding, and insight into these great quandaries. If that applies to you, then I invite you to follow this meticulously chartered ancestral route that I have now mapped out before you.

A large and varied number of different aspects of this complex and intriguing story have already been told in great detail. Within this more modern and scientific era the greatest emphasis has been placed upon the physical and material evolution of the universe, the planets, and the Darwinian theory of evolution by natural selection. Yet, this is no more than a record concerning an intellectual inquiry into a single strand of what is, in fact, a double stranded story. Such an inquiry would be tantamount to our unravelling a single strand of our DNA in our search to unveil the mysteries of our genome and the manner in which it is expressed within our biological makeup.

As with our DNA, there is a second strand to the nature of our humanity, and to its historical unfolding. Likewise, as with our DNA each of these strands mirrors, and complements, the other strand. It is only when both elements are interwoven, and placed together into a unitary structure, that we can begin to apprehend the extraordinary nature, interdependence, and complexity, of the subject of our inquiry. The history of creation, of life and humanity, is more than a physical, chemical, and biological event. These events must be placed within the context of what it is that defines humanity and of what it means to be truly human. The answers cannot be found purely within the scientific and biological terms of reference. The spiritual evolution of mankind is the second, and by far the more important, strand of this great and awesome story.

Having said that, I am not suggesting that human evolution constitutes a biological process within which there is a spiritual strand or elemental subset. On the contrary, I am explicitly, and uncompromisingly, stating that the evolution of humanity is, in its very essence, a unique, and fundamentally spiritual process. The biological element is but a mechanism, and a material means, by which this mystical process would unfold within the parameters that define the material, and the mortal nature of life, and our living universe. Consequently, the task demands the use of more than the left brained language of science, logic, and intellect. We must also resort to the primacy of the right cerebral hemisphere, to the use of metaphor, allegory, imagery and imagination. Most of all we must be able and willing to engage with our human intuition in order that we may recall and recollect that fundamental wisdom which we have long since surrendered to the archives of our subconscious and overwritten with cognitive arrogance. It would appear that we have inadvertently capitulated to the dictates of our intellects and our ego minds.

No doubt, but that some individuals will object to the very thought or idea that this story has a second strand that relates to the spiritual or metaphysical. Despite such objections, the full truth regarding this story must be told and will continue to unfold in word and deed, in truth and in reality, until the end of time. What precisely is this authentic reality? Do we actively seek to fully acknowledge and embrace it? Are we far more preoccupied in our efforts to create and live out some alternative version that is grounded only in the material, the intellectual, and the scientific?

At the core of our inquiry lies the fundamental question of what it is that defines our humanity and what precisely does it mean to be human. The scientists will insist that humanity is simply defined by a unique cluster of biological properties that have been encoded within our D.N.A. throughout the evolutionary history of this planet. Like all forms of life we date back to some specific, and as yet unidentified, primordial ancestor – *LUCA: the Last Universal Common Ancestor*, some 3.8 billion years ago. Life is no more than "self- replication with variation". Thus, Darwin's theory is restated in a contemporary scientific nutshell. Yet we must ask if these genetic expressions are the sole determinants of our humanity. Might our humanity have more to do with the non - molecular, the non- organic, with the nature of our mind and that illusive quality which we describe as human consciousness? Might the phenomena of mind and consciousness be something far greater and far more enigmatic than a neurological expression of the biological workings of our human brain? Might it be that these uniquely human properties are not simply generated by the complex neurochemical and electrical interactions located within our craniums?

Furthermore, we might ask the most vital and elementary question within this evolutionary process. At what juncture did the primate, from whom we have presumably evolved, become uniquely human? What precisely was it that became the all defining factor or event? Was it simply the consequence of some final and critical evolutionary alteration, variation, or mutation within a small portion of our D.N.A.?

Yes, we will be challenging some critical aspects regarding the interpretation which we have traditionally applied to Darwin's theory of evolution. We will also challenge a number of closely related scientific facts as they are presumed to apply within the historical unfolding of our ancestry and of our human nature. The term "presumption" serves as a useful reminder not to assume in advance that our mental (i.e. mind- full) faculties are exclusively confined to, or the necessary consequence of, our cognitive intellects.

We share nearly 99% of the same DNA sequence as chimpanzees, from whom we split 6 million years ago. If at some future date we were able to reconfigure the 1% difference that exists between these two species using genetic engineering techniques, would we confer the property of humankind upon this primate relative of ours? Would such a species be classified as human, or perhaps within the subcategory "Chimpanzee Humanoid?" Most importantly, beyond the visible, the microscopic, molecular, or behavioural, would such a "creation" be devoid of some illusive property that we recognize as uniquely human? Alternatively, if by some accident or incident a segment of the human population's DNA was to mutate in a retrograde manner that critical and approximate 1% so as to match that of the chimpanzee, would they lose their humanity and become no more than animal? Would we still refer to them as human or reclassify them as something less than that: such as "Human Chimpanzoid"?

While the likelihood of either, or both, scenarios may appear highly remote, they are not theoretically impossible. Most of us might find it impossible to arrive at some absolute and definitive answer. Despite this I will venture to say that in the former instance the humanoid creature would more likely resemble Neanderthal man in nature, behaviour, and form. I will be proposing that this primate, and many other "Homo" classified species, were devoid of the facility of human consciousness and were never destined to become a human being. But that is another issue which we will address in due course.

For the moment these questions have been posed so that we might seek to fathom the ultimate depths of the nature of human kind. Are we no more than intelligent monkeys with the facility of speech and language in addition to some fairly obvious anatomical and physiological variations? It is at this level of consideration that many, if not most of us, would intuitively feel that there is another strand to the story of humanity beyond the material and the purely biological. Regardless of the purity of one's scientific intellect, and any measure of aversion to the philosophical, psychological, and spiritual, I would hope that I can provide supportive evidence for the popular contention, and deeply held belief of many, that we are more than the expressive intellectual and emotive sum of our evolving molecular and biological parts. In due course we will revert to the beginning of this epic story. We will attempt, hopefully without undue prejudice or prejudgment, to reconstruct a more holistic framework that is inclusive of the second strand.

Un Faisceau de Lumiere

CHAP 1A. THE AIR OF CONTEXT

As in all things,

What one sees is there.

What one fails to see,

Is not,

For now,

Until our eyes are opened.

From "Our Paradigm ", by the author.

If there were three odd little words to describe the keys that could help to magically unlock the doors to an authentic vision and understanding, of ourselves and our universe, they would be "context", *"primacy", and "synergy"*.

These are the keys that can open the Doors of Perception to the reality of life within our world. These are the keys to the acquisition, and ultimately to the sharing, of genuine knowledge. In fact, these are three of the master keys that help us to define both the purpose, and the implicit meaning, of the term "human consciousness". Without these "Keys of Wisdom", we are reduced to gazing at life through the uncorrected, and imprecise, prism of our intellect. This is a ground glass prism that refracts, disperses, and dims, the source of our genuine human enlightenment. Such is the nature of the spiritual light that is essential to illuminate our perception, and provide us with a clear and authentic vision of life and our shared reality.

Yet, there is a fourth, and final, word that describes the unlocking mechanism to this reality. This is the word that finally releases the entrance bolt, and inscribes the circle of knowledge. This is knowledge that once shared, will revert to its source of origin. It is knowledge crafted, guided, and directed, upon the wings of the golden key-ring of Consciousness. It is concealed within the term "reciprocity", and is of such vital importance that it will be considered as a separate entity. Within its terms of reference resides the critical interchange, the crucial act of sharing, and the ultimate returning. It is within the act of sharing that synergy can be realized. Additionally, it is in the faithful return of its content to its primacy that reconciliation is acquired for, and on behalf of, every one of us.

Reciprocity is the fundamental unit of transactional exchange, and of spiritual and conceptual intercourse. In its absence, the acquisition of knowledge would be no more than a self-indulgent and futile mental exercise. In due course, you will come to appreciate the manner in which this specific form of interchange is reflected within the enigmatic relationship that exists within, and between, the content of our mental and cerebral capacities.

In addressing a wide range of issues that pertain to the nature of our humanity within the following chapters, the fundamental importance of all four of these defining characteristics, as they apply to the topics under our consideration, will become clearly evident in every instance. Regrettably even these irritating little brats of words are invoked so often in the text that I honestly do not wish to see, nor hear again, from either "primacy", "context", "synergy", or even "reciprocity", for a very long time. In the meantime, be assured, if not forewarned, that I will make every effort to follow my own directions, as herein expressed, with regard to the sharing of knowledge, and as it is seen to apply to the pursuit of our individual and collective human enlightenment.

In so far as it is conceptually possible to do so, each of the core issues that are addressed within the text are placed within the context of their spiritual and material (i.e. scientific), primacy. In other words, we will revert to address these issues in terms of what we will variably refer to as their "Scientific Laws", or "First Principles". We will also refer to them within an alternative allegorical form of language that is elaborated and expressed within a "Primary Thesis", (The primacy of the Word), or as expressed within the meaning of the term "Sitz im Leben" (The original life setting).These fundamental issues are also considered from a synergistic perspective that attempts to reconcile the invariable conceptual polarization as it is expressed within the language of science and that of the metaphysical.

This cognitive conflict is, to a large extent, an inherent feature of the discordant nature of the dominant metaphorical source from which these propositions, and beliefs, are derived. The misappropriations of terminology, and the conceptual extrapolation of scientific theory into the domain of the nature of life and the lived experience, are additional contributing factors.

Very little of anything that we attempt to communicate to each other has any value, use, or relevance, in the absence of context. As you will understand more clearly in subsequent chapters, what the word "context" is to syntax is what that activity is to the right brain. A major function of our right cerebral hemisphere is the provision of a primary allegorical (or metaphorical) substrate for intellectual analysis by the left brain, and to contextualize the cognitive material that is subsequently returned to it from that side of our analytical and logic brain. This synergy of effort provides us with a perceptual product that can be integrated, and applied in a meaningful way, to the external world in which we live.

The right hemisphere, as provider of the original substrate, underwrites the material that is presented to the left hemisphere. Only our right cerebral hemisphere can perform this synergistic feat of allocating concepts within a specified context. This is because the format of context has already been preconditioned by the implicit nature of the substrate initially provided to the right hemisphere.

The primary substrate of all our concepts is allegory and metaphor. Metaphor, by definition, is a means of comprehending something new in terms within which we are already familiar, and within a context that has been previously known. Everything that we come to know is like something that is already known. The source of the primary, and allegorical, substrate to which the right hemisphere is in receipt, is derived from the collective unconscious. These primary allegories, in common with all forms of intuitive, and archetypical, allegory, are implicit in the sense that they have not been subject to cognitive abstraction and explicitness by the left analytical hemisphere. In other words, explicit concepts and ideas are dependent upon the provision of the implicit, and the collectively intuitive, for their generation and their expression. Consequently, all our conceptual constructs derive their primacy of context from an implicit and intuitive source that is shared by all human beings.

These primary allegories, or metaphors, are representative of "intuitive precepts", or "first principles", that are derived from pre-existing concepts with which we, as man within a celestial domain, had once been familiar. These pre-existing concepts have been retrieved as recollections that were originally archived within our "unlived memory". These are the ancient remnants of the authentic and perfectly conceptualized memories of man, (as we shall define the term "man" later within this chapter), as he initially existed within a celestial domain of the first creative event as described in the Book of Genesis.

These "first principles", as originally imbued within the essence of the Spirit of man, are derived from the Holy Spirit. They are expressions of the Will of the Spirit, and are representative of the spiritual life force and the spiritual knowledge that was imparted to man as first created. Within this context we refer to the content of these first principles within the terminology of the "Wisdom of the Soul". "Wisdom of the Spirit" is the term that we apply to describe the nature of these "first principles" within the broader context and as they refer to that which constitutes the authentic source and the fundamental essence of all that exists within creation.

The nature of the units or "first principles" may also be considered as "monads", as defined by the eighteenth Century German philosopher, Liebniz. Monads are considered to be immutable, and "true substances", that are individually "programmed" to act in a predetermined manner. Each program is coordinated with all others He defined these substances as metaphysical points, or "universal units", that are both "exact and real". Liebniz considered monads as the metaphysical units that constituted the "perpetual living mirrors of the universe". As so defined, monads are representative of the authentic, and metaphysical nature of the universe within which resides a material correlate that is amenable to our sensory senses of perception. Within those limited terms of reference, where "exact" also implies absolute perfection, this is an appropriate descriptive term that may be applied with reference to the "first principles" of the Wisdom of the Spirit. However, the fundamental philosophical context in which Liebniz applied the term "monad" is considered to be inherently flawed.

The term "Wisdom of the Soul" more specifically refers to these "first principles" as they pertain to the life force that animates the mind of man and provides humanity with the primary substrate to all knowledge. These properties are conveyed to our collective unconscious through the agency of the "breath of life" to which we commonly refer within the definition of the term "consciousness". The Wisdom of the Soul is now reciprocated within the neurological functionality of the brain where the content of its "first principles" are cerebrally reformatted within the construct of a symbolic template that we can identify, and to which we can cognitively relate. In effect, these symbols constitute a form of imagery that is both strangely familiar, and exists within a context that was once known (i.e.as derived from unlived memory). These images are now represented within a new, and different, format. In this sense they are, by definition, "Primary metaphors". This is the term by which we will refer to them throughout the remainder of the book. The use of this terminology will also help us to distinguish these primary forms from those which we describe as "Secondary" metaphors. These latter types refer to metaphorical concepts that are derived from living memory and through the explicit constructs of our intellect.

The preconceived Primary metaphors are initially presented to our left hemisphere so as to augment the content of our Secondary metaphors that reside within our living memory and which, in turn, contribute to the progressive formulation of our conceptual thoughts (i.e. reformatted Secondary metaphors). In this manner, the Wisdom of the Spirit, and the Word, may become manifest as our thoughts and deeds are subsequently expressed within the context of our lives upon this earth. Ultimately the interpretative construct that we apply to our Spirit of Wisdom, and / or the intuitive belief that is contained within its implicit contents, may also be shared, as knowledge, with others, in our thoughts, in our words, and in our deeds.

The validity of our perceptions is accurate to the extent to which we have authentically incorporated the content of our Primary metaphors, within the formulation of our concepts. It is however, of critical importance that we constantly bear in mind that the nature, and the implicit content, of this archetypical repository is originally derived from the Wisdom of the Spirit. That particular transcendental substrate, from which all authentic knowledge is derived, is universally accessible to the mind of all mankind.

I must make it clear that this is not to infer that all knowledge, as human concept, is an accurate reflection of the "Wisdom of the Spirit". It is only the primary substrate of knowledge to which I am referring. Obviously, that substrate may, or may not, be authentically integrated, or linguistically applied, within the synergistic construct of our cognitive concepts. For the greater part, as it pertains to us as rational individuals, that is an issue that pertains to the exercise of our free will.

One cannot but reflect upon the observation that the process, as described, mirrors that of the Incarnation of the Word on earth. The Virgin mother of God conceived within the mentality of her soul, and by the power of the Holy Spirit, as a consequence of her absolute belief and submission to the primacy of the Word. Yet, because of the flawlessness of her reception of the Word, the Word became flesh, rather than being reflected as a mere image that was conceived within the content of her thoughts, words, or deeds. The preconceived Word was delivered in the flesh to dwell among us. The content of the Primary metaphor, as it was validly expressed within the world, was manifest as a living perceptual entity that was both "perfect and real". This event exemplifies the magnitude of the surrender of self in total gratitude for what had been received, and that of the act of reciprocity in the giving back to its origin, and source:

Love begets love.
Love is reciprocity.
Reciprocity is love.

Within the construct of our concepts, the intuitive "feeling", and implicit context, come first, the conceptualized thoughts and ideas then follow. By way of contrast to the content of our collective unconscious, our cognitive concepts are derived from Secondary metaphorical constructs that have been retrieved from our living memory. These secondary metaphorical concepts are largely dependent upon the provision of their Primary metaphors. However, these are also further integrated into the accumulated product of our observation and experience over our lifetime. As a consequence, these Secondary metaphors may be inherently flawed, particularly since a significant proportion of them have been constructed within the content of our childhood experiences, and thus recorded within our memories. (We will be discussing the formation of memory in Chap.8). The resultant outcome is such that the content of these Secondary metaphors may be transmuted to an inauthentic form, so that when retrieved from memory, (so as to be integrated into the construct of our concepts), they may have lost their intrinsic validity. In addition, any, or all, of our total aggregate of Secondary metaphors may be simply misappropriated within the construct of our language. As you may have already guessed, and pre-empted, what I might say in regard to language, yes, it is indeed the final form of metaphor. The verbal, or written, expression of our thoughts constitutes our "Tertiary" metaphors.

Spoken words are sounds that symbolize that to which we wish to specifically refer. Likewise, the written word is composed of symbolic units which we inscribe to achieve precisely the same purpose. The language of the poetic verses quoted within this book is probably a more accurate, and authentic expression of what I wish to convey than is that of the written and more explicit text. What has been relegated to poetic expression is not intended as a celebration to the beauty, and the nuances, of the King's English. Indeed, it is more configured within the manner of the Gaelic (Irish) tongue. This is a language that expresses the imagery, the feelings, and related emotional content of the collective unconscious through the medium of its rhythms and its sounds, its tones and the richness of its textures.

A large amount of what is conveyed through the medium of Gaelic is communicated within a spiritual context and a related mode of expression. For example, one greets another person, not with a "Hello", but with the words "Dia guit", which translates to "God be with you". The courteous reply is "Dia, agus Muire guit", meaning "God, and Mary be with you". This form of dialogue permeates the manner in which people relate to one another, and in how they express their thoughts and concepts in the Irish language. It is a language of the spirit and of the earth. As such it is a reflection of the spiritual and the mortal aspects of our humanity. The Gaelic language is both musical and lyrical. It flows as does a river run through forest, bog, and pastureland, and onwards towards the sea of our collective conscious. It is borne upon the sounds of living water as it cascades down in streams of consciousness. This is a river that arises from the archives of our unlived memories. This is the reservoir, of all that is authentic in respect of our humanity. Its primary substrate, and its source, is the Wisdom of the Spirit. It is in this sense that we should consider all our thoughts, and their linguistic expression in any tongue, as a means of conveyance of the all that is implicitly valid, dignified, and sacred as it applies to the nature of our humanity.

Our thoughts, as agents of the Holy Spirit, may survive in the smithies forge of our intellect as words of enlightenment, or they may decay, and fade to ash in the process of their conceptual transformation. Yet, everything that is authentically expressed, in thought, word, and deed, is once more raised up to be redeemed. It is transformed as an act of prayer since it is reciprocated with the Spirit that is its primary source.

It is within this intuitive mode of imagery that I have always thought since my childhood days of conversing "as Gaelige" (i.e. through the medium of Irish). Yet, those days are now long gone since I converted to English in my teens. However, the acquired mode of conceptualizing through intuitive imagery has been retained. Evidently, despite my teenage act of ingratitude, and unfaithfulness, my memories continue to be recorded, stored, and retrieved, "as Gaelige". However, once intuitive imagery has been redeemed within the explicit, and the conceptual, format of language, therein resides the potential towards its being misconfigured within the content of its cognitive, and linguistic, expression. This is a manifestation of the human potential which we all share, to varying degree, as rationalizing beings.

The reconfiguration of the implicit to that of the conceptually, and verbally expressed, explicit format, is seen to be a critical issue as it pertains to the manner, and the means, by which we endeavor to communicate. We shall be addressing this issue in some considerable detail, particularly as it applies to intellectual knowledge, and specifically in relation to that of the scientific variety. We can also fully appreciate that the conceptualized content of our accumulated cognitive material enlarges and expands with the progressive acquisition of our insight, and understanding, over time. Nevertheless, we acknowledge that the primary archetypical metaphors that we commonly employ within the conceptual terminology of much of our modern language have long since been appropriated, and linguistically expressed, within a specific identifying reference that defines their implicit meaning.

Even at this early juncture, I must make it quite clear that what is frequently referred to as "intuitive thinking" both by members of the general public, and by trained psychologists, oftentimes does not constitute intuition per se, nor does it apply as a descriptive means towards accessing intuitive knowledge. Regrettably, this terminology is often misappropriated as a means of describing rapid access thinking (i.e. thinking fast), and emotionally charged thoughts that are commonly typified by reflexive statements or verbal outbursts. These forms of thinking are based upon the rapid, or reflexive, retrieval of secondary metaphorical concepts in the absence of more careful consideration, and re-evaluation, in respect of their validity and their appropriate context. Consequently there is the attendant risk that such thinking may be inherently flawed, or over-ridden by irrational and emotive arrogance. Indeed, it has been proven that such "fast thinking" is far more likely to be flawed than the "slow thinking" form of concept formulation and related cerebration.

A prerequisite to the furthering of our knowledge and enlightenment,(with respect to the process of unveiling elements of the objective truth), is that our current concepts remain firmly anchored within the primacy of context as it refers to the precise nature and identifying reference of those specific terminologies that had been previously conceptualized, and verbalized in the past. It is only when this interactive, and continuous dialogue between past and present remains grounded within its contextual primacy that it retains the authenticity of its linguistic meaning and expression. The coherent integration of current intellectual and scientific insight necessitates that it is applied within the parameters that had originally defined the implicit meaning of the term to which we wish to refer. These are the parameters that served as the identifying reference for that specific concept as it is had been expressed in language.

In effect, it is imperative that we retain continuity between the progressive acquisition of knowledge and the contextual primacy of the concepts to which such knowledge is applied. Authenticity necessitates the maintenance of continuity within the conceptual and linguistic core dynamics of our continuous dialogue between past and present. Likewise, it is imperative that metaphors are carefully chosen, and authentically reproduced, within the construct of new and innovative concepts.

Regrettably we have the human propensity to uncouple our intellectual concepts from their contextual primacy. We are predisposed to claiming intellectual and autonomous mastery over our cognitive abilities, while denying the imperative contribution that had been derived from the source of their contextual primacy. In addition, we all share the human propensity to corrupt, or misappropriate, metaphor within the conceptual and linguistic expression of our intellectual endeavors. These inherently human traits are frequently motivated, and inspired, from within the psyche as a means of claiming mastery and control over the primary substrate and its designated contribution to the expressed content of our mind. The Emissary conspires to enslave its rightful Master. We will be explaining, and describing, all of these issues within the forthcoming chapters as each of them pertain to our mental faculties and their cerebral correlates. We will discuss these intriguing processes in relation to the initial source of our inspiration, our artistic creativity, the formulation of our thoughts, and to their conveyance to the world at large through the medium of language.

As so defined, it is this "primacy of context", from which all subsequent concepts have been derived, that both literally, and metaphorically, brings all things to life within the world in which we exist. It is the air and oxygen that sustains us. It brings meaning and purpose to life. In the absence of this primacy, our conceptual paradigm becomes an inauthentic construct of our intellect, and a denial of the truth in respect of the nature of our humanity, and of our entire universe. The authentic nature of anything, including that of our humanity, can only be apprehended when it is considered within the primacy of its context. In this particular instance, the term primacy of context refers to the conditions and circumstances that are relevant to the essence, and the source, of those aspects of our nature that are distinctly human. In this sense, context and original primacy are intimately related.

Primacy refers to the original substrate from which all subsequent features, or manifestations, of that which we are investigating are derived. All of our concepts refer back, and are dependent upon, a primary source within a specified context. Even while we may have been able to identify the atomic and subatomic particles within matter, we cannot yet say that we fully comprehend its nature unless, and until, we can comprehend the context of its original primacy, i.e. the nature and behavior of the specific properties that define its original substrate and its source .In effect it is what we term the "first principle". In the Greek language this term is expressed as "arche". The significance of this term as it applies to primacy of context, and to our understanding of archetypes, will become apparent when we address the issue of the collective unconscious in the latter part of this chapter.

In the instance of our humanity, primacy refers to the nature and the spiritual properties that define its substrate and its source. I will borrow a theological term *"Sitz im Leben"* (which refers to the original life setting of Scriptures) from Geoffrey Wainwright, and Scott Hahn, to describe this identifying feature. The use of this term has similar implications with regard to the source of that which renders us human, and the impact which it has upon our lives. This original life context is more than a historical recording concerning our biological evolution. It is more than a scientific narrative regarding the origin of species. It is more than a human legacy that may be either acknowledged and evoked or refuted and forgotten. It is precisely the "Sitz im Leben" facet of our nature that animates the mind of man so that we may achieve actualization and genuine self- fulfilment. Human life becomes a meaningful event because of its primary source, its "arche", or spiritual principle. Human life becomes a purposeful event because of the inexorable and teleological movement and direction of that universal principle. Indeed, the determinants that apply to the meaning, purpose, and path of progression of the entire universe within the cosmos, have been set, and sealed, within the context of their primacy.

If you have a brief glance at the bibliography that denotes the sources of reference material for this work you will notice that they are predominantly of the

THE KEYS TO THE DOORS OF PERCEPTION

contemporary scientific type, or of an assorted mixture of the non-scientific that represent a diversity of subjects and far longer historical time frames

By and large, these scientific texts are devoid of meaningful context in respect of their failure to acknowledge the contextual primacy of the source of their subject matter. On the other hand, the primacy of context that once pertained to the spiritual, and which provided these texts with the capacity to enlighten and inform, has faded from our minds and memories. Beyond all doubt the scientific references that have been accessed are superb academic pieces of work from a purely analytical, and intellectual, point of view. Yet they abjectly fail to represent what is essential knowledge, and truth, in regard to the holistic nature of our humanity. Consequently these scientific propositions lack the inherent capacity to demonstrate, or specify, how this nature can, and ought to be applied in any meaningful manner to our lives.

Any person might well argue that the disciplines of science and physics pertain only to the application of our left hemispheric faculties towards our comprehending the laws that govern the behavior of the physical properties that constitute life and our universe. Spirituality is not part of their fundamental brief. Similarly, we might conclude that spiritual beliefs are predominantly the preserve of right hemispheric activity such that they cannot be relegated to the left hemispheric analysis of our rational intellect. Such a contrived, and aberrant, imposition of this left and right hemispheric segregation is prohibitive of the vital, and essential, process of bilateral cerebral synergy, reconciliation, and the penultimate process of right hemispheric contextualization. As a consequence, cerebration is reduced to a split brain, or bipolar and schizophrenic- like mode of activity that cannot relate to the fundamental nature and reality of the living world. This regrettable process of what is referred to as "de-contextualization", is to a large extent, the consequence of our spurious, and ever changing paradigm of linguistic, cultural, and intellectual terms of reference that presume to authentically redefine the nature of our humanity, and expand the parameters of our knowledge.

Knowledge and our comprehension of truth, inevitably changes, as it should, with the progression of time. However, in order that it may retain authenticity, it must always remain loyal to the source of the original contextual primacy from which it derived its substrate, and its implicit meaning. Perhaps because I am predominantly left-handed, (hence right brained) I have chosen a task that I feel is within my remit. Likewise, since I am not an intellectual genius, I felt that I had best avoid applying undue burden upon my rational left brain. All that was required from my left cerebral hemisphere was some interpretative work that would provide me with a large lorry load of facts carefully extracted from the treasure troves of their relevant bibliographic sources. This motley cargo of explicit facts was then represented to my right cerebral hemisphere in order that the delegated task, for which it is designed, could be effectively accomplished.

THE KEYS TO THE DOORS OF PERCEPTION

The overall objective of this bi-hemispheric synergy of effort was to provide the scientific material with some meaningful context, and restore some fresh and vibrant context to the remaining material. The ultimate goal is to resuscitate what was originally dead, and resurrect what once had lived, but had long since faded, or even died. Within this renewed context you may acquire some useful insights into the nature of your humanity so that they may be applied within the context of your own life in some meaningful manner. So, we can now breathe on!

CHAP 1B. LANGUAGE AND BELIEFS

Language, mankind's Tertiary Metaphor: That which distinguishes man from beast: That which provides access to the contents of another's mind, motives and intent, both individually and collectively; That whose power may reside more within its interpretation and reception, than in its utterance and delivery; That which may enlighten, and inform, comfort and entertain; That which may proclaim the gross profanities of our human nature with deception and lies, distortions and illusions that corrupt and deprave both mind and spirit.

The common currency of language is the word. Many people often casually, and inadvertently, misconstrue words as representing a range of various name tags which we have invented as a convenient means of describing something specific. This may be a particular object, quality, activity, or experience of some kind or another. The recent introduction of the word "Selfie" into the dictionary is a typical example. This word is now accepted as the term which we may employ to describe a photograph which an individual has taken of one self. However, the truth of the matter, as well we know, is that language, as conveyed within its terminology, structure, and syntax, is a symbolic, or metaphorical, means of expressing concepts that we have generated within our minds. Since the instigation of the word as a mode of communication its use and meaning has expanded and evolved over time.

In everyday conversation, most of us are not consciously, and cautiously, choosing each word in sequence within a tightly self-audited conceptual framework. The words seem to spontaneously emerge and flow in a steady stream of banter. No one is consciously performing a verbal analysis on the content of our every word and its precise meaning. Occasionally we get caught out when a listener casually trips us up in the knowledge that what was stated was erroneously expressed. No, it is not always due to a Freudian slip, a lesion within the Limbic system that is affecting our memory, or injury to Brocca's area such that we are having difficulty in expressing ourselves. Neither is it necessarily the consequence of an alcoholic hangover, or a sign of pre-senile dementia. Invariably it is simply the consequence of our subconsciously thinking in the fast mode. We just grab the most convenient metaphor that emerges from our memory, and it is not always the correct choice. Most of us would find that to do otherwise would interrupt the natural rhythm and the flow of our stream of consciousness. Inner city Dubliners are so well aware of this that they attach a postscript to every other statement that they make. This verbal attachment takes the form of "you know what I mean". Therein, all forms of verbal nuances, or human error, are dismissed. But even Dubliners are astute and known to apply appropriate discernment, particularly when it comes to politics. For example, there is the infamous story concerning a particular politician who was canvasing for support in regard to his election as the major of the city. He was heard to proclaim that he would "put shoes on the footless children of the city as a first priority". Yes, he was tripped up by the multitudes, and he fell down upon his incredulous mouth. Perhaps he should have amended his sentence with the "magic words", just like the rest of the good citizens. But then, that would have been perceived by him as being infra dig for a man of his position, and status.

Within Dublin city, and to some extent even nationwide, the opening remark is often typified by the phrase "what's the story?". The story is what matters, (in Gaelic that's the "sceal, agus an sceal eile": this story, and the story that inevitably must follow), and not the precision commentary of historical facts. But then, in that Fair City, life is strung together like a well- worn set of rosary (prayer) beads. These beads are all looped together like a recurring mantra on a never- ending storyline. Unlike the images captured on camera or camcorder, these are living memories, tales from the salt of the earth, that are being expressed and are recorded. For these Dubliners, this city is the home soil, and the life setting, in which their own personalized stories will unfold. Their beads are the four majestic keys that unlock the doors to a true reality. In time their stories will become part of the collective conscious among its city dwellers. They will become part of the fabric of daily life. Inevitably, they are enshrined within the rites and rituals of their shared community. These are the prayerful sounds of a people in communion with each other.

No doubt, but you will better appreciate the implications of these allegories when we consider the nature of consciousness, the collective conscious, and unconscious, within a later point of this chapter. So, consign this paragraph, (and the Master Key words of Primacy, Context, Synergy, and Reciprocity), to the fore front of your memory, and it with aid you in due course. Meanwhile, plan a visit to Dublin City and you will get to know "the story". Then you will surely hear what it is that I am saying here "You know what I mean!"

However, many are far more cautious in their wording, particularly when they are expressing themselves in a professional capacity. Explicit precision is an inherent feature of their work. This particularly applies to science (physics, chemistry), medicine and law. Within those disciplines the words employed are invariably carefully chosen. What is stated within the context of each word is intended to convey the explicit fact of the matter. However, one must be cautious in their listening. What is expressed is not always accurately placed within the implicit context, and intuitive meaning, of their chosen terminology.

What was once implicit within the word as it was first coined has in many instances become progressively obscured. Indeed it has oftentimes been forgotten to the extent of its extinction. We now employ words for the greater part within what we perceive as an explicit context. They are truthful expressions in so far as they are perceived to be conceptually accurate within a rational and scientific context. That is to say we can prove their validity through a logic that is based upon scientific theory that constitutes actual and irreconcilable "fact", and such fact constitutes "truth". Ergo – the language of science conveys the truth, what is not scientific is an illusion, a deception, and a lie.

The meaning of any word is based upon our understanding and experience of the concept that underlies that specific choice of verbal description. The formulation of our thoughts and the nature of our related responses are governed by the nature and content of our concepts. The concepts are in turn derived from enlisted and selected allegorical and metaphorical concepts that have been drawn from memory. What is selected from within the memory bank is determined by a subconscious process of categorization. The act of categorization occurs as an incessant process of frenetic mental activity. Mental categories differ from group classifications in that they are related only in so far as they may be loosely linked as entities or situations that belong to a pre-existing category within one's mind. The essential linking factor of the categorization process is analogy. Consequently, analogy is central to the conceptualization of our thinking, our thoughts, and ultimately to our behaviour. The essence of analogy, but most specifically of metaphor, is that of understanding and experiencing one kind of thing in terms of another. It is a means of comprehending something new in terms in which we are already familiar and within a context that had previously been known.

The cognitive scientists and linguistic experts now inform us that each concept within our mind owes its existence to a long succession of analogies (i.e. allegorical or metaphorical concepts) that have been generated unconsciously over many years. Some unspecified primary analogies gave birth to a concept and thereafter further analogies continued to enrich progressive concepts over a lifetime. Analogies are derived through a process of categorization of related material that has been relegated to memory. Consequently all existing concepts are dependent upon their antecedents. The conceptual present is grounded in the conceptual past. Without concepts there can be no thought, and without analogy there can be no concepts. It is abundantly clear that our entire cohort of resident analogy, allegory, and metaphor have been conceptually constructed at some previous historical moment in time. That is to say that they are all of a secondary type. They are secondary allegorical or metaphorical concepts that have been formulated from some pre-existing, or "pre-conceptualized substrate". Their source of origin must have been derived from some primary, and elementary, constituents. That primary substrate is the "first principle", or "arche", to which we most commonly refer within the context of the term "archetypes", as originally coined by Carl Jung. We shall discuss the nature, and the source, of these "first principles" in some detail in due course.

In tandem with these linguistic theories most modern philosophers consider that our entire intellectual life consists in the formulation of concepts or beliefs and in the passage from one belief to another through the use of reason and experience. They are obviously talking about cognitive beliefs that are grounded in the intellectual logic of the left cerebral hemisphere as opposed to the spiritual kind that are based on faith rather than on human intellect. The content of such concepts are described as propositions. They interpret this entire cognitive process as one of searching for knowledge (fact) and error (untruth) so that conceptual beliefs are vehicles of truth or falsehood. Yet there is a general consensus that this can be no more than relative truth since absolute truth and objectivity are impossible to discern. We are constrained within the subjective parameters of biological self and our own minds such that the necessary perspective to achieve objectivity is prohibited.

You will also recollect that with regard to our universal and enduring quest for knowledge (as alluded to within the Forward) that the ultimate objective is "to unpack its contents so that it may be applied to, and within, the context of our humanity, and the world in which we live. We are motivated to realize its fruits in order that we may experience a sense of happiness, self –fulfilment, and meaning, in its actualization". It is apparent that the cognitive and philosophical theories in respect of the construction of concepts and beliefs as a means of acquiring knowledge with regard to what is valid, have been construed (as one would expect) through the application of reason and intellect. These cognitive facilities are predominantly left brained activities. Consequently, each issue has only been considered within the limited context of left hemispheric cognition. So, let us look at each step of the process within a wider and more complete context:

Any idea, thought, or concept first arises in response to an inquiry or question of some sort or another. The inquiry is instigated by a sense of wonder, fascination, puzzlement, or awe and admiration.

A question is essentially a plea, a calling out for inspiration, for understanding, and wisdom, that will provide a response towards assisting in the satisfying of that need.

The left analytical brain cannot always respond to this plea since it is limited and constrained by virtue of its dependence on the right hemisphere for its primary substrate. The left hemisphere can only do more of the same with whatever it has already acquired from the right. In this sense the left brain can only retrieve analogies from past memories and so can only reconfigure pre-existing concepts. Obviously there is a limit to the number of meaningful variations that can be constructed from any fixed number of pre-existing allegorical concepts that reside in memory. So this description is no more than an example of the recycling type of processes that the linguistic academics have described. It is no more than a system of recall and replication with some added variations. It also fails to explain by what means the initial allegorical concept was generated.

The brain cannot create that which is a prerequisite, and a precondition, to the process of creativity. The cognitive brain cannot conceptualize, and allocate to memory, that which is required in order to conceptualize in the first instance. That is an oxymoron. Interestingly, the modern linguistic concepts with which we have been propositioned mirror that which defines evolution as a process of "self-replication with variation". The defining hallmark in both cases is one of Darwinian fundamentalism. In each instance the relevant context of original primacy has been side tracked or ignored. In neither instance is there an acknowledgement, or acceptance, of the primary substrate or spiritual essence that is an intrinsic and unique feature of our human nature. The recycled concepts as described are no more than the common garden variety that applies to our routine or mundane daily thought processes. They abjectly fail to account for neither original and creative thinking nor human enlightenment. Intellect it would appear exists within an autonomous void, bereft of intuitive wisdom.

Original, creative, and innovative conceptualization is derived through the contribution of new substrate from the right cerebral hemisphere. The essence of that substrate is derived from the same source as are all our beliefs, be they of the conceptual or the faith based variety. It is abundantly clear that regardless of how long, or how often, a mature and well trained ape (or any other animal) may observe or experience the phenomenon as described by $E = MC$ squared, it will never be capable of formulating an allegorical concept from the content of this abstraction. Consequently, it can never be conceptualized as an idea or a meaningful thought. The response to the human plea for knowledge and wisdom is retrieved from an archetypical and unlived memory that is grounded in the original domain of our pre-existence. It is derived from what we have called the metaphysical LUCA or simply the spirit of our humanity. Carl Jung, who originally coined the term "archetype", originally referred to it as the "collective unconscious"

Archetypical memory is what provides us with intuitive awareness or human intuition. Because of its source of origin, which resides beyond the domain of subjectivity, it is objectively true and authentic. By its very nature, since it has not been pre-conceptualized nor retrieved from living memory, it does not have the configuration that is the hallmark of our left hemispheric analytical processes. Rather archetypes present as a symbolic yet familiar unlived allegory. We often describe this spontaneous experience in terms of an "intuitive feeling". However, such a term is confusing and misleading. A clear distinction must be made between emotional feelings, which are instinctual (i.e. instinctual feelings) and intuitive awareness. The former is biologically grounded and error -prone, while the latter is derived from the spirit and has authentic permanence, is independent of living memory, and transcends all mortal conceptualization. It is implicitly singular and sacred. It is described here as the "Wisdom of the Spirit". This constitutes the primary substrate, or the "first principles" upon which all of secondary metaphorical concepts are ultimately dependent. Consequently, the content of our archetypes constitute what we may now refer to as our "Primary metaphors".

This will be considered in further detail with respect to the acquisition of the Wisdom of the Spirit as an entity that animates the mind of man with a form of "living knowledge" in addition to that of the phenomenon of inspiration and imaginative creativity elsewhere in the text. While this specific form of spiritual wisdom is not derived from the senses, it may indeed manifest itself in a variety of sensory modalities inclusive of feelings (i.e. emotive experience). It may also be visual, auditory, or even of the taste or smell variety. This then is the primary substrate of all knowledge, of creativity and inspiration that is acquired by the right cerebral hemisphere. It will be surrendered over to the left brain to be analyzed and grasped within the limitations of our intellect and our recourse to the analogies of memory. Even so, we retain the prerogative to acknowledge and accept as valid that for which there are no resident analogies. That is what constitutes faith. For example, we cannot formulate a concept of God since God does not belong to a category of anything. Consequently we cannot provide a related analogy. Neither is there any suitable "identifying reference". Faith, without recourse to proof by intellect, is an acknowledgement of the implicit truth that abides within the archives of our intuition. We will revert to related aspects of this subject matter in our later deliberations with regard to the evolution of the brain, and the nature of consciousness, mind, and spirit.

From a purely practical standpoint the purpose of choosing specific words is to assist us in our efforts to specifically identify something to which we wish to refer. To identify something is to be able to make it apparent to others amid an array of particular things of the same type as that of which we wish to verbally refer. We refer to this as the "identifying reference". This process of individualization begins where the process of conceptualization (i.e. predication) leaves off. We individualize only if we have first conceptualized and we do so with a view to clarification of the subject or something to which we wish to allude. It is because we think and speak in concepts that language (in terms of structure and syntax) must repair the deficit of specificity within the concept. However, since our concepts may be interpreted in a vast range of possible ways, so also may every individual word have an unlimited range of meaning. Obviously, the context within which the word is used within a sentence, while also having due regard for the context of time, place, and culture, will invariably provide us with interpretative direction.

Regrettably, there is a great array of words that are of critical importance to our ability to communicate in a coherent manner whose meaning has been mutated, and / or whose context has been transmuted beyond their characteristic parameters. That is to say that these words have been relegated to a new and explicit status that infers specificity, accuracy, and scientific validity. In the first instance the analogies from which they have been derived have been manipulated by scientific theory to the extent that they have been stripped of their primary identifying reference. In the second instance, the context within which they have been relocated extends beyond the defined parameters within which the term had been originally contained. The identifying reference that had been implicit within the meaning of the word has been rendered obsolete. In many instances contemporary philosophy and psychology have contributed to this explicit linguistic process. As we will discover in due course, this global trend is largely driven by the academics and is a manifestation of the undeserved glorification of the human intellect. It is in fact a manifestation of what we shall refer to as a "Left cerebral Hemispheric Shift" or left brain dominance. As a consequence of this cognitive realignment and scientific distortion, what was once implicit in the intended meaning of the word has become progressively obscure or perhaps entirely forgotten.

These facts must be borne in mind when using a pocket dictionary as a convenient means of cross checking the meaning of a word. The handy reference may fail to include the implicit definition of many commonly used words. When the meaning of a word is altered or corrupted so also is the concept and the analogy upon which it had once been crafted. Since the right brain has primacy over the left, it is proposed that all primary analogies are ultimately dependent upon a source of archetypical and intuitive knowledge that contains fundamental elements of truth and validity. Consequently, to the extent that the word is subject to distortion, so also is the truth within which it had once resided. The progressive shift from the implicit to the cognitively explicit has reduced language to a hollow and mechanical echo, a mere collection of sounds that are devoid of substance, of wisdom and validity. While science has the capacity to assist us in the pursuit of the truth, it is not the only valid means of doing so. Academic scientists in particular often establish their reputation and status on refuting the theories of their contemporaries and their predecessors such that scientific truth is ever changing.

There is a perception that, as humans gain increasingly sophisticated knowledge, science rewrites the facts of what we thought we had previously known. In reality, the truth is not necessarily embodied within all that is scientifically new and innovative. Indeed, most of what is valid and essential to the purpose of our lives resides within the ancient archives of our unlived memory and our mind. These must be salvaged and retained as living memories and memorials to the sacred dignity of our humanity. The words within which they are encrypted and encoded must not be forgotten or profaned. Alteration of the intended context within which the word is applied also contributes to the progressive decay of specificity of the identifying reference attributed to the word in the first instance. Such decay occurs in an exponential manner relative to the extent to which these forms of descriptive liberties are taken and applied. In due course, the word becomes disembodied and dismembered as a once meaningful and functional unit of articulation. The essential essence of the word may be extrapolated beyond its critical event horizon. This is the point past which both sky and land dissolve beyond the subjective limits of our optical resolution. It then ceases to provide us with a reliable source of reference as to our conceptual location in time and space. It has expanded and dispersed like an imploding star into the endless void of the firmament. Inevitably it fragments and fades, beyond recognition as any valid, or specified, form of conceptual expression. It ceases to serve its intended purpose as a means of verbal communication, transmission, and conveyance. In a word, it becomes a non- sense. The once implicit meaning from which the word had arisen vanishes forever from the memory of our minds. Many well- crafted, and inspired, words have fallen victim to such a fate.

A great number of words, which are used in everyday language, refer back to the intuitive knowledge that molded their implicit meaning, and their verbal expression, in the first instance. Most of us have forgotten these historical roots. These are what help us to retrace the progressive emergence of our humanity upon the planet. These represent the verbal fossils of our creative imagination, and of the spirit of humanity. These are the treasured artefacts that were once retrieved from the archives of our collective unconscious. It was this process that provided us with the means by which we could express, within some form of conceptual terminology and imagery, what it is that we refer to as "authentic knowledge", spiritual beliefs, or simply Faith. Examples of these linguistic artefacts are scattered through the pages of the Old Testament, particularly within the words of the Prophets and the Psalms of David, They are vividly expressed through the words of Christ, and in the Book of Revelation. These ancient words also abound within the universal imagery of mythology. The identification of such linguistic origins is like a journey back through time. It is a journey into the shadows of our ancient memories as originally written and recalled within the spiritual, social, and cultural evolution of the human mind.

The superimposition of intellectual concept, particularly through the medium of philosophy, and ultimately through the sciences, would usher in the inevitable linguistic transition, from the intuitive and implicit, to the rational and explicit form of verbal communication. Regrettably, within this era of science and global communication this indiscriminate abuse of language has become a common and acceptable mode of articulating the inauthentic, or of expressing the conceptually corrupted version of the word. All too often, this misappropriation has been deployed as a delusionary means towards expressing that which is intellectually beyond human comprehension. Words that had been finely crafted within the wisdom and the memory of the past have been consigned to the hands of the perfidious and profane. In a great number of instances some of our most priceless verbal treasures, enduring symbols of our human dignity; have been condemned to the chambers of their inevitable extinction. With feathered quill, and poisoned tip, these precious jewels are being transmuted to cheap and worthless sound bites. They are fast fading from the content of our living memories. Unless this process is reversed, all mankind might subsequently, and surely, speak in hollow words, mere drivel, and meaningless babble.

Subsequently, within the context of this discourse and this missive it has become necessary to reinstate the implicit as it applies to a variety of core words where they arise within the language of the subject matter. Some examples of words, or related descriptive terminology, whose meaning has become obscured or misaligned, many of which are linked in pairs, include the following: Man and Human; Evolution of Man and Evolution of the biological Human precursor; Consciousness and Conscious (aware-alert);Intuitive and Instinctual (Inherent) ; Implicit and Explicit: Mind and Psyche; Mind and Soul; Soul and Spirit; Religion and Faith ; Church and Religious Institution. In addition I have found it necessary to resort to the use of a number of recent neologisms which are primarily of the gerund type (i.e. creating a verb from a noun). These include words such as contextualization, "ensoulment", trans- symbiotic, and humanization. I am seeking to identify a common language that will permit clear and meaningful rapport between psyche and soul, between our left and right cerebral hemispheres, the material and the transcendental. I have sought to apply the familiar and contemporary forms of conceptual metaphor (inclusive of the language of science) that pertain to the logic and rational mind of the psyche in an attempt to convey the pre-conceptual and archetypical imagery and metaphor that pertains to the spirit or the soul. In effect, what is required is to represent the ancient and the traditional forms of metaphor, as they have been represented in Scriptures, and within the language of religion, within a format that can be understood and interpreted by both psyche and soul. I can only imagine that an equivalent effort had to be applied in the process of creating the English language. In that instance a common root that had been long established, particularly those extracted from Latin and Greek, was used in the formation of a new language. Other elements would be grafted on as Anglo Saxon, then Middle English, terminology evolved. Finally, modern English, as now spoken, would become the common currency of a dialect that we would learn to speak and understand. So perhaps you can appreciate that this linguistic task is an essential and critical prelude to the body of the written work so that it may be read and interpreted in a clear and comprehensible manner.

The superiority of man over animal is not only linked to his cognitive and language skills. Perhaps of equal, or indeed of greater importance, is his ability to Reflect. The term as used herein does not refer to cognition, memory, recall, nor any aspect considered to be related to left sided cerebral activity. It is in fact the inverse of these processes being more aligned to what we commonly refer to as transcendental meditation. We will explain the process as one in which the power acquired by Consciousness provides the means by which we can turn in upon Self or oneself to take procession of self as an object endowed with its own particular consistence and value ; no longer to "know", but to "know that one knows". This introspective ability provides us with the facility of experiencing an awareness of authentic self which resides beyond the realm of the biological creature. This unique human facility is a characteristic feature of our mental qualia. Qualia provide a reference point of objectivity as it applies to the relative validity of the subjective sensory and cognitive perceptual experience. It is what we describe as an "authentic intuitive awareness" of the potentialities, the wisdom, and the power that are derived from the Spirit. This form of objectivity may be most acutely experienced within the content of insight meditation and most dramatically within that of a near death experience (NDE). In the latter instance the intuitive objectivity of the mind (as soul) can witness and observe the interpretative subjectivity of the psyche.

These qualities are enfolded within our Primary metaphors. Our ability to reflect in such a manner is representative of our spiritual awakening and "ensoulment". It is what enabled mankind to arise, or be raised up, beyond the material world and to a higher order that is far above the ancestral primate. It is precisely because mankind was endowed with the ability to reflect in such a manner that he was enabled to believe, and to trust in the potential of his human spirit. Moreover, it was this gift that allows us to apply this trust to, and within, the world in which we exist.

We will argue that it is this intuitive wisdom, and power, that served to bring about the transformation of the biological hominid so that the human species would emerge upon this earth. What had been but a primitive hominid, endowed with a primordial mental and cerebral capacity would be utterly, and entirely transfigured, and transformed, by means of a spiritual process. This, in turn, is what was to serve as the final, and magnificent, impetus that was necessary for the evolutionary emergence of a new, unique, and sacred species which we have chosen to ignominiously classify and refer to as Homo Sapiens.

CHAP 1C. THE AIR OF CLARITY

You were almost there not so many years ago,
So near the Truth, the Light, our Hope,
forevermore.
Then you circumscribed the margins,
wandered to and fro,
Crossed through the very centre, and passed
by the vital core.

From "Almost Enlightenment",
by the author.

PART ONE: DEFINITION OF MAN & HUMAN

Any interpretation that may be applied to the wording of this missive must be preconditioned by the definition, and intended meaning, which has been applied to the terms "man / mankind" and to "human / humanity" within the content and the context of the text. Human "consciousness" and human "mind" are also specific identifying references that are of fundamental importance within the terminology that we apply as defining properties, or features, that are unique to our species. Consequently, we will now endeavor to define these terms within the proximity of their implicit contextual primacy. With respect to "man" and "human", we will instigate our deliberations by placing both of these terms within their respective and original, primacy and context. This may be considered as representative of a Primary Thesis upon which the conceptual, and linguistic, account of the evolution, and the emergence, of humanity are described within the overall content of this book.

Most people are familiar with the notion that humanity is an imperfect rendition of a previous state of immortal perfection. All those who relate, and identify, with Judeo-Christian beliefs envisage our earthly existence as a form of a rebirth, or transition, from this original state of perfection to one of a mortal nature. Ultimately however, it is generally understood that we will revert to a state of immortality within some infinite domain following our mortal death and expiration as a living creature. Many other religions also share in this belief, albeit within a context of recurring rebirths and alternative forms of life on this earth. In either event, there is but one beginning, and ultimately but one end, whether it be seen to be either absolute at mortal death, or immortal (as eternal life beyond mortal death). Consequently, this conceptual format will be adopted, and applied, within the terms of reference that pertain to the topic that is under our current consideration.

IN THE BEGINNING – A PRIMARY THESIS

"In principio erat verbum: And the Word was with God and the Word was God"(John 1.1.).

As the Word unfolds, man, as a perfect and immortal spirit, is created in the image and likeness of God. The term "Word" denotes the expression of the mind and will of God. All that came to be was derived from Him and by Him. The term is also commonly applied within the context of the incarnation. This refers to the event wherein the will of god was made flesh in the person of Jesus Christ. Of greatest concern for us is the fact that the totality of the spirit of mankind was originally created from the divine essence of this same, one, and only God. This celestial spirit, named "man", was made in the image and likeness of God. Consequently, the spirit nature of man is perfect, everlasting, and eternal:

"The Lord created me at the beginning of his work, the first of his acts of long ago. Ages ago I was set up, at the first, before the beginning of the earth". Proverbs 8: 22-23.

Yet, the Word was refuted and rejected by the free will of man. This was to render man incompatible with his essence and his source. The bond of unity, of loving trust, knowledge, and understanding that had existed between man and god was broken. Pride, lust, and envy ushered in the loss of perfection and immortality. Man had removed himself from the perfection, and the context, of his primacy. Separated from the life source of his essence, and from within the context of his original life setting (Sitz im Leben), man was doomed to change, to age, die, and ultimately to decay. This degradation, and self- inflicted exclusion, of man from within the context of his primacy, is fundamentally one of a process of "de-contextualization". Yet, the divine essence of the spirit of man would continue to reside within the domain of the Kingdom of Heaven. In the interim, the image of this essence, as a "spiritual principle", would be imbued within the reconstituted form of man as he is reborn within a second Genesis.

The universe, the earth, and all that dwells therein were created some 14 billion years ago from the decontextualized substrate, or debris, of what had once been contained within the domain of eternal perfection. Scientifically, this moment is described as the "Big Bang". Was it simply the beginning, or did it also signify the end? It could just as well have been both the explosive death knell that accompanied the destruction of a first "celestial universe", and the loss of mankind's paradise, while heralding the birth of the material universe within a second creative event. These concurrent events would express the combined wrath, and mercy, of a loving god within a single act. The story of matter, time and space, and of the rebirth of man, emerges within the context of a second Genesis. A new soil is prepared, a "primordial soup", within which the seed of life is sown anew. In time, a biological entity will emerge within a new creation, an ever changing realm of life, death, and decay that is governed by the laws of nature and science this biological seed of mortal life is resuscitated, and revitalized, with the spiritual breath of eternal life. Consciousness was breathed forth from the substrate of the spirit that is the Word, and it would imbue all humanity with its animating spiritual principle throughout every age.

"The Lord God formed man from the dust of the ground, and breathed into his nostrils the breath of life, and the man became a living being". Gen.2: 7-8.

The story of evolution upon this earth describes the slow, and progressive, incubation of this seed, and its coming to its predetermined fruition with the emergence of the spiritual creature that is humanity. This biological creature, and its spiritual principle, is granted a Devine reprieve. Such an act of love, mercy, and forgiveness, permits all of humanity to retain the potential of being raised up once more to its former glory and state of perfection. The biological human creature, and its spiritual beacon, or soul, must await their intended reunification with their original spiritual essence. In this manner the Kingdom of God may be ultimately realized upon this earth –as it is in Heaven.

The soul is that immortal facet of the mind of man which is animated through his consciousness. It reflects his true nature and identity as it is contained within his spirit. The soul of our humanity yearns constantly in hope, and with trust in the promise, that it would be finally reunited with its spirit. This is a promise that was made, and sealed, within god's covenant. The Kingdom of God is only unfilled within the mind and heart of our mortality here on earth. In the sense that the spiritually collective, or "unified body" of man, from whom our humanity is derived, fell from grace through an act of defiance in the face of God, so also have all of us fallen from perfection. This form of spiritual inheritance, or imperfection, is what is commonly referred to as "original sin". In addition, within the mortal context of the sacrament of marriage we reaffirm this original unity of body and of spirit as it becomes established between man and wife. The story of man and of humanity begins in eternity and from infinity. It is, and never was, constrained within any given timeframe. It is everlasting, even while it continuously unfolds within its current material and earthly context. The physical and the metaphysical strands of which we are ultimately composed are inexorably bound, and interwoven, within the very fabric of our being, and the history of our human evolution upon this planet.

Life first began to emerge upon our planet 3.8 billion years ago. Yet our spiritual "evolution" continues to unfold while it has concurrently molded and directed the specific manner in which we have mortally evolved as human beings. This alone would dictate our uniqueness, the conditions and the timeframes, out of which humanity would emerge within the chain of life. The once immortal form of man would be slowly reconstituted as a mortal being through a process of nature, and spirit, in evolution over a span of many millions of years. The biological element of humanity evolved progressively in complexity and stature, ascending within the Tree of Life. We might also envisage his spiritual aspect descending such that each would merge, and fuse, to establish a perfect unity of being. It is when this unity, and its related spiritual reawakening, has been accomplished and fulfilled, that humankind emerges as a unique spiritual being. The spirit of man would have lain in slumber to await the day when the mind of humanity had been adequately prepared to acquire the full measure of the facility of consciousness. As described in Genesis, man was put asleep while being prepared for the creation, or "birth", of woman. What had been originally united as one in spirit was to re-emerge as a divided entity within a mortal realm. Within that specific account of this asexual reproductive -like event there is no reference to an immediate reawakening:

"So the Lord God caused a deep sleep to fall upon the man, and he slept; then he took one of his ribs and closed up its place with flesh. And the rib that the Lord God had taken from the man he made into a woman and brought her to the man." Gen 2. 21: 22.

From a biological perspective, the rib could be seen to represent an accessible source of marrow which contains a rich supply of stem cells. These are the biological precursors of all human cells, and possess the potential to form a complete human being. The reawakening would not occur for billions of years. It would be a long time after cellular division (mitosis), and sexual reproduction, had been firmly established within the Tree of Life before this dramatic spiritual, and biological, phase of evolution would come to fruition. The acquisition of consciousness is what would finally reawaken humankind to an awareness of his true identity. In such a manner, humanity has been raised up to a new level of life. While the anthropologist, Carl Linnaeus, has described, and classified, our species as "Homo Sapiens sapiens", we shall endeavor to correct this inadequate and deficient terminology. This dramatic and unique event, of "ensoulment" warrants that the title "Homo Sapiens Spiritus sapiens" is officially conferred upon the human species. These events are presented as the Primary Thesis to the content of this book. They form the prelude to the story concerning the spiritual and biological evolution, from the beginning, to the current time, within the total history of humanity, and of our universe.

DEFINING THE TERMS "MAN" AND "HUMAN":

"Man" is the term which has been used as the identifying reference which describes the spiritual nature, and related properties, of this First Creation or the first beginning, as it exists within the domain of eternity. This is the term which is used in the Vulgate (Latin) translation of the Book of Genesis: The Vulgate is a Latin version of the Holy Bible which was composed by St. Jerome (Eusebius Sophronius Hieronymus) in 382 A.D.

"Faciamus hominem ad imaginem et similitudinem nosrtam;" (Gen.1: 26).

i.e."*Then God said: Let us make man in our image, after our likeness*"

And

"Et creavit Deus hominem as imaginem suam: ad imaginem Dei creavit illum, masculum et feminam creavit eos" (Gen.1: 27).

i.e.: "*God created man in his image, in the divine image he created him ; male and female he created them*".

It will be noted that both man and God are referred to both within the individual and the collective, within the singular, and the pleural contexts of each of these terms. God and man are referred to as "us", and as "them". In the second story of creation God is again referred to in the pleural context: "*See! The man has become like one of us*" (Gen3. 22.)

The term "man" is also obviously pleural since it is further qualified by the use of the term "them" in relation to the duality of their opposite, yet complementary, natures (i.e." male and female he created them"). The term "man" is applied in the same manner as we more commonly refer to "mankind" within the collective context of its meaning.

Within multiple contexts throughout Scriptures, man and God are referred to as both individual, and collective, mirror images of each other. I am in him / them, as he is in me / us. Such a thought, the very idea, that god and man are mirror images of each other is utterly amazing, awesome, and astonishing, beyond all form of words. The term "man" continues to be used in the second account of creation. Perhaps it would be easier for us to distinguish the spirit of man as described within the first story of creation, from that of mortal man (i.e. human), as referred to within the second story, if the term "man" was confined to the first account only. Herein it describes the ancestral spirit of the mankind which is truly representative of our last universal common ancestor (LUCA). This ancestry has also been described as that which pertains to its original life setting or its "Sitz im Leben" (see "Air of context").

The human spirit, or spiritual nature of mankind, is both perfect and immortal since it was created from the essence of God and in His image. While the spirit of mankind was derived from Him, and off Him, it is not God. The Spirit of man exists as a discrete and distinct co-dependent, entity which is spiritually bound to, and within, the mystical body of Christ. This entity was created, empowered, and inspired by the Holy Spirit of the triune godhead.

The Second story of creation is interpreted as relating to the recreation, or rebirth of "man" as a mortal creature within an imperfect and material domain. Herein, mankind has been separated from the perfection of his spiritual essence and from his celestial domain in eternity:

"The Lord God formed man out of the dust of the ground, and breathed into his nostrils the breath of life, and the man became a living being" (Gen. 2: 7).

This "breath of life" is interpreted as the means whereby the image, or reflection, of man's original spiritual nature has now been incorporated as a fundamental spiritual principle within his material and mortal form. We generally refer to the "soul" as being a functional aspect of this spiritual image.

This Second story of creation, in effect, is part of the allegorical description of the creation of the material universe, the earth, and the initiation of the process of our biological and spiritual unfolding, or evolution, in time and space. It would probably be more appropriate if we were to reserve the use of the term "human / humanity" when referring to man reborn again within a mortal and material context This variation of the term "man" serves as a specific identifying reference which indicates that the spiritual phenomenon, and spiritual nature, of the first created "man" has now been transmuted and modified in some manner. We have described this transmutation as having been instigated through a process of "de-contextualization" from within its original perfection, and permanence of substance and of form. As a consequence, first "man" reemerges within another form that is imperfect, and within another context that is embodied within a mortal temple and a material earthly setting.

The word "human", when used as an adjective, is derived from the Latin term "humanus" meaning earth or soil. The origin of this word is derived from the Latin noun "humus" which means earth, or soil. In this interpretative instance, "human" would translate to convey a nature that embodies both Earth and Spirit: "hum (us)-man". From an intuitive perspective, such an identifying reference would confer absolute specificity and authenticity in the coinage, and application, of this unique and distinctive term. Moreover, the name Adam is derived from the Hebrew noun "ha adamah", meaning "earth/ ground". In Arabic, the term Adam also means "earth/ mud/ clay". You will note that the word Adam is only mentioned in the Vulgate version of the Bible within the second account of creation in the Book of Genesis. To this extent, the St. Jerome version of Genesis reserves the name Adam to indicate a creature that is distinct from that of the nameless "man" (hominem) as referred to in the first story of creation. The use of the name Adam, within the second story, serves to distinguish this specific "man" as being an "earth –spirit". In other words Adam is "earth –man", or "human". Such a statement, places him within a mortal context both in nature and location. He has been transformed from pure spirit, and reborn in an imperfect and material form. Moreover, he emerges alone, as a single and isolated male, who is initially unaccompanied by his female counterpart. He has been separated from the original, and complementary, spiritual unity that had been a feature of man's nature within the first creation.

The fact that this creature, required to be resuscitated back to life with a "breath" that was blow into his nostrils (i.e. airways) also defines him as having been dead to his original spiritual perfection. In point of fact, where Saint Jerome had specifically applied the name Adam in the Latin Vulgate of the text (382 A.D), this has been replaced in a number of instances by the word "man", or "mankind", in the English translations.. All of this only serves to compound, and reinforce, the current, and historical, lack of clarity in relation to the interpretative distinction that ought properly apply to the nature of "man" as referred to within the first story of creation, and that of the human creature, "Adam", who emerges within the second version. However, what can be implied with some certainty is that this rebirthing event, which is described in this second story of creation, may be simply restated as saying that the human creature is born as "the son / daughter of man". Adam, as derived from the soil, in both name and nature, is but the son of original celestial man. His primary spiritual ancestor, or LUCA, is the perfection of the first created and spiritual "man".

Interestingly, this is the identifying reference, (i.e. "son of man") by which we are informed that Jesus Christ repeatedly alluded to himself as an individual human person. However, in the specific instance of Jesus, the spiritual principle was not an imperfect image, as reflected within the soul of our mortal nature. Rather, the spirit of Jesus was that of the true, and perfect, essence with which he was consubstantial, and of one within the divine nature of the Father, and the Holy Spirit, of the triune God. Yet, he humbled himself to unfold as the Word made flesh, and thus incorporate himself within the biological, and the evolutionary, history of humanity. As a consequence, he could state that he existed within the world as we mere mortals do. We are also, individually and collectively, clearly identifiable in nature, and in terminology, as the "sons and daughters of man". To this extent we may envisage Jesus as the first, infinite, and perfect "man", or "Adam". Mankind, on the other hand, now exists as "humankind" The once immortal spiritual nature is retained only as an imperfect image, or beacon, which we refer to as the soul.

In common modern parlance we interchange the two descriptive terminologies, man and human, while also applying the more formal term "Homo sapiens" whenever it is deemed appropriate to do so. I have also taken these same liberties within the descriptive content of this text. However, you will none the less fully appreciate that in each and every instance, even though separated from his original spiritual essence, humanity continues to retain the image of this essence (as soul and spiritual principle) as he exists on this earthly planet. Likewise, his beginning, or his primacy, since there can ever be but one, refers back to that last universal common ancestor, whom we have identified as the immortal spirit that was the first created "man".

I have purposely avoided the use of any alternative metaphorical concept, or imagery, to describe man / mankind or human / humanity so as to try and avoid misrepresentation and confusion. The traditional and historical description of our spiritual ancestry as being an Adam and Eve seems to be a reasonable use of allegory as long as it is confined to the Second account of creation, as did the Scribes within their written testament of these events. However, it is apt to be very misleading when we casually apply these names within the descriptive content of the first story of creation. This has inadvertently led most of us to conceptualize two individual people, represented in the form of a man and a woman, as existing within a celestial domain. However, it is abundantly clear that the ancestral spirit of humanity cannot be conceptualized within any material context whatsoever. There are no three dimensional bodies, no x or y chromosomal sexual determinants of gender or genital form. Even though some form of complimentary male and female natures was spiritually unified within the first created man (kind), we are not really fully justified in our applying a concept that conveys a human image of a man and a woman. There was no physical and biological him and her, no time, or any specific geographic location. We must assume that the Scribes reserved the titles "Adam and Eve" in order to specifically identify, and describe, man reborn within a different context of their nature, form, and their material location upon this earth.

If we were to try and conceptualize our original spiritual ancestry within the first story of creation, it might appear to be more appropriate to employ such terms as "animus and animo" or perhaps "Yin and Yang", rather than those of "Adam and Eve". These terms more accurately convey the idea of opposite yet complementary principles, or forces, which are intimately bound together and united as a single unified entity. The terms "male" and "female", as they are applied to man within the descriptive text of the first story of creation in the book of Genesis, denote a complimentary bond of unity, in essence and in spirit, as originally intended within their celestial domain. The terms refer to the perfect nature of the bond that is united in love, with love, and through the divine power of love. The spirit of mankind may be considered as such a perfectly integrated entity. However, there are some serious, and obvious, drawbacks to the use of such alternative allegories as animus / anima, or their conceptual equivalents. In the first instance, they lack any sense of a property of existing as a living being, or of an individual personality in possession of an intrinsic worth, value, honour, and dignity. They are devoid of any distinguishing characteristic traits, or qualities, beyond that of a fundamental, and enigmatic, source of original vitality. Once again, the application of such terminology would be similar to the intellectual, and linguistic, pitfall wherein God has been conceptually described as a mere "possibility" from one particular theological perspective. Furthermore, up until the nineteenth or twentieth centuries, very few people would have been able to relate to this type of imagery as representative of their human ancestry. Some form of human counterpart was necessary. In fact many even found it difficult to relate to Darwin's theory of evolution when it was published in1859, and to the idea that we had evolved from a lower species of primate life. For many these difficulties still persist. This missive will help to explain the precise, yet largely justifiable, logic that forms the basis of this problematic issue. Most of us have long since felt that we had matured intellectually, if not spiritually, to overcome what are often seen to be quaint, outdated, and unscientific objections. So, perhaps it was inevitable that people in general would adopt the human portrayal of our "first parents", an Adam and an Eve, as the only viable, and acceptable, option to which they could easily relate. It would also serve as a means of maintaining an identifiable continuity of characters within both the celestial and the earthly domains. This familiar duo, an ill-fated and tragic version of a Romeo and Juliet, would subsequently reemerge in the Second act within the context of a new covenant and the promise of a reprieve. Most people now accept as "Gospel" the theory of evolution according to Darwin. This Gospel will be seen to represent nothing more than an account of the biological strand of human evolution.

Adam and Eve are introduced within the context of the second account of creation as representative of our "first parents", but also as the first archetypical human beings within the tribe of Israel to have acquired the full measure of consciousness and of ensoulment. In this sense they are the first of the "chosen people" of god. There is no doubt that other humans within various tribes were beneficiaries of this phenomenon at a similar phase in the evolution of the human species. These would be "descendants" of the multitudes of the early homo species that had migrated out of North Africa and dispersed throughout Eurasia. We will refer to these, and Neanderthal, within the context of our human evolution in a later chapter. Examples of such individuals may include the Nephilim who are referred to within the context of the aftermath of the great Flood and the children of Noah. This awakening is what would identify the human species as separate and distinct from all other forms of life. It is a process of progressive cognitive and spiritual enlightenment. Such a degree of evolutionary complexity is evident with the emergence of key indicators relating to man's consciousness, his sense of morality, justice, and spiritual dignity, in addition to those which relate to his mental, intellectual, and creative skill sets. These include the emergence of art, religion, science, and agriculture. All of these are variable manifestations of the human facility to comprehend abstract thought. They provide us with the ability to reflect and to consider authentic self within the broader context of metaphorical concept and allegory. Such extraordinary talents lie beyond the boundaries of the instinctual and primordial senses that can only inform us with regard to the physical and material content of the world.

The reawakening of spiritual awareness is what constitutes the emergence of a moral conscience and recognition of the natural and moral law. In this manner we become fully human. We have been transformed as a spiritual being with a sense of justice and morality. Freedom of choice acquires a meaningful context within which it is to be exercised and executed. Mankind procures both intellect and intuitive insight in addition to the awesome responsibility that these endowments entail. The contents of this primary thesis represent the primary conceptual truths upon which the holistic reality of mankind's existence, his mission and purpose, are founded. Within the content and context of the remaining text we will investigate some of the more relevant biological facts, particularly those of the neuro-scientific, physiological, and genetic types, in addition to the metaphorical and metaphysical consistencies that underpin all of these primary conceptual truths.

PART TWO: CONSCIOUSNESS & MIND – AN EXPLICIT CONTEXT

> The fire of Love ignites all Wisdom,
> All knowledge burns within this blaze.
> It is released, it is set free,
> Within the seven flames of the Trinity.
> The humble heart it will surely raise,
> Of those who yearn the Truth to see.
>
> From "Seven Flames", by the author.

It is within the nature of man to reflect upon himself. We have an intuitive desire, and perhaps a sense of need, to try and comprehend at least the fundamentals regarding our human nature and the world in which we live. We search to find some level of understanding, some meaning and purpose, to our existence and our lives. This is a process that inevitably draws us to consider the nature of self and others within the context and circumstances of our living. The inescapable focus of attention invariably falls upon a final common denominator. It is the consciousness of the mind of man.

While it is abundantly clear that the brain is not the mind, it is also clearly evident that the brain is where mind and matter appear to meet, interrelate, and reciprocate in some manner. From a purely functional perspective the neuroscientist considers mind and brain as synonymous, the rational being that if you damage the brain, the related mental correlate is similarly afflicted. Most of these scientists also consider that the mind is a product of our cerebral activity (i.e. cerebral primacy in relationship to mind).

The term "psyche", derived from the Greek word "psukhe", meaning life principle or soul, has long since been divested of its spiritual connotations within the disciplines of psychology and psychiatry. The term is currently employed as referable to the mind solely within the context of its neural (cerebral) correlates. As we will soon explain, this is but a partial truth.

The terms "consciousness / conscious" are applied to describe the state of awareness and alertness as registered, and perceived, within the content of both cerebral hemispheres (cerebral cortex). The rational in this particular instance being based on the fact that if the cortex is denied input from the brainstem regions of the thalamus and limbic systems (which are within the reticular activating system), consciousness is extinguished. It is in this overall biological and cerebral manner that, from a scientific perspective, we are provided with the experience, the sense of being, and of an "inner self", as existing within the world.

All of these scientific facts are entirely logical, well founded, and valid, but their validity is strictly limited to within the explicit meaning of their scientific language. The validity of the scientific paradigm, as linguistically expressed, disintegrates when it is redefined within the implicit meaning of its terminology, and the contextual primacy of the relevant subject matter. It will be demonstrated that such a language is intrinsically flawed. It is a misappropriation of the terminology that defines the implicit, and precise, meaning that applies to the identifying reference that characterizes the nature of what these vitally important words are intended to convey.

Despite the fact that a clear, accurate, and concise definition of both consciousness and of mind remains elusive, we will attempt to ascribe some sense of identifying reference to these terms as a preliminary. We will subsequently clarify, and enlarge upon, these particular faculties within the specific "context of their original primacy". This task will be undertaken as we progressively scrutinize, and probe, into the depths of our human nature within the finer and interrelated details of the subsequent chapters. We will explore the mysterious nature of the affiliation, and alliance that exists between mind and brain. In addition we will seek to explain, and account for, the incessant conflict that rages within our minds with regard to the choices and decisions we regularly make within our daily lives. For now, let us first and foremost, carefully examine the phenomena of consciousness, and the human mind, in respect of their explicit definition, expression, and their scientific terms of reference. Then we will be in a position to begin to redefine them within a more implicit and intuitive context.

The human mind is intimately associated with consciousness. Indeed it is consciousness that is considered to be the fundamental animating factor that energizes our mental faculties, and our brain, to a state, or condition, of operative functionality. In an earlier chapter "Language and Beliefs" we discussed how a variety of terms, including those of "consciousness", and "mind", have been corrupted, and misappropriated, as a consequence of their explicit transmutation, and revision, within the common currency of our language. As in the instance of several critical terms that are of major relevance to defining the fundamental nature of our humanity (e.g. man, human, soul, spirit, and evolution), they have been stripped of all of the meaningful content, and context, that properly belongs, and applies, to their identifying reference. They have been mutated to an order of explicit fundamentalism.

As presently defined and applied within a wide range of academic disciples, the terms "consciousness" and "mind" are invariably expressed within the sole context of a neural and cerebral correlate of our mental capacities. This biotechnical approach has evolved to a degree that it has greatly encroached upon our perception of these human faculties as being the product of our neurological activities as they interact with, and within, the material content of their internal and external environment. These are the interpretations that are invariably applied to these words in the instance of general medicine, anaesthesia, neurology, neuroscience, psychiatry, pharmacology, and evolutionary and clinical psychology. For the greater part, they are now commonly equated with the faculties of awareness and alertness, (and the nature of our related emotional and intellectual responses to them), within a highly technological milieu of super computerized data processing, and related electrochemical events. This mechanistic, and biotechnical, perception has broadly overflowed into the psyche of the general public.

Once more, as in a great variety of other instances, our academic mentors have largely succeeded in their efforts to contribute to the configuration of an inauthentic, and humanly denatured, perception of our personhood and of our global paradigm. Our vision, and interpretation, of reality is at risk of succumbing to the status of the inane, the banal, and the incongruous, as that which is reflected in the current content of our tabloid press and related sources of our popular information media. Medical science has long since applied the abbreviated version of the word consciousness, in the form of "conscious" and "unconscious", as a clinical means of classifying and quantifying levels of mental arousal. More recently, conventional science has applied a number of specific criteria which it considers as representative of the identifying qualities, or enigmatic features, that define the human mind.

These include the following:

1. Qualia or the nature of the "inner life" which we perceive as the subjective experience.
2. Unitary binding of spatially distributed activities into a single vision and coherent sense of "self"
3. Transition of pre-conscious processing to consciousness
4. Non-computability (of the classical type)
5. Free will.

Let us first consider the nature and content of the biotechnical elements as they apply to consciousness and mind. Then we will discuss the issues concerning the definitions of awareness and alertness as they may apply within some specified, and limited, context to our understanding of the implicitly valid meaning, and nature, of both consciousness and of mind.

It has been proposed that neuronal circuits oscillating synchronously at high frequency (called 40 Hz.) within the thalamus and cerebral cortex may explain how these mental and conscious events occur within our brains. As we shall subsequently illustrate, the thalamus, limbic system, and related basal ganglia, which are present within a region of our brainstem (called the "reticular formation") are critical elements for the maintenance of awareness and alertness. However, we will also demonstrate that these cerebral functions do not fulfil the conceptual, or linguistic, criteria that define either of the terms "consciousness" or the human "mind". These descriptions do not refer to the specific phenomenon, or to the substantive content, of that which these specific terms were originally intended to convey to our minds and memories. As currently applied within these scientific contexts, these interpretations are a reflection of our efforts to describe the manner, and the means, by which consciousness of mind is deployed in, and by, the brain, to mediate, and impart, it's phenomenal and unprecedented effects, within the human organism. They are excellent indicators of the means by which consciousness, and the content of the psychic aspect of the human mind, may be encrypted within the brain, and might be functionally expressed, within a theoretical module, as human specific traits and acquisitions.

We will illustrate in due course how the psyche aspect of our mind is derived from a primitive instinctual awareness that is uniquely embedded within the ancestral component of what we now refer to as the brainstem. As a consequence, the fundamental, and biological, template that is representative of the psyche is encoded within our human DNA. Our genes are simply composed of an intricate collection of chemical molecules, which we have identified and described as DNA. Genes are not sentient beings. They are clusters of molecules that are configured so as to survive, replicate, and adapt to their own advantage in response to changes within their environment. In this sense they may be described as "selfish", since there is no inherent sense of empathy in relation to another. Indeed, there is no real sense of self-awareness within the context that this term applies to the individual person. The integration and alliance of such a selfish quality within the empowered and intellectual content of a facet of the human mind largely accounts and contributes to the self-serving, and egocentric, nature of the psyche. However, the psyche, as an empowered facet of the human mind, is no more than an emissary which is functionally dependent upon the substrate of consciousness. In other words, consciousness has "Primacy of Affect" over that of the psyche. This fact is directly mirrored within the cerebral correlate of our mental activities within the context of the primacy of affect which is attributed to the right cerebral hemisphere over that of the left hemisphere.

All of these mental and cerebral concepts, and their related descriptive terminology, will be discussed in detail, as our story unfolds, within the relevant chapters of the text. As a consequence of these facts, the explicit use and definition of consciousness and mind, within both the scientific and the popular public domains, is fundamentally flawed. In neither instance do they refer to consciousness or the human mind within the valid context, or the content, of their original primacy. All that can be inferred from an intellectual, or scientific perspective, is that there is some theoretical evidence to suggest that a rather vaguely integrated combination of neurotransmitters, electrical, sonic, and quantum computation, are likely candidates that may explain the manner in which the enigmatic phenomena of consciousness, and mind, are materially and biologically mediated and expressed within the human organism.

At the present time innovative research, led by the highly regarded, and publically respected, Roger Penrose, is seeking to unravel the mysteries of consciousness. The Penrose –Hameroff "Orch-OR" model is proposing a quantum computational – biological module that may, in theory, explain the precise location, and the possible means by which consciousness, (within the explicit meaning of that term), could be generated, or functionally mediated and expressed, within the human brain cell. The underlying theory presupposes that tiny organelles, called microtubules that exist within the cytoplasm of all of our cells function as self-organizing quantum computers within our brain cells. An organelle is a specialized subunit within a cell that has a specific function, and is usually enclosed within its own membrane. Human cells have a large number of these highly complex units, some of which contain their own DNA (e.g. Mitochondria), and others that do not. The function of a protein is closely related to the organelle in which it resides. For our purpose, and at this point of time, we will only consider three closely related types of organelles. These are the microtubule, endoplasmic reticulum, and ribosomes

FIG. 1

THE CELL

A NEURONE (BRAIN CELL)

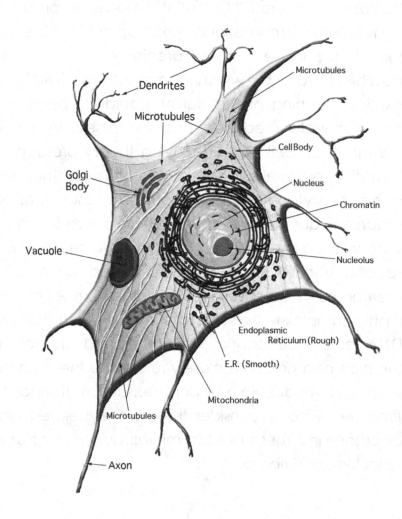

The abbreviated title, "ORch OR" of the Penrose – Hameroff study refers to "Orchestrated objective Reduction". Microtubules are only present within the cells of Eukaryotes,(i.e. multicellular organisms), and are tiny dynamic, and hollow fibres, that are components of the cytoskeleton which supports and gives strength to cell. The cytoskeleton formed by the microtubule is essential to the architectural structure and form of the organism's development. They play a critical role in the formation of the nervous system and the development of the brain's neuronal base of brain cells. They can also elongate or shrink, and by so doing can generate a force such as that which is required for the flagellated propulsion of sperm or for the separation of cellular elements during cell division (i.e. mitosis). Curiously, the switch from growth to shrinking of the microtubule is called a "catastrophe". These characteristic features of growth and recovery, and of shrinkage by catastrophe, which are continuously occurring at any given moment within the same cell, account for their dynamic instability. Also, of critical importance is their role in the transport of motor proteins and other organelles within the cell, in addition to their role in the regulation of gene expression. A large variety of drugs can bind to the microtubule so as to interfere with its dynamic action particularly that in relation to cell division. This has been applied as a means of creating anti-cancer agents that lead to the inevitable death of the cancer cell.

There is another organelle within the cell called the "endoplasmic reticulum", (abbreviated to ER), which is like a complex system of canals that runs from the nucleus, through the cytoplasm, out to the exterior margins of the cell and onwards to the extracellular environment. These channels play a related role in the transport of proteins within the cell. Some of the E.R. is also closely allied to protein synthesis, sorting, and folding, which occurs in tiny clusters, called ribosomes that line the margins of some ERs. Because of the grainy appearance that these ribosomes give to the E.R. at these sites, these portions of the system are referred to as "rough E.R." The remaining elements of the endoplasmic reticulum, which lie more to the perimeter of the cell, are called "smooth E.R.'s".

Only properly folded proteins are transported from the endoplasmic reticulum, marked with a specific address tag called a "signal sequence", to their targeted destinations. Messenger RNA transports a copy of portion of DNA, encoded for a sequence of amino acids, from the nucleus to the ribosome. There it is translated back into a matching sequence of amino acids to form a protein molecule.

All life could well be described as "protein in action". Since all activities of human life are performed, regulated, and dependent upon proteins, such as neurotransmitters, enzymes, hormones and all our bodies essential chemicals, you can appreciate the central roles which both the microtubules and the endoplasmic reticulum play in the preservation, maintenance, and expression of the human life form. Together they also provide a means through which the genetically encoded material within the DNA of the cell's nucleus may be transmitted to the individual cellular cytoplasm, then into the wider environment that communicates with all of our cells. Finally the gene is expressed in some specific manner of action, or identifiable trait, within the environment of the external world which we inhabit.

The microtubules, and the endoplasmic reticulum, are the microscopic lungs, and heartbeat, in addition to the final pathway that is a delegated expression of the biological movement and action of both our brain and physical body. In effect these two vital systems within our cells are what largely mediate the expression of the totality of our consciousness of mind, of our brain, and of our physical body, within the environment within which we exist. Moreover, since they can contribute to the alteration of the genetic expression of our protein molecules, so also may they alter the physical and emotional expression of our bodies or minds.

Disturbances of metabolism within the ER, or the over-expression of proteins can lead to ER stress. This is a state in which the folding of proteins slows with the subsequent build-up of malformed, or unfolded, proteins. This kind of ER stress is emerging as a potential cause of large number of fundamental disturbances that are commonly expressed within a great variety of specific disorders and diseases that afflict the human species. At one time within the very recent history of medical science and psychiatry, this clinical observation was expressed as a "psychosomatic" phenomenon. This was the module largely applied as a means of explaining the role in which stress and worry became manifest as a physical or mental ailment. Many physicians, and also by extension, most of the general public, considered that heart disease, high blood pressure, stomach ulcers, asthma, and depression, were all of a purely psychosomatic origin. This perception only started to fade out of the academic mind-set in the mid nineteen seventies. That at least is one example where the explicit definition of a scientific concept fell into general disrepute and has, for the most part, faded from our living memories. However, it would now appear that there was in fact a significant element of truth, as we can more clearly comprehend it at this time, within the dynamics of the biological relationship that exists between stress and the genetic alteration that can be effected in the synthesis of our protein molecules. The stressors need not be confined to the realm of our emotions. They may be of a far more pervasive nature such as arises from within our internal or external environment (e.g. infections, chemicals, toxins, drugs etc.) However, the manner in which our bodies respond to these various types of stressors is often dependent upon our overall emotional status and our sense of vulnerability. What may be viewed as stressful by one individual may be what motivates and empowers another. In any event, such changes as we have described within the ER, or related DNA encoding, may account for the common pathway by which many, or most, diseases and conditions of ill health are expressed within the human organism. We will consider these issues again when we address the manner in which epigenetic changes can affect our health and behavior.

These biotechnical propositions with regard to the manner in which consciousness, and the human mind, may exert their influences upon the human organism at the brain – body interface are of immense interest, and of great potential value to the health and wellbeing of all of us. Our scientific understanding with regard to the relationships that exist between mind, brain, body, and our environment, are only in their infancy. However, I suspect that unless, and until, we have a far greater understanding with respect to our human nature, meaningful enlightenment and purposeful application to the experience of our existence, and our individual lives, will remain beyond our highest aspirations and our conceptual grasp.

Our primary concern is in regard to the nature, and the source, of consciousness. By what means did we come to be the beneficiaries of such a facility; in what manner did it evolve; how can we account for the invariable sense of inner conflict that is a feature of our human nature; what determines our predispositions towards either good or evil; in what manner did we acquire a moral conscience; and to what purpose are we in receipt of the enigmatic powers of this amazing mental acquisition?

AWARENESS AND ALERTNESS

Consciousness is not a facility that awakens when we arise from slumber, and, vanishes when we go to sleep. It is not something that can be anaesthetized by anesthetic agents, chemicals, or drugs. Be it in common parlance or medical terminology, when we apply the term "loss of consciousness" (i.e.unconscious), it should explicitly mean "loss of biological ability to express, or apply consciousness". An alternative way of describing such a state or variety of states, (with regard to loss of ability to apply consciousness) is to say that there is loss of awareness and of alertness to the degree that is indicated by the level of difficulty to arouse. (See under neurological states & cerebral location, in regard to "Coma").

However, it will be also be shown that there are a great variety of conditions in which the facility to express consciousness may be functionally impaired in the absence of any loss of awareness or alertness. Most of these are the consequence of localized brain injury (such as the frontal lobes and specific regions of the right brain) that are essential to the neurological expression of consciousness. But of far greater importance are those frames of mind that reflect a blatant disregard, and ambivalence, for the "primacy of affect" as it pertains to the integration of consciousness within the context of both our mind and its authentic cerebral expression. We will discuss these particular types of mind-sets in a subsequent chapter entitled "Confabulation".

The familiar expression of being "consciously aware" of something is an appropriate description used to convey the common synergy of activity that may exist between the consciousness of mind and the awareness of brain. In this instance the expression is intended as another means of conveying the idea of being "intuitively aware" which, in turn, implies that such an awareness has been imparted by means of a primary process that is independent of the rational intellect and of our facility to construct thoughts and concepts. Incidentally, the realignment of the expression "loss of consciousness" to that of "loss of the ability to express or apply consciousness", would also require that the definition of "subconscious" was modified to mean "subliminally aware".

The following list of mental states will give you some indication of what I mean by "awareness" and "alertness", and in what a variety of combinations and states we are most familiar with them. I have also provided you with some indication as to the regional location within the brain that is allocated to the maintenance and control of each these neurological states. As a preliminary it is necessary to understand what areas of the brain are most concerned with maintaining and controlling our levels of awareness and alertness. Since this is not intended as an introduction to neurology, I will address these issues in broad generalities and simplistic terms of reference. Do not be too intimidated or perplexed by the Latin terminology.

The essential anatomy of the modern human brain of Homo sapiens has only been in existence some 200,000 years. That was within the period when Neanderthal existed, and subsequently became extinct as recently as 28 000 years ago. However, it would appear that a far greater degree of neuronal complexity and configuration of the neocortical circuitry, particularly in respect of the Frontal lobes, has evolved far more recently (i.e. 10,000 years). This most recently advanced brain, which typifies our species, evolved as three distinct brain entities which are described as the brainstem (most primitive), the midbrain, and the cortex or new brain (neocortex).

FIG 2.   BRAIN STEM/ BASAL GANGLIA
         & RETICULAR FORMATION

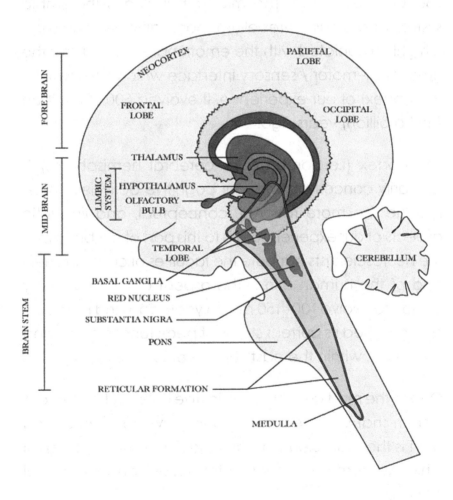

The brainstem controls the basic essentials relating to being awake, alert, asleep or aroused. In addition, it controls the rhythmic and reflexive aspects of our biology including those of our stereotypical vegetative movements (yawning, sucking, chewing etc.). Its origins date back to a period within the eukaryotes domain approximately 750, 000 years ago. The midbrain includes the limbic system, thalamus, cerebellum, pons, and medulla, and is highly associated with the emotional aspects (and the emotional–motor / sensory interface which is relayed to the cortex) of our experience. It evolved 500,000 million (half a billion) years ago.

The cortex (i.e. forebrain or cerebral hemispheres) is primarily concerned with our cognitive activities. These include the more rational, conceptual, and linguistic aspects of our experience. It is to this part of our brain that the neuroscientists attribute the faculties of consciousness and of the human mind. This aspect of our brain only began to evolve 100- 150 million years ago and probably only reached its current status of peak functionality, and efficiency, within the past 10,000 years.

One of the most critical and primitive areas of the nervous system that is related to our being awake, aware, and alert is the brain stem. In particular it is within that region which we term the "reticular formation" and the "basal ganglia".

FIG 3. HORIZONTAL SECTION THROUGH BRAIN

THE BASAL GANGLIA

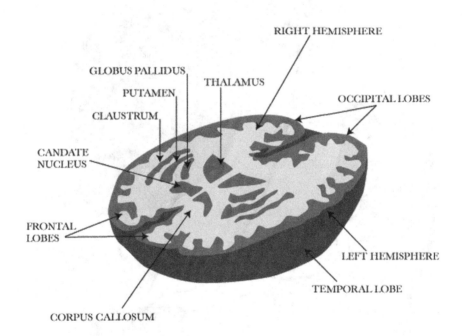

Fig. 4   Basal Ganglia and Connections

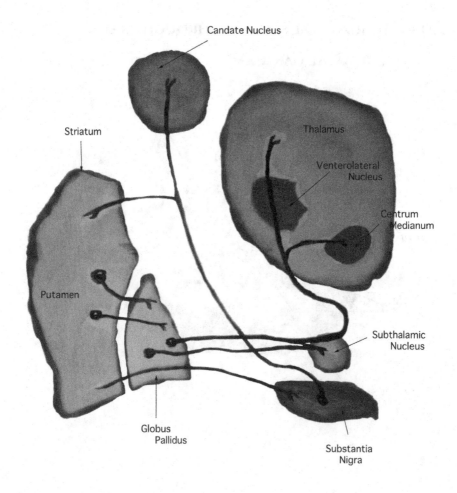

This is the area that first geared us for survival functions. It is commonly associated with the "fright, flight, or fight "responses to threat. However, it may also be seen as the means to a heightened alertness in response to either the possibility of pain or pleasure. Their sources may be represented by what could be lurking in the forest: a dinosaur (pain), a deer (food), or a darling (mate). Of course these are also related to survival, even within the mindless context of the "selfish gene". But then, who amongst us is so mindless?

For the sake of simplicity, it may be assumed that the brainstem and reticular formation is inclusive of everything below the level of the cerebral hemispheres. In addition to the diencephalon, its component elements include the striatum, basal ganglia, limbic system, midbrain, cerebellum, pons, and medulla. This region of the primitive brain functions as an interconnecting system that relays its collective information to the cerebral cortex via the diencephalon, (the "in between brain" of the thalamus and hypothalamus).

The diencephalon behaves as a rudimentary unconscious mind, generating emotions, pain, hunger, thirst, sexual arousal, depression, and rage. There is no concern for consequences, other than satisfaction of internal needs. The basal ganglia mediates reflexive motor activities such as heart rate, breathing, reflexive stereotypical movements (yawning, sucking, chewing, swallowing, walking movements, and mating posturing). In addition the brainstem controls the rhythmic cycles of sleep, and arousal. These elements of the brainstem cannot think, reason, or feel love or sorrow. All sensory input (except smell) is first projected to the brainstem, and relayed directly to the diencephalon. In this sense, the brainstem may be considered as the basic provider of data to the cerebral cortex in respect of much of our primordial, personal, and self- centred, physical and emotional needs, and desires. This particular form of information is primarily relegated to the left cerebral hemisphere.

On the other hand the limbic system facilitates all aspects of emotional, social, motivational, and sexual identity. These include the ability to feel love and sorrow, as well as pleasure, fear, anger, hate, and rage. In addition to its role in maintaining hormonal homeostasis, the limbic system enables us to form, and recall, memories that enable us to process, analyze and to learn and retain complex information for future reference. In turn, it can transfer this information to the neocortex which it may impel to act upon its desires and its fears. This form of data is preferentially relayed to the right cerebral hemisphere which is cerebrally more aligned with our subconscious mind.

However, while all of these subcortical regions of our brain contribute to the maintenance of awareness and alertness, there are no indications that they have the facility to experience consciousness in terms of the capacity to comprehend self (intuitive self-consciousness), nor engage in self-refection (i.e. to know that one knows). For the most part these primitive subcortical regions of our brain function on a reflexive, subconscious, homeostatic, or on an "I need", and "I want", conveyance basis. The information content of the basal ganglia, (and their related connectivity with the diencephalon), is more aligned to the agenda of the left hemisphere, whereas that of the limbic system is predominantly lateralized to the right hemisphere. The localization of the limbic system appears to be related to its social-emotive content, particularly in respect of empathy and compassion. Together with its contribution to memory and recall, and to motivation and intent, these attributes must also be of significant relevance to the type of broad based and inclusive type of attention which is a characteristic feature of the right cerebral hemisphere. We will consider the relevance of these primordial related issues again as they pertain to the more recent evolution of the brain, and to the related acquisition of human consciousness, in a later chapter.

The basal ganglia are intimately connected with our involuntary (autonomic), or reflex, nervous system. This system controls heart rate, respirations, body temperature, pupil size, and muscle tension and stance. In effect, it controls the flow of nerve impulses to those parts of our body that prepare us for some form of action. (We will consider the autonomic nervous system as it pertains to stress and relaxation in more detail in a later chapter). In addition the reticular formation and basal ganglia are intimately related to alertness, sleep and arousal. For example, the cerebrum lapses instantly into sleep when major areas of the upper reticular formation are destroyed. Our overall state of awareness and alertness is otherwise determined by the general interconnectivity of these regions with our cerebral cortex and its various lobes (particularly the Frontal and Temporal lobes).

The reticular formation represents most of the grey matter in the medulla, pons, mesencephalon, and even parts of the diencephalon. The basal ganglia include the caudate nucleus, the putamen, globus pallidus, amygdaloid nucleus, and the claustrum. The thalamus, subthalamus, substantia nigra, and the red nucleus all operate in close association with the basal ganglia and may be considered as a functional part of the basal ganglia. (See diag. of basal ganglia connections)

STATE: LOCATION OF BRAIN REGION

1. Awake, Aware, & Alert:
Integrated activity of Cerebral Cortex, Frontal Lobes, and Brainstem, particularly reticular formation, thalamus, limbic system, and the basal ganglia.

2. Asleep:
Suppressed activity esp. of the brainstem regions.

3. Meditation: (The "Relaxation Response", and T.M.):
Suppressed cortical & thalamic activity where cognitive awareness is suppressed but alertness is heightened.

4. Stages of Coma:
These are indicators of loss of awareness, alertness, and ability to arouse to varying degrees. This may be due to various levels of suppression of cerebral cortical activity and brain stem, including reticular formation and basal ganglia, either alone or in combination. It can present as being dazed and confused, to a state of deep and unresponsive coma.

5. Loss of Awareness (as an isolated phenomenon):
Result of general or localized cortical impairment, attention and / or memory, e.g. Epilepsy, dementias, schizophrenia, psychoses (inclusive of drug induced psychotic states.).

6. Loss of Alertness (as an isolated phenomenon):
Due to suppressed frontal and temporal lobe activity, (without coma), including the basal ganglia in more advanced cases.
e.g. fatigue & sleep deprivation, mild to moderate alcohol or sedative ingestion. Disorders associated with reduced Dopamine activity e.g. Parkinson's disease

7. Loss of global motor activity:
A state known as "locked in syndrome", results when there is selective injury or disease to basal that control muscle activity. While one is unable to speak or move they remain awake, aware, and alert. It may be misconstrued as a vegetative type of state.

We can now appreciate that the biological activities of the primitive brain, particularly those associated with the brain stem, confer a fundamental level of awareness and alertness to the living organism which we may describe as an "instinctive awareness". This primitive self- survival mode is further refined and enhanced in proportion, and in parallel, to the level of integrated neurological complexity within the organism as a whole.

IMPLICIT DEFINITION OF CONSCIOUSNESS & MIND
(and the evolution of the Psyche and Ego):

> Contained within the simplicity,
>
> Of its sacred sanctuary,
>
> Wherein God's Love resides,
>
> Beyond the greedy grasp of man,
>
> And of every human intellect,
>
> Therein true genius lies.

From "Seven Flames", by the author.

THE ANIMAL PSYCHE:

The central nervous system of our ancestral primates had evolved to a significant level of complexity and sophistication such that their level of instinctive and biological self and other (non self) awareness may be reasonably described in terms of a primitive, and instinctual, mind or psyche. This instinctual awareness, and alertness, (or psyche), is grounded within the genetic template of the primitive brainstem and the basal ganglia. As a consequence it is, by its very nature, entirely preoccupied with the needs of self as a first and absolute priority. These include self-preservation, reproduction, food, and shelter by whatever means necessary within the competitive imposition of available resources. Empathy, compassion, concern, and respect for the dignity of others, are not part of its fundamental brief. This form of instinctual, and biological, awareness does not constitute, nor adequately qualify as, a "mind" within the linguistic, and conceptual, context that it is applied in human terminology. It is no more than a biological extension that is grounded within the neurological activities of the primitive brain (presently our human brain stem).

How do we get to know about anything? How do we acquire knowledge? You may surmise that we acquire it through the application of our rational human brain in regard to our observations, and experiences. So, can animals gain knowledge, as something known, albeit to a lesser extent than we do? Animals are not in procession of a memory bank of secondary conceptual metaphors from which they can retrieve, and select, relevant characters from amidst a host of associated allegorical categories. In effect, an animal is not in procession of a mind that is capable of the process of constructing a thought. They are dependent upon an entirely different process of assimilation of data.

An animal simply accrues, and relegates to memory, a series of closely related associations and relationships as a means of survival and reproduction. They may also acquire certain skills and abilities in response to a wide variety of reinforcing stimuli. These are usually in the format of reward (e.g. survive, eat, and reproduce) or punishment (e.g. starve, die, and become extinct). The most critical, and fundamental, of these associations have long since become genetically embedded as instinctual awareness within each species. These properties are neurologically located within the midbrain and the limbic system. Within this system there is a primitive form of memory that has genetically evolved within each species. We will consider the intricacies of these primitive neurological components in a later chapter (Chap. 7).

This species specific template may be further augmented, and refined, through the acquisition of specific forms of learned and conditioned, responses. In time, these acquired behavioral traits may be genetically transmitted to the offspring. This is the basis for selective breeding so that specific traits are propagated within a chosen cohort. It will become increasingly evident, as we proceed with our deliberations within the coming chapters, that it is only to the animal kingdom that Darwin's theory of evolution can be applied. In this context an animal does not learn to acquire information in the manner of a human being. They lack the facility that is necessary to extrapolate information from data. In effect an animal is unable to conceptualize. As a consequence they are devoid of the facility that is necessary in order to acquire knowledge.

Within the animal kingdom there is no process of metaphorical conceptualization in relation to the formation, storage, and retrieval of memories. The learning is not an intellectual, nor a conceptual process of cognitive neurological activity. There are no primary metaphors, nor stream of consciousness upon which the substrate of all knowledge may be conveyed. Consequently, there are no secondary metaphors from which concepts may be constructed, and no language whereby any thought could be conveyed. There can be no sharing of meaningful knowledge. There are no obvious means by which gratitude may be expressed so as to give glory and praise to the source that gives life to all of our endeavors. In short, there is a fundamental deprivation of consciousness. Consequently, an animal in not in procession of the Wisdom of the Spirit, and has not been endowed with a soul, as have each and every member of the human race.

THE HUMAN MIND:

It was the acquisition of consciousness that was the transforming event within the evolutionary process that resulted in the creation of the species that is uniquely human. Consciousness, as the "breath of life", serves as the agent that imparts to all mankind the primary substrate of all knowledge, of all that is known, and of all that ever will be known by mankind. This includes knowledge concerning the authentic nature of our humanity, in addition to all intuitive and intellectual forms of knowledge.

Consciousness is the means by which the Wisdom of the Spirit is conveyed to humankind. The Wisdom of the Spirit is the "life force" that is embodied within the essence of the Holy Spirit. This life force, of which we as humans are in receipt, is that which once resided within the spiritual essence of man as first created within a celestial domain. The life giving property of the Wisdom of the Spirit is imbued with authentic knowledge, and unfathomable power, in respect of all things, spiritual and material, in heaven, and on earth. It is through the agency of consciousness that all humanity is in receipt of an intuitive awareness with regard to the Wisdom of the Spirit. It is by this means that we acquire an intuitive awareness in respect of our authentic spiritual nature. The procurement of this facility is what we describe as "ensoulment". The specific content, and the measure, of this spiritual wisdom is allocated, and revealed, in accordance with the Will of the Spirit.

Humankind has also been provided with a means by which he may seek to gain access to the content of this spiritual wisdom. As we shall soon explain in some detail, this wisdom is archived within our collective unconscious. Within that domain we shall refer to it as the "Wisdom of the Soul". The content of the "first principles" contained within this Wisdom is conveyed to us by means of archetypes. Archetypes are the symbolic, or metaphorical, means by which the intuitive awareness of the Wisdom of the Soul may be brought into the realm of our conscious awareness. It is by this means that we may choose, (or refuse), to apply this pre-conceptual knowledge within the context of our lives. It is also the means by which we may share this Spiritual Wisdom with others.

In addition, the acquisition of consciousness, and hence of conscious awareness, and "ensoulment", is what animated,and empowered, the mind so as to provide the evolving brain with the stimulus towards progressive neurological complexity and greater cognitive abilities. It was this specific sanctifying and humanizing event that would elevate, and greatly empower, what once had been no more than a primitive, and instinctive, awareness of a biological self-identity, to the magnificent status of conscious and cognitive awareness. This is the fundamental basis on which our ability to conceptualize is founded. It is what renders us as a unique, sacred, rational, and intelligent, species of life upon the earth.

The metaphysical process of the procurement of consciousness describes a process wherein the mystical transfiguration of a selected, and evolving, species would result in the emergence of a unique and sanctified creature. This is a creature that has been endowed with a transcendental, and spiritual, nature. Even while that aspect of the human mind which we refer to as the "psyche", remains grounded within a primordial animalism, this once primitive, and instinctual, awareness has been raised up to a higher status which is now shared with an intuitive spiritual awareness, Henceforth we shall refer to this spiritual awareness as being a property of the soul. We have also described the procurement of this unique facility as one of "ensoulment".

The acquisition of this newly acquired collaboration, and fellowship, between psyche and soul is what we now collectively refer to as "the human mind". The spiritual seed, or potential to reacquire our perfection, resides within the "soul of the mind". The mortal, and material seed of imperfection , imbued with a genetic affinity that is confined to self-preservation and self- enhancement, resides within the psyche of the mind of our humanity. In other words, our potential towards selfishness and egocentricity, which by its nature is devoid of love, compassion, and concern for another, is embodied within our material and biological nature from which the psyche is derived. When such an inherent propensity is empowered by the intellect, it acquires the awesome potential towards the extremes of selfishness from which all evil is ultimately derived. As metaphorically alluded to as the "Serpent" within the book of Genesis, it is relegated and reduced to this level of material degradation:

"On your belly shall you crawl, and dirt shall you eat all the days of your life" (Gen. 3: 14).

Evil can only be sustained, and nurtured, by the substrate of the psyche which is embedded within the biological substance of our humanity. It is a manifestation of our use of reason and free will when we choose to delegate control of our mind-set to the governance of the ego directives of our psyche. In stark contrast, the soul is sustained by the "mana" that is derived from the spirit of the Word. It is accessed through our intuition, and through our archetypical Primary metaphors. We may also gain access to The Spirit of the Word by way of Scriptures and the liturgy. However, the propensity toward evil would be permanently retained within the psyche of the human mind-set:

"He will strike your head, and you will strike his heel" (Gen. 3:15).

And finally, that aspect of our mind, as a functionality of the soul, would not be released from this source of inner conflict until the death of our psyche, and the physical body within which it is grounded:

"Until you return to the ground, for out of it you were taken, you are dust, and to dust you shall return". (Gen. 3:19).

What is of utmost importance is that the psyche must continue to depend upon the functionality of the cognitive brain from which it is historically derived in order to exert and manifest its power base. In tandem with all mental activities, from a functional perspective, this is a reciprocal relationship that exists between psyche and cognition.

Within the realm of motive and intent, the agent of the psyche is the ego mind. It is to this aspect of the psyche that mastery and control over its entire complement of cognitive and intellectual abilities and skills has been inadvertently delegated and transferred. Such was the magnitude and the scope of these awesome capabilities that the mind of man, through the agent of the psyche, could rise up in conflict to claim mastery over its primary provider and its source of power.

Perhaps it should come as no surprise to us that, given its newly acquired status, the ego would be tempted to usurp its gracious and loving master, and seek to claim unto its own "the tree of life and knowledge". The mission, and the ultimate goal, is to subvert and enslave the essence and the spirit of humanity in defiance of its source. The history of humanity is the history of this incessant mental conflict that forever wages between our psyche and our soul.

The psyche and the ego are devoid of power in the absence of cognitive and intellectual awareness. The psyche holds no sway within the mind of a new born infant or an individual whose cognitive awareness is in slumber or is otherwise impaired. The governance within such states of mind is the unfettered soul. This is invariably the case within such instances as deep coma and severe dementia. It is also evident within a variable measure in any form of mental and intellectual retardation be it of the congenital or acquired variety. Within all these persons the fullest, and the greatest measure of humanity, as a sanctified and spiritual individual, still resides.

In direct contrast, the human Spirit, and consciousness, are not dependent upon the biological integrity of any region of the brain. The Spirit and the soul live on even while the psyche is destined to expire with brain death. The fuel of the soul is derived from the Spirit (i.e. mana) while that of the psyche is derived from the cognitive brain (i.e. rational thought).

CONSCIOUSNESS AND COGNITION

The facility of cognitive awareness is primarily a function that has been elevated from its once primitive status of instinctual awareness within the brain stem, and neurologically relocated to the left cerebral hemisphere. We have referred to its corresponding mental correlate, and newly endorsed mental facility, as the "human psyche". On the other hand, the primacy of conscious awareness, (as distinct from "cognitive awareness"), whose substrate is conveyed by consciousness, is predominantly reciprocated within the functionality of the right cerebral hemisphere. We have referred to its reciprocal provider within the mind in terms of the spiritual principle or the "soul". The acquisition of conscious awareness provided the critical stimulus, and the impetus, that was essential to evoke an explosive neurological response within the evolving human brain. The outcome was to result in a gigantic surge of both the neuronal content and related interconnecting complexity within the brain, particularly within both cerebral hemispheres and its frontal lobe regions. Consciousness is the facility to apprehend the authentic essence of self, without and in advance of, the evidence of the perceptual senses. It is a spiritual discernment which empowers and animates the mind so as to enable access to this fundamental and essential truth. The terms "Wisdom of the Spirit", or "intuitive wisdom of being",(of authentic Self), are appropriate descriptions that may be applied to the content of human consciousness.

Consciousness is the vehicle, or the means of expression, of the living presence of the Holy Spirit within the world. This is the Spirit who, as emissary of the Word, proceeds from the Father, and the Son, since all eternity. The Holy Spirit entered the world since the beginning, as the Lord, the giver of life. It is he who would instigate, and orchestrate, the evolution of all life towards its purpose and fulfilment. The Spirit was to prepare a biological, and living, temple for the reinstatement of its own sacred image, as humanity upon this earth. It is he who would imbue the clay from which this sanctuary was composed with the breath of life eternal. It is the Spirit who now speaks to us upon the wings of human consciousness so that we may become aware of the essence, and the source, of our being. We are invited to listen, and respond in praise, and in thanksgiving, for our reprieve and ultimate promise of redemption.

What is of utmost relevance is that we clearly acknowledge that consciousness is not the consequence of a mental activity. Neither is it the product of a neurological process within the brain. It is not derived from the psyche, or from the activities of the brainstem, or any of its synaptic connections. Neither is it a feeling nor emotion. The brain cannot create that which is a prerequisite to the process of creativity. That is an oxymoron. The brain cannot create that which is required in order that a process, that is dependent upon creativity, is possible (e.g. imagination, belief, and concept). That is an absolute and fundamental contradiction. The source of the primary creative substrate must be extrinsic to the brain. This is consciousness, and it imbues the mind via the soul. The single and most essential feature with regard to consciousness is that it provides us with the mental facility, and hence with the cerebral cognitive ability, to become aware of the nature of our being. We acquire an intuitive knowledge with regard to the identity of the authentic self.

Consciousness constitutes the essence of the spiritual principle which defines the nature of humanity. "Ensoulment" describes the acquisition of the mental facility of awareness with regard to the spiritual nature of self. Consciousness provides the substrate that enables us to become consciously aware of our true identity. Ensoulment describes the means by which consciousness becomes a functional property within the mind-set and the cognitive domain of mankind. Ensoulment is what provided the impetus that was required to empower and elevate the mind to a higher state of comprehension. This is reciprocally reflected at a biological level within the evolutionary development of the neocortex (particularly of the Frontal lobes), the augmentation of our complement of "mirror neurons", and the related neurological complexities, that are specific to the species Homo Sapiens. To be more correct, we will apply the appropriate title to this humanized primate. Henceforth, he is deserving of the title:

"Homo sapiens Spiritus Sapiens".

It is evident that Wallace, Darwin, and Linnaeus, failed to see what resided beyond the mere fossils and the bones. Blind vision inscribed their paradigm.

Mankind, by virtue of his conscious and cognitive facilities would be the ultimate master of his earthly domain. Now reason and intellect could reciprocate such favors as had been granted by the consciousness of mind. The self-proclaimed master, and commander, of mortal and biological self then entered into world of mankind. The human Ego was born. The fate of humanity would remain forever crouched within its shadow. Each and every one of us would be subject to its dictates, its ambitions, and desires, for the remainder of all time. The true Spirit of mankind, and its creative source, would remain as the only definitive hope of salvation from the inevitability of our own permanent self-destruction. Arrogance and pride of intellect, as it is orchestrated by the psyche, and humility of Spirit, as expressed by the soul, would remain forever locked in mortal combat. The history of humanity, individually and collectively, is the history of this lamentable and bitter conflict. We will place all of these complex issues within their relevant and proper contexts, as we proceed to trace the evolution of mankind in body and mind.

CONSCIOUSNESS- THE BREATH OF LIFE

A scented candle in your room
Flickers gently in the glass.
The summer air is sweet and warm
With scenes rekindled from the past

It burns with scents of love and peace,
To fill aching hearts so grim.
These sacred scents could fill your heart,
If you would only breathe them in.

From "Scented Candles", by the author.

This word, this Royal word, falls so casually and carelessly, from the lips of man. The term is derived from the Latin "conscious", meaning the "sharing of knowledge". It may be best conceptualized within the material world as a "breath", or a "breath of living knowledge". This is the breath that was blown into the inanimate clay at the creation of humanity in order to give it "life". Such an act, as a form of resuscitation, was required in the aftermath of man's spiritual death through his separation from the original perfection of his first celestial creation.

FIG. 5a   IN THE PATHWAY OF CONSCIOUSNESS

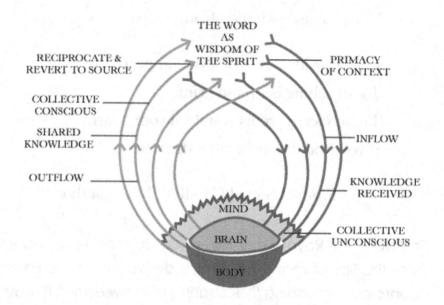

THE WORD
AS
WISDOM OF
THE SPIRIT

RECIPROCATE &
REVERT TO SOURCE

PRIMACY
OF CONTEXT

COLLECTIVE
CONSCIOUS

SHARED
KNOWLEDGE

INFLOW

OUTFLOW

KNOWLEDGE
RECEIVED

MIND

BRAIN

BODY

COLLECTIVE
UNCONSCIOUS

HUMAN BEACON
MENTAL / CEREBRAL SYNERGY
& RECIPROCITY

THE BIBLICAL MENORAH
AND THE
PATHWAY OF CONSCIOUSNESS

THE LIGHT OF THE HOLY SPIRIT / SEVEN GIFTS

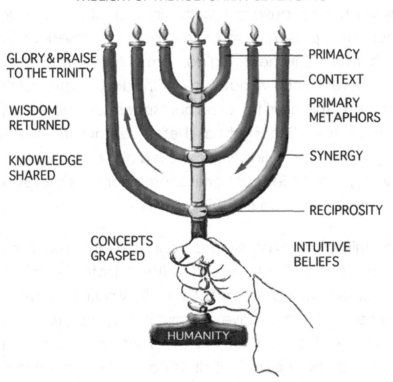

GLORY & PRAISE
TO THE TRINITY

WISDOM
RETURNED

KNOWLEDGE
SHARED

CONCEPTS
GRASPED

PRIMACY

CONTEXT

PRIMARY
METAPHORS

SYNERGY

RECIPROSITY

INTUITIVE
BELIEFS

HUMANITY

"THE FIRE OF LOVE IGNITES ALL WISDOM
ALL KNOWLEDGE BURNS WITHIN THIS GLOW"

The neurological terminology that is applied to describe the functional configuration of the circuits, and their pathways, within our nervous system, provide us with a perfect analogy as to the "flow" of our human consciousness We can envision consciousness as having both a sensory inflow (i.e. afferent) pathway, and a motor outflow (i.e. efferent) pathway. The single, and the universal source of the Wisdom of the Spirit, is what defines the nature and the essence of our consciousness. This is what is conveyed to the individual mind, which in turn, is representative of the receptive "beacon" of our humanity. In neurological terms, this is the sensory and afferent "Inflow" pathway. Within the location of the "beacon", this input traverses our "sphere of thought" as it reciprocates with our right and left cerebral hemispheres, our psyche, and is finally reconciled (i.e. as a process of synergy) within the right hemisphere prior to its expressive transmission out into the living world.

The animated expression of our thoughts represents the motor, and efferent, "Outflow" pathway of our consciousness. The content of the Inflow path is conveyed by means of the collective unconscious. Upon its reception within the "beacon" of our mind we may choose to listen and take heed so that its content is authentically reconfigured within the substance of our thoughts and their expression within the world. Alternatively, we may choose to ignore the implicit content of this knowledge so that it is reconfigured through the sole agency of our psyche and our intellect. The reconfigured content of the outflow is transmitted as the "sharing of knowledge" within the sphere of the "collective conscious". In this sense, consciousness provides us with an ear with which we may listen to the Wisdom of the Spirit, and a medium through which this Wisdom may be shared. In this reconciliatory manner, it may revert to its source, as a true reflection of its primary content. It is returned to the Holy Spirit, as an act of love, humility, and gratitude. In the absence of such a process of synergy, and reconciliation, it would decay, as a manifestation of our conceptual materialism, and a product of our intellectual arrogance.

Consciousness is the "air" we inhale and exhale. It simulates, quite vividly, the two phases of our respiration. Within this excursion of our chest wall there is a brief pause. It should serve as a reminder to us all to hesitate, and contemplate, as to the relevance of this rhythmic movement to our lives, and to our every thought and deed. It should also serve to remind us of the fundamental sanctity contained within all words. All language is sacred. We ought to be more aware of what it is we say, and of the manner, and the context, within which it is said. This applies to every thought expressed, be it in writing or in the spoken word. Consciousness, in effect, and by implicit meaning, is knowledge shared ("conscious"). Someone, somewhere, surely will be listening. Someone, perhaps one that is vulnerable, one young and innocent, or perhaps one who is just eager to learn more, may take heed.

In this allegorical sense, we inhale consciousness as we inhale fresh air that is saturated with oxygen. This form of transcendental "air" is saturated with the oxygen of intuitive knowledge, the fundamental source of our every breath of "inspiration". Such knowledge, or wisdom, is that which is essential to sustain all human life. Just as oxygen fills our lungs, and diffuses into our bloodstream, in a similar manner, intuitive knowledge flows inwardly to permeate our entire being. It is the primary source of all human inspiration, our every concept and thought. This is the archetypical substrate, the mana and the food, of our creativity. It is the fuel that provides the intuitive insight that is required for all of our spiritual, intellectual, and artistic forms of enlightenment. Consciousness, as with oxygen, bursts into flames in the presence of a mere spark. That spark is empathy, compassion, and understanding. That spark is love. Within these flames, these tongues of fire, all knowledge burns incessantly:

> "The fire of Love ignites all Wisdom,
> All knowledge burns within this blaze".
> From "Seven Flames", by the author.

It will yield its sacred essence within the domain of the human mind. In turn, this wisdom of the Spirit will be surrendered to our intellect to be reconfigured as our human concepts. Finally, it is expressed within the world in which we live. It is within the context of this world in which we share, and the air we breathe, that our words are brought to life. Our human word, enveloped, and contained, within the sanctuary of our consciousness, will inevitably return in sacred plumes to the source that is the Spirit of the Word. This is The Word that is the breath of life, now, forever, and eternally. Yet, if our words are corrupted and profane, they will choke and die enroute for lack of air and oxygen. Meanwhile, our intuitive knowledge reverts, and contributes yet again, to the repository of our shared and collective unconsciousness. This is the vast reservoir of enduring truth that is the source of life, for all, and for all eternity.

Within the second phase of our breath, we exhale carbon dioxide as the residue, and waist product, of our respiration. In like manner, we may consider that we exhale the used debris of our intellectually constructed concepts. These are the allegorical contents that contributed to formation of our thoughts and concepts. These functional templates, or scaffolding, are now returned to memory whence they had once been beckoned and retrieved. All human concepts, be they of the intuitive or intellectual variety, are the building blocks of our perceptual reality. When the essential substrate, or material, from which these blocks are made is composed of the intuitive knowledge derived from the Spirit of wisdom, we may be assured that the structure will endure. On the other hand, if our perceptions are derived from intellect alone, being devoid of Spiritual wisdom, they will corrode, rust, and collapse into a pile of rubble. In such case, and perhaps within some era yet to come, these fragments would exist as ancient relics within the museum of our virtual reality.

These exhibits might well serve as a vivid memorial, and testimony, to our human folly and our intellectual pride. The intuitive knowledge of consciousness, like oxygen in air, is essential to maintain cerebral and mental vitality. Deprived of air, and the brain will cease to function. Inevitably, and within a brief interlude, we die. Likewise, human consciousness sustains all mortal,(biological, and spiritual), life. Without this sacred breath, the vital air and oxygen of consciousness, surely we would also die. We would die the awful, and eternal, death of both body and of spirit.

THE COLLECTIVE UNCONSCIOUS

A young man journeys to his ancient core,
Where cymbals chime to a silent beat.
A flock of doves drift slowly bye,
And moonbeams shine through an open door
To dance brightly at his feet.

Kneeling by an open gate is an angel from on high.
Reaching out with outstretched arms,
The young man rises towards the sky.
In a blaze of light the Spirit flies,
Into his longing soul.

From "Epiphany of Doves", by the author.

Archetypes are projections, or impressions, derived from the "first principle" of our inspirational faculties. The term is derived from the Greek compound of "arche" and "tupos". Arche means "first principle" which cannot be represented or seen directly. This universal principle is representative of all that is real, perfect, and authentic. It has primacy of affect over all that is subsequently experienced, comprehended, and perceived, within a conscious or subconscious state of mind. Tupos refers to "image", all of which have shared, and similar, characteristics. (i.e. a "type").

The arche, or "first principle", is not derived from any prior experience within the individual, personal, or collective, lifetime of our biological humanity. We regard the content of these principles as representative of the agency that provided first created man with a perfect form of "living wisdom". We refer to this perfect wisdom as the "Wisdom of the Spirit", as it was provided by the Holy Spirit for the benefit of man. As a consequence, we also consider these universal principles as representative of the content of our "unlived memory".

The nature, and the content, of archetypes are embodied within the term "living wisdom". There are two interrelated, and interdependent, properties that are inherent within the content of our archetypes. The first of these that we will address is that of wisdom. The second is that which relates to the actualization of that wisdom within the lived experience of our human existence. These universal primary principles are initially imbued within the human mind through the agency of consciousness. Their contents are archived within the potential cognitive accessibility of our collective unconscious. *The living wisdom* of these principles is subsequently encrypted, within an empowering symbolic format, or animating perceptual impression, (i.e. image-"tupos") within the neuronal circuitry of our precognitive, and subcortical, regions of the brain. In this manner archetypes may be transferred, into the experience of human life from our collective unconscious. They may emerge within the realm of the subconscious, or that of the conscious (cognitive) domain, in a variety of ways.

In the subconscious realm of dreams archetypes may present within the context of various symbolic representations of repressed thoughts, and feelings that reside within the psyche. These may be random clusters, or disorganized fragments, of living memory that have originated from the region of our limbic system and dispersed past the diencephalon towards the cerebral cortex. Anatomically this would include the Hippocampus, Hypothalamic, and Thalamic, locations of the midbrain. These repressed memories are in turn infused with the creative substrate of our archetypical imagery that is derived from the facility of human consciousness. The resultant dream content is representative of the outcome of these two interactive sources that are derivatives of both living and unlived memory.

Within the domain of conscious and cognitive thought, archetypes are the common substrate of all that we finally conceptualize, perceive, and experience within the context of our lives. Archetypes are intuitive, not instinctual, inherent, nor acquired through experience. Intuition is a facility derived through human consciousness. As such, archetypes are representative of what may be retrieved through our ability to reflect inwardly upon the archived repository, and the implicit content, of our intuitive wisdom. This is the wisdom of authentic self, the "Wisdom of the Soul", that is derived from the essence, and the spirit, of man as originally existing within the domain of the first creation. (The use of the term "man" is as has been defined within the Chapter 1 "The Air of Clarity" Part 2). Consequently, we consider archetypes as being derived from our "unlived memory" since they refer to the recollections of first created man. These unlived memories, as with those which we term "living and evoked memories", (as originally described by Doctor Wilder Penfield in 1951), are experienced as real, living, and felt events within the current moment of their unfolding. The "unlived memory" content of our archetypes is experienced as a living phenomenon within the current context of our lives. (We will discuss the details in respect of Penfield's research, and evoked memories, in Chapter 8.).

The knowledge content of our archetypes is the substrate of our imagination and of our creativity. It may be either artistically expressed in music, myth, spiritual belief, fantasy, drama, or the visual arts, or it may be presented in the form of an intellectual proposition. (See chap. 3 "The Sphere of Thought & Artistic Creativity"). Primary metaphors are derived from the first principles contained within the Wisdom of the Spirit. As a consequence, all human works inspired, and created through the faithful conceptual reconfiguration of the content of our Primary metaphors are highly imbued with the qualities of authenticity, and universality. These are works whose intuitive content has not been subjected to the manipulation, or self-deceptive reconstruction of the psyche and the human intellect. Neither have they been subjected to, nor debased, within the related facility of their expression through the medium of language. The measure of their integrity is the degree to which they remain firmly loyal, and true, to the content of their Primary metaphors, and do so within the implicit context of their original primacy.

The value that is inherent within our work is a reflection of our dedication, commitment, and the extent to which it is imbued with this form of integrity. This provides us with a firm foundation in regard to our work ethic in all that we do, and in every walk of life.

Some examples of human works that most closely approximate, and authentically reflect, the content of these Primary metaphors include those of "primitive" art, (including children's artwork), ancient mythology, Holy Scriptures, and spiritual Revelation. You will recall that it is within this form of authentic context, as it relates to Scriptures and Revelation, (which fully reflect the authenticity of their source) that we identified this observation as being one of the two most important statements contained within the content of this entire work.

The specific manner in which the archetype is expressed, and interpreted, may well be a reflection of the culture, and tradition, in which the metaphorical content of the individual living memory is contained. The metaphors contained within this living memory have been subconsciously, gleaned through a combination of genetic inheritance and individual observation and experience since, or perhaps even prior to, the moment of birth. Within this context it could be said that the expression of archetypes have an inherited and an acquired contribution. However, the archetype itself is not an inherited form of instinctual, or primordial, memory that is derived from the ancient psyche of the human mind.

Inevitably, and regrettably, something in respect of the original perfection of the living essence of all things is lost when it's intuitive, and implicit, nature is redeemed within the realm of the conceptually explicit. By way of analogy, something vital is lost at the instant that a flower is picked, or when a butterfly, or a bird, is captured and removed from the freedom of its natural environment. Likewise, something is lost at the instant that one attempts to convey an emotion or a feeling within the content of a verbalized expression. When intuitions are extracted from their living, or felt, context, some critical element of their intrinsic beauty, and meaning, dissolves within the coarse grasp of our conceptual and linguistic expression. When we gaze upon some work of art, or listen to a great piece of music that stirs our deepest emotions, we simply absorb the felt experience, and dwell within the magic of the moment.

Once there is any attempt to engage the analytical brain to extract the content of that which we perceive, the enchantment of its holistic perfection fragments into an array of granules that are devoid of its living beauty and vitality. This same dilemma is inherent within my efforts of striving to convey to explicit language the meaning, and the content, of that which, by its very nature, is both implicit and intuitive. While the archetypical symbolism conveys the interpretative meaning that is implicit within their content, it is also imbued with the spiritual content of the Word of God.

The Italian liturgist Salvadore Marcili attributes a process of actualization to the proclamation of the Word. That is to say that the expression of the Word, through the medium of the Wisdom of the Spirit, has an affiliated "event character". Jeremy Driscoll O.S.B. refers to this "event character" of the Word within the Forward to Scott Hahn's book "Letter and Spirit", as it is manifested, and conveyed, within the written text of Scripture, and as expressed within the Eucharistic liturgy of the Word within the Catholic rite (i.e. at the celebration of Mass). In other words, the proclamation of the Word of God imbues it with a spiritual form of life. In a similar manner, the human expression of the Word, as conveyed within the content of the Wisdom of the Spirit, becomes a living, and experiential phenomenon when it is authentically, and conceptually, expressed within the context of our lives. The Word may be expressed within the content of our thoughts, words, or deeds (be they physical, intellectual, or artistic). It is in this precise manner that the conceptualized construct of our perceptual paradigm acquires the potential to become an authentic rendition of the reality of our human nature, and of our purpose, within the lived experience. Within the daily routine of our lives the fruits of our every thought, and of our every action, become animated, and imbued, with a Spiritual form of life.

The ultimate, most dramatic, and most meaningful example within which such an actualization of the Wisdom of the Spirit was to become manifest was that of the incarnation of Christ Jesus. Within a biological context, the womb is the temple of the seed of life. Within a spiritual context, that "seed" is the "Seed of Life" embodied within the "first principle" of the Wisdom of the Spirit. Thus was the Word made flesh, having been conceived within the mentality of the soul, and subsequently expressed as a living event within the womb of the Virgin Mary, Mother of Christ. The archetype that first presented to Mary so as to mentally prepare her within the domain of her soul was that of the archetypical angel whom we refer to as the "Arch Angel Gabriel". This form of premonition, or foretelling, was a familiar feature of the manner in which the prophets of the Old Testament received the message of the Word of god. Yet, the Word was never revealed within the flesh, but only within some form of conceptual imagery, act, or ritual. Once again, within the New Testament there is an archetypical example, within the person of John the Baptist, of this manner of foretelling, and of the need for human preparation in advance of the coming of the messiah. In the instance of the Virgin Mary the Wisdom of the Spirit was not simply conveyed, nor reciprocated, within the format of a Primary metaphorical concept. The power of the Holy Spirit and the perfection of the manner of Mary's response were such that the Word became a conceptual reality within the flesh. This reality was conceived within the content, and the living presence, of the one whom we call Jesus.

I had been restless and uneasy these past several days. A great sense of frustration enveloped me because I could not find the words that would allow me to translate into language that which I knew and felt within my soul to be true. And what I believed to be true did not concur with the language of those whom I perceive as my spiritual antagonists, while I yet regard them as the greatest among those of my intellectual mentors, and my leading cerebral protagonists:

Charles Darwin and his Origin of the Species, (1858); C.G. Jung in his dissertation regarding the psychology of the unconscious,(1912); and Crick and Watson's, (1953) interpretation of the manner in which the structure of our DNA may be applied towards our understanding of our human nature. The current cohort of scientific intellectuals, from Hawkins to Dawkins and their like-minded contemporaries goes without saying. Together, these intellectually gifted, and influential, individuals have contributed in great measure to the shaping of the global paradigm concerning our human nature. Yet, it must be stated unequivocally, that this scientific gospel is deficient, and implicitly untrue when extrapolated into the domain of life, and the nature of our humanity. The spiritual, and authentic, nature of humanity has been excluded, and erased from the equation. And the record has not yet been formally corrected, nor the error of omission ever been acknowledged.

Today my preoccupation had to do with the issue of the collective unconscious. With all due respect for C.G., I felt that the scientist had silenced the mystic that resided within him, and done so at a most critical juncture of his personal enlightenment. Perhaps it was because he felt that his scientific reputation, his credibility, and professional career, were at stake within the halls of academia. He did not wish to be aligned on the wrong side of the intellectual paradigm. Some had already begun to refer to him as a mystic. This was an identity that he rapidly refuted and dismissed. I have no doubt but that he had been enlightened in regard to the truth: that individuation has to do with striving towards wholeness through reconciliation of psyche and soul. That this is a spiritual process of transfiguration rather than one of a psychological transformation achieved through the integration of the psyche. But then perhaps Jung chose to use the term "psyche" with the implied understanding that this was inclusive of the soul! Either way, it was clear that he believed that archetypes were not a human creation, or invention, nor a derivative of metaphorical concepts that are retrievable from our living memory. He stated that they existed in their own right, and independently of man. Archetypes were seen to be representative of elementary truths endowed to man, but not of man. Furthermore, Jung believed that a fundamental trust in the validity of such truths is what constitutes a primordial faith. He also stated that belief in Revelation and the incarnation of Christ as the son of God is what raised this primordial faith to a higher level. In other words Jung believed in the idea that archetypes were the source of what we are describing as "Wisdom of the Spirit", and "Wisdom of the Soul".

The psyche is the "false self". It is no more than the transactional persona that is a projection which presents within, and to, the world in the masquerade of authentic self. It is in continuous conflict with the soul. Integration of the psyche could never be equated with a holistic integration of the human mind. The soul is master and has primacy of context within the mind of man. The psyche is but the emissary, and the intellectual mouth –piece of the soul. Besides all that, archetypes are not inherited primal instincts that have been encoded within the ancient fragments of our DNA. Archetypes represent an intuitive, metaphorical, and spiritually empowering form of knowledge, to which we all have access by virtue of our human consciousness. It was the acquisition of consciousness, together with the spiritual principle that describes "ensoulment" that constitutes the nature of our humanity. These are the qualities that have the potential to facilitate the configuration, and perception, of an authentic paradigm of reality in regard to ourselves, and the universe. However, it is quite evident that Crick and Watson failed to discern this aspect of our nature in 1953 when they identified the structure of our DNA within our biological genome. Likewise, Darwin failed to identify the evolution of the spiritual nature of man when he was inspired to write about the origin of the species. In all, the scientific, and the intellectual, have silenced the intuitive, and the spiritual, within many a great and brilliant mind. It brings to mind some distant echoes of the story of Dorian Grey. Did some among these gifted individuals betray authentic self in subservience, and in gratitude, to the directives of their mental emissary?

CHAP 1D. THE SUBJECT MATTER

PART ONE: THE AIR OF TRUTH & SYNERGY

There is poverty and starvation of Spirit,

Hunger and thirst for Truth.

There is despair for need of Love and Hope,

Death to a resurrection and salvation

That was gained for each one of us.

From "Life- Mirror of the
Soul ", by the author.

It is a strange anachronism and curious oddity when the study of mankind, of his evolution, his fundamental nature, his mind, and his journey through the ages, is solely confined to the realm of intellectual logic, and the laws of the biological sciences. Such an investigative approach to this particular subject matter is tantamount to dissecting and discarding the more important half of the very substance of your inquiry from the very onset. It is an incomprehensible paradox and a tragedy when these limited terms of reference are imposed. It holds little, if any, prospect that the outcome of the study could further a deeper insight, and an added the measure of genuine enlightenment, with regard to our humanity or the purpose of our existence.

Rejoice, take heart. We are already living in an age of profound personal enlightenment. This is the age of great scientific discovery, of knowledge and understanding, and of freedom of expression. Alas, if only this were true. We are gazing out at life through the blinded eye of self- deception in the hopes of seeing a better and more perfect tomorrow. To a great extent this illusion has, and continues to be, perpetrated by many of our most celebrated and accomplished scientific writers and academics. Amongst my greatest causes for concern is the fact that, without exception, mankind has been portrayed as the sum of his biological parts, and the evolutionary products of the human brain that can mastermind his destiny. Indeed some will even insist that humanity is but the outcome of a selfish gene. Equally infuriating and confusing, is that theories regarding the evolution of mind and brain, in addition to descriptions regarding the attributes and functions of both these human properties, are often casually interchanged without notice or forewarning.

Most of our current scientific literature concerning the nature of humanity states, or infers, (within the confusing language as described) that the human brain is the agency and the source that provides us with motive, purpose, intelligence, creativity, choice, agenda, and goal. Nothing could be further from the truth. These are the primary attributes of the human mind. It is the mind that underwrites the substrate of thoughts, ideas, inspiration, and creativity. It is the mind that motivates to inquire in search of knowledge and truth. It is the mind that makes the choices, plans the strategy and determines the goals and objectives. This, as we shall come to understand, is a highly relevant and critical distinction that requires our most careful and detailed attention. Besides all this, mankind is presented devoid of any spiritual contribution, at least beyond the level of fantasy and wishful thinking. I recall reading somewhere with respect to science, and its hallowed truths and realities, that scientists usually insist that their perception of the world is valid based upon their incontrovertible evidence. And they ask, indeed expect us, to have faith in the subjective authenticity of their flawless objectivity. The fact of the matter, despite our occasional and periodic verbal protestations and denials, is that we do acknowledge, accept, and respond to the content of these scientific and intellectual gurus. The consequences are clearly evidenced and reflected at every level within society: in our arts and culture, our national institutions, and in our political and social policies. These scientific doctrines, as they are most commonly proclaimed in relation to the nature of our humanity, are finally reflected in our attitudes, values, priorities, and beliefs. Of greatest concern is the manner in which it influences how we relate to ourselves, and seek to communicate to each other in the routine of our daily lives.

PART TWO: IN SEARCH OF WISDOM

Have we become a contemptuous race
With hardened heart and flint like face?
Chosen ones, hah! we wander, lost in desert sands.
We stumble in the darkness with no prophet
for a guide.

No one to hear our voices
Nor meet our harsh demands.
No one to grant safe passage,
Nor in whom we can confide.

From "Exodus 2000 ", by the author.

Most of us have little doubt about the human potential for intellectual ingenuity, knowledge, and understanding concerning ourselves and our universe. However, to claim that it is infinite and potentially all-knowing would be regarded by most as an overstatement. I have little reason to believe that science, philosophy, or psychology could ever fathom the ultimate depths of our human nature. Specifically, it seems highly unlikely that any scientific metaphor, or collection of secondary metaphors, could ever be provided to fully explain, or adequately account for, the human mind, the nature of self, or of consciousness.

It is unfortunate, if not highly regrettable, that so many great intellectuals are under the illusion that they will finally comprehend the totality of the human condition by adopting a new and more radical form of rational thought, theory, and concept. Indeed, Raymond Tallis author of "Aping Mankind", stated that he was trying "to understand what we are in a way that dispenses with the supernatural (non) explanations without succumbing to the kind of naturalism that I espoused when I was fifteen and had just shaken off my religious beliefs." Furthermore, Tallis quotes Gerry Fodor, (with whom we shall later acquaint ourselves) and refers to the observations of Max Planck (the physicist who coined the term "quantum" in 1900) and the current concepts of quantum theory to support his contentions. I can well understand and appreciate the logic of his line of thinking. As we shall discuss, the emergence of these innovative scientific theories with respect to the behavior of subatomic particles could be seen to have brought us a step closer to the threshold of the spiritual realm. Paradoxically, despite the fact that Tallis, and many like- minded academics, refuse to step across this threshold, it is evident that something more than pure reason can accomplish this particular movement of the mind. The truth of the matter is that the keys to the Holy Grail of wisdom and understanding are already within easy access, and within range of the hungry grasp of every human being. This radical, and profound, source of enlightenment resides within our collective unconscious. One must be motivated to seek, and knock, to acknowledge, listen, and respond to the content of this archived treasure. Many will fail to concede the wisdom of their intellect to such a rival and potentially challenging source of knowledge and insight.

While I have great regard and admiration for all of these people and their contemporaries, it appears that such faith in intellect and disregard for faith of the spiritual kind is unwarranted, misjudged, and misplaced. Perhaps, the kind of radical rethinking that is initially required as a first priority is of the non- thinking variety with submission, humility, and trust at its very core i.e. meditative soul searching. It is unclear to me whether some of these academics consider such an undertaking to be above or beneath their intellectual dignity. Either way, there is little doubt that it is not beyond the boundaries of their humanity. Such an undertaking would ensure that the intrusion of our existing scientific paradigm were at least temporarily restrained to accommodate an entirely new entity that is derived from a different, and higher, source of wisdom! On the other hand I applaud these gifted individuals who have the capacity to elaborate with such eloquence and insight upon the mystery of the human condition and on how it defies our ability to define it within the disciplines of biology, neuroscience, and evolutionary theory.

In stark contrast, there are those among us who accept and appreciate that in order to more fully comprehend our humanity we must acknowledge the limitations of our reason and intellect. Such an approach describes a spiritual mind set or the application of a transpersonal psychology to the task of seeking to understand human nature and the purpose of our existence. Transpersonal psychology extends beyond the personal self and personal identity. It involves a recognition, understanding, and realization of intuitive, spiritual, and transcendent states of consciousness. (Lajoie, D.H. & Shapiro, S.I. "Definitions of Transpersonal Psychology", pub. 1992). If you pause to think for a moment you may come to appreciate that all human endeavor should rightly be of the transpersonal variety. This is regardless of whether it is manual labor, or of the intellectual and artistic variety.

Ideally our efforts should extend above and beyond self, inclusive of the spiritual aspect of our human nature. Sometimes this is what we refer to as "true dedication" or "selflessness". Long ago it was often described as a "vocation in life", particularly as it applied to the nature of an individual's work, and the attitude which they adopted towards the realization of their efforts. Perhaps work might be more aptly described as an "invocation", since that in effect is what it truly represents. We are calling out in hope that through our efforts we may experience genuine meaning, purpose, and self-fulfillment in our lives. Yet, whether it is within the limited context of work, or the overall nature and content of the activities of our daily lives, there is a great diversity of opinion as to what it is that constitutes happiness, and self-fulfillment.

Professor Paul Dolan, behavioural scientist, has defined happiness as the experience of both pleasure and purpose over time. ("Happiness by Design" Paul Dolan. Allen Lane. 2014). He states that what matters most are the individual differences in what we personally find to be joyful and fulfilling. But we are usually so preoccupied in doing what we feel we ought to be doing in order to address or own perceived needs, and expectations, that we fail to pay attention to what is most important in regard to our pursuit, and acquisition, of happiness. He suggests that in keeping a diary of our everyday experiences, and scoring each of these in terms of pleasure and purpose, that we will come to recognize the hidden wisdom contained within the subconscious domains of each of our minds.

However it appears that Professor Dolan over looked the fundamental task of attempting to adequately define the concept of the term "human purpose". This is purpose as it applies to the proposed reason for our existence. It is that entity that serves as the ultimate guide to the objectives sought within the experience of our living. The term has been removed from its primary context, and relocated within another spurious domain. Despite this glaring omission, what he does propose would seem to be sound and practical advice. Yet, there are inherent dangers, most of which are as a direct consequence of his failure to clearly define the implicit nature of human purpose.

This strategy fails to address the nature and source of the revelations contained within those subconscious intuitions. There is a risk that their meanings, and significance, may be misinterpreted. There is a risk that within the process of our analyzing the value-quotient of our experiences, that we will engage in what that region of our mind, (the psyche), and of our brain, (the left cerebral hemisphere), can do with great proficiency. It can confabulate (Chap.8). Self- delusion misconfigures our perceptual reality, and does so in a highly ego centric manner. We could all too easily be misled so that we would revert to the pursuit of our own perceived needs, desires, and expectations at any cost.

The truth of the matter is that the answers cannot be gleaned from the conceptual content of our left brain. The answers reside within the content of our intuitions.

We must first learn how to access, and relate to these so that we are not misled by the directives of our ego mind. In fact, one of the literary critics who reviewed Paul's book stated that within 48hours of having read, and applied the suggested strategy, that the quality of her life was improved. She resigned from "a voluntary project that was eating up time and energy", joined the London bike scheme so she could cycle across London, and allocated more time to "eating and talking with people I most liked". Such people may well be her kids, or perhaps her children's friend's parents or guardians. However, she still feels that the 90 wearisome minutes at the hairdresser is unavoidable.

Now, I might just have a small dog's bone to pick with Miss Money Penny. It would seem that this dear lady knows quite well how to look after herself. Neither am I certain as to whether this would necessarily typify the kind of rapid response that Paul might have anticipated or advocated. Overall, it is unclear as to whether one could say with any real certainty that Miss Penny applied right judgment. Given the brief timeframe, there would have been little opportunity in which to reflect upon one's core attitudes, values, priorities, and beliefs. But then, only Paul may be able to answer the former question, and Ms. Penny the latter.

There are two identifying feature that are characteristic of genuine happiness and fulfilment. Firstly, they are rarely experienced as an instant sense of gratification. On the contrary, they are invariably accrued over the extended period, and demand time, effort, and commitment. Secondly, the immediate beneficiaries are usually other than one's personal self. Consequently, the diary should (a) be recorded over a minimum of several weeks prior to the instigation of any action. (b) the information recorded should include the identification of the immediate to medium term beneficiary. This second item is deserving of a score out of 20, (in contrast to the 10 allocated to those of perceived pleasure, and purpose), being down-graded if the beneficiary is oneself, and up-graded if it is otherwise. In the interim, perhaps a public health warning should be included with each copy of the book to the effect: "Chew slowly before swallowing; may induce Visual Impairment or even Blindness".

Had Professor Paul Dolan been operating entirely within a "Left Hemispheric Shift" mode of cerebration (Chap3.) while composing this material? Might yet another historic epiphany be forthcoming from the Right Hemisphere in that particular regard, and as it is applicable to both Paul, and many other British academics? Is Penny more guided by her Limbic system, particularly her cingulate, or hypothalamus, (Chap.7) than she is consciously aware? I would gladly give a penny for each of their thoughts.

Consequently, the content of this book considers the mind of man within the context of his biological and spiritual elements or "natures". It is clearly acknowledged here that the inference of such a duality is purely for the purpose of illustrating the atheistic denial of the spiritual within mankind and its exclusion from their academic deliberations concerning the human condition and human nature:

> *"The human person is a being at once corporeal and spiritual.*
> *The unity of soul and body is so profound that one has to consider the soul to be "the form" of the body. (Council of Vienne 1312).*
>
> *"It is because of its spiritual soul that the body made of matter becomes united, a living human body. Spirit and matter, in man, are not two natures but rather their union forms a single nature""*
>
> *(Catechism of the Catholic Church.; article 365. Veritas 1994.)*

Specifically, it is this unity that renders human life sacred. It is sacred, deserving of great reverence and awe beyond any other form of life because it transcends nature and mortality. Sanctity is neither a property nor a part of the language of science. Sanctity is what the real and ultimate value of human life is based upon.

Since the dawn of mankind there has always been a conceptual abyss between what constitutes the nature of the material world and that of the spiritual realm, inclusive of our souls. Matter, and spirit, was an issue of hard fact and reality on the one hand, and a vague mythological folklore on the other. With the advent of science, this perceptual distinction was further copper fastened. To a large extent the discoveries of Isaac Newton in the seventeenth century, and those of Darwin in the nineteenth, were to incontrovertibly unhinge all pre-existing spiritual concepts concerning the nature of mankind and of the universe. The perception was that spirituality and religious beliefs were contrary to common sense, human intelligence, and the facts of a scientific rationale.

Prior to 1900, when Rutherford discovered that the behavior of atoms was random, as opposed to predictable, the deterministic nature of science was seen to be absolute, and reproducible, in fact or in theory. Finally, with the advent of quantum theory and its further advancement through the work of Albert Einstein, Arthur Compton, Max Plank, Richard Feynman, and many more in recent decades, the demise of this traditional scientific predictability and our reliance upon common sense, was to be laid to rest.

Quantum theory has to do with probabilities, and the laws of chance, rather than with the absolutes of predictability or the application of common sense. According to quantum theory, an atomic particle can be in several places simultaneously, at one location and every location at the same time. it can also move from one place to another by exploring the entire universe simultaneously. Likewise, it has become increasingly evident that what distinguishes mankind from his ancestral primates cannot be simply attributed to the laws of biological evolutionary theory. The nature of the mind of man, of self and other, in addition to that of consciousness and morality, cannot be explained away by either Darwinism or neuroscientific theory alone. Science has moved forward from the hard-core concepts that once separated physical matter, and the non- matter of the spirit.

What now separates the scientific and the spiritual paradigms may in fact be a far thinner line than many atheistic intellectuals may care to contemplate or seriously consider. It may never prove possible to fuse these paradigms within a single and inseparable unit. This is because, like the encrypted contents of our two cerebral hemispheres, they differ in their content, and their mode of attention towards their subject matter. They also differ in their fundamental objectives and their specified goals. Yet, the content of each of our cerebral hemispheres must be reconciled within a synergy of effort so that a higher order of subjective truth can be applied within the context of our lives. So also might our intellectual concepts, and our intuitive beliefs, be guided towards a higher order of mutual coexistence, respect and cooperative harmony.

CHAPTER TWO: THE BRAIN—HOW IT IS DESIGNED TO FUNCTION

THE HUMAN BRAIN

The pregnant snail within our shell
Crawls through the dirt and slime.
The worm has breached our sacred well
And drank our Wisdom dry.

The shadow lurking in our mind
Is the one that came from Hell.
The shadow has released its kin
From the Eve from whom it fell.

From "Exodus 2000 ", by the author.

When I first saw a human brain it was floating in a large jar of formalin that was perched upon a shelf along with a large variety of other internal body parts. It was dull and grey, grooved and convoluted, rather like I imagined a portion of an elephants tongue or an aged chunk of contorted tire, might look. That was obviously a very dead brain. It looked so simple and basic, so rudimentary and benign. To think that that dull mass of tissue was what rendered me capable of thinking, analysing, planning, memorizing, dreaming, loving and feeling, or creating anything of any beauty, use or value whatsoever, seemed incomprehensible. Thankfully, I no longer entertain such dubious misperceptions.

All of these higher cerebral processes are first instigated, and animated, within the mind through the facility of our human consciousness, and that of our collective unconscious. In this respect, the mind has primacy of context (as previously defined) with regard to the intellectual, creative, and uniquely human content of our cerebral faculties .These mental activities are simultaneously replicated, and encoded, within a complex, and highly integrated, electrochemical and architectural format that is the defining feature of the neurological circuitry, and anatomy of the human brain. In order to maintain continuity of scientific terminology, we will rephrase this proposal regarding the mind's "primacy of context", by stating that the mind has "primacy of affect" in relation to the source, and cognitive content, of the brain.

A unique form of reciprocity exists between mind and brain which facilitates the exchange of their encoded data content. In addition, there is a form of neural reverberation within the substance of the brain that refers the neural signals in a retrograde manner back towards their source of primacy as it is represented by the Right Cerebral Hemisphere, and that aspect of the mind to which we have ascribed the facility of "ensoulment". We shall discuss these issues in more depth when we consider the nature of the reciprocity that exists between mind and brain in the next chapter. Intelligence, artistic creativity, and genius, will never be discovered within the brain. They may, at least in theory, be reflected in the functional configuration and electrochemical activity of its neuronal networks. None the less, this astounding lump of neurological tissue is capable of a vast array of complex functions. These have been genetically engineered and fine- tuned over time so as to connect us internally to both mind and body, and externally to the world outside.

The brain has the amazing capacity to translate, format, configure, and respond appropriately to a massive diversity of various forms of "information stimuli". Some of this data is derived from within the mind and internal physical milieu, and some from the external world with which it communicates via our sensory modalities. These include our special senses (e.g. sight, hearing, taste, smell) and all the other sensations that are conveyed from our skin, bodily tissues, and internal organs. The initial reception of this data is dependent upon a vast array of highly specialized "receptor sites" which convey their encoded messages, (from their respective mental, and biological locations), along their corresponding networks of individual nerve fibres to their target locations within the brain. This is the means by which this rather strange and mundane looking lump of tissue provides me with all my highly sophisticated mental and sensory faculties via the gigantic network of tentacles, and specialized probes that allow me to connect with the essence of my spirit, and the world in which I exist.

What is most astounding is the manner in which the brain can translate, and encode, the complex contents of the mind, and of that which is derived from the external sensory input, into an electrochemical format that is then relayed to specific interpretative locations within our brain. The only means by which the brain, and its neurological network, can convey, and interpret data from the interior domain of our mind, or from the external environment,is by way of a process of encryption. The brain is not the source of the content s of the mind, nor of the external environment. The composition of these two sources necessitates that it is first translated, and encoded, as units of data within the electrochemical format that comprises the computational neurological modus operandi of our brain and nervous system. This massive array of complex data must then be relayed to specific sites within pre-delegated lobes of the brain so that an interpretative analysis of its content may be performed. Each of these lobes contain highly specialized regions that are custom designed to decode certain types of information depending on their source and content. Within these delegated sites these signals are translated into a related, and functionally active, format that is designed to illicit a specific neurological response. It is the integration of these responses, from their multiple and varied sources, both internal, and external, that provide us with an interpretative, and holistic, composite of our perceptual reality. This decoding system involves a process of decryption, and reconfiguration, into a "user friendly", and interactive mode of identificatiiion, managemennnt, and manipulation.

The 1981 Nobel prize winners, David Hubel and T.N. Wiesel, scientifically demonstrated the manner in which these interpretative and encryption functions apply to the Occipital lobes in regard to visual perception. The neurons within this lobe are inherently configured as a basic visual perceptual template from birth. Visual sensory input within the first two weeks of life is essential to the establishment of the integrative functional networking of these neurons. Inhibition of this optical input,(e.g. by congenital cataracts), during this critical time results in permanent blindness. It also accounts for the phenomenon of induced blindness in one eye,(Amblyopia),that can result from childhood squint. ("Brain and Visual Perception". Pub. Oxford University Press. 2005.).

Furthermore, the volume of traffic that is relayed through any given part of our brain's interconnecting network serves to influence the level of activity within that specific portion of the circuitry and its target destination. That activity is, in turn, repeatedly reciprocated with the mind. It is in such a manner that we may reinforce certain thoughts,(as they are conveyed from our mind), and their related patterns of behavior, so that they become habitual and predictable features of our personality.

We will discuss the details of this entire encoding, and decoding mechanism, in addition to that of *"reciprocity"*, in Chapter 3 when we are dealing with the issue of our thought processes. In Chapter 10 we will address the issue in regard to our personalities. You may now come to understand, within the content of the following chapters, that whenever it appears that I am attributing a mental function to any of the brain's neurological anatomy; it is only intended as a personification of the corresponding aspect of the mind of which it is a biological representation. The mind provides the essential "seed" while the brain serves as the "soil" in which this seed is sown. The harvest will reflect the synergistic interactions of these two vital components. They will do so in terms of specificity, range, quality, and quantity. In effect, the higher brain centres comply with the instructions provided by the mind. The quality of the response will reflect the inherent capacity of any specific brain, or any part thereof, to translate and expedite these commands in the format of neurochemical messages and directives. Under the normal conditions of good health, the brain will respond, for the greater part, to the instructions of our will. It will do so as would a loyal and faithful servant with the single exception of those instances where the will is overridden, or bypassed, by an instinctual reflex, or a repetitiously engraved emotive response. Beyond these willful and voluntary controlled parameters, the brain functions autonomously, as does any other bodily organ, in the completion of its "in house chores". Likewise, the quality of these complex, and autonomic, chores are dependent upon the biological composition and functional integrity of the related nervous tissue. It is only the higher brain centres that are located within the cerebral cortex and neocortex that mirror and reproduce the specialized skills and functions that we associate with human intelligence and creativity. Most of these activities have been identified as been localized to specific anatomical locations within our cerebral cortex. Specific names, which we describe as lobes, have been delegated to each of these regions. They are the Frontal, Parietal, Temporal, and Occipital lobes.

Fig. 6

Lobes of The Brain

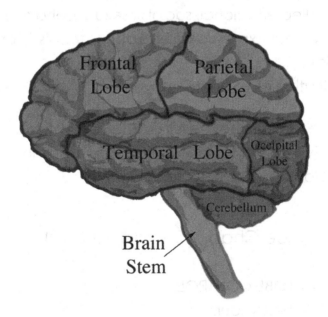

FRONTAL LOBE CONTROL:
Attention: Aware & alert within our environment.

Decision making: Responding to our environment. Motivation.
Judgment, Problem solving, and
Sequencing.
Emotional, social, & sexual control.
Expressive language & meaningful verbal expression.
Motor integration. & Voluntary movement.

FRONTAL LOBE DEFICITS:
Difficulty with attention: Inability to focus on a task.
Loss of spontaneity & flexibility in thinking.
Persistence of a single thought. (Perseveration)
Difficulty with problem solving & sequencing of multi-stepped tasks.
Personality changes Emotionally labile.
Uncontrolled emotional, social & sexual behaviour.
Loss of Verbal Expression (Left Lobe- Broca's Expressive Aphasia)
Poor initiation of Voluntary movements.

Left lobe deficit may result in Rt. Hemispheric Shift & Savant Syndrome. Rt. lobe deficit may result in L. Hemi. Shift & Confabulation Syndrome.

See Chap.8. Sectors (a) & (d).

TEMPORAL LOBE CONTROL:
Aggressive behaviour.
Short–Term Memory & Face recognition. Categorization of Objects. Location of Objects.

Musical Awareness.

Receptive Language & language comprehension.

TEMPORAL LOBE DEFICITS:

Excessive aggression.

Short- Term Memory Loss. Difficulty recognizing faces. Disturbance in selective attention to what is seen or heard. Difficulty identifying, verbalizing & categorizing objects. Difficulty understanding spoken word (Wernicke's Receptive Aphasia)

Persistent Talking

Changes in level of sexual interest

PARIETAL LOBE CONTROLS:

Academic skills.

Awareness of body parts.

Eye- Hand coordination.

Touch perception & Visual attention.

Object naming & manipulation of objects.

Right / Left organization.

PARIETAL LOBE DEFICITS:

Difficulty with academic skills

Lack of awareness of body parts. Impaired Hand-Eye coordination.

Impaired processing of touch senses & poor Visual attention. Difficulty naming objects & problems with reading.

Right / Left confusion.

OCCIPITAL LOBE CONTROLS:

Visual perception

Visual processing

Perception & recognition of printed word.

OCCIPITAL LOBE DEFICITS

Visual field defects.

Difficulty in visually locating objects.

Inability to detect object movement.

Word, visual Pattern, & Colour blindness.

Difficulty reading & writing. Hallucinations & Visual illusions

BRAIN STEM CONTROL

Arousal & Level of Alertness

Sleep regulation

Breathing, Heart rate, &Temperature, Swallowing & Startle reflexes.

Balance & Movement.

BRAIN STEM DEFICITS

Impaired Arousal & Alertness

Poor Sleep regulation (Insomnia & Sleep Apnoea).

Impaired regulation of Breathing, Heart Rate, & Temp.

Difficulty Swallowing impaired Startle reflexes.

Difficulty with balance & Movement.

Dizziness & Nausea (Vertigo).

CEREBELLUM CONTROLS

Coordination of movement & Equilibrium.

Eye Movements.

Balance & Postural control.

CEREBELLAR DEFICITS
Impaired gross & fine motor movements.
Slurred Speech.
Impaired Eye movement.
Loss of ability to Walk.
Tremors & Dizziness.

See Fig.6A & related text Fig.6B which illustrates these lobes of the brain and the related functions / deficits that are ascribed to them. From our particular perspective however, we maintain that these specialized anatomical regions are dependent upon the substrate that is provided by the human mind in order that these instructions may be transcribed, and functionally implemented, by the human organism. In this regard we must maintain a critical level of awareness with regard to the fact that what is conveyed by the mind to the brain may become deeply ingrained over time. Eventually, it may be faithfully, and automatically, reciprocated back to its source upon the slightest prompt. We become skillful at what we practice diligently and repetitively.

What we think, and do, repeatedly is what we in turn become in respect of our personality, attitudes, values, and behaviors. We have all encountered the sinners and the saints in one guise or another throughout the course of our lives. We may have raised-up our voices in condemnation or in praise. But how often have we sought to identify these same traits in some measure within ourselves, be it large or small, or perhaps more subtly expressed within a different context?

We all share in the same propensity to do good or evil. That is the nature of our humanity. To think otherwise is a denial of this fundamental reality.

This reciprocal, continuous, and recurrent feedback, between mind and brain serves to reinforce patterns of thought, feeling, and responses that become embedded in the form of personalized habits or traits that can be stubbornly resistant to change. In effect, what transpires is that the Primacy of the Spirit is delegated to the psyche and its biological counterpart,(the left cerebral hemisphere), so that it progressively acquires a status of functional autonomy that becomes increasingly independent of the human spirit. More often than not, this situation evolves subconsciously, and by stealth, and beyond the conscious surveillance of our intellect. Better to remain constantly vigilant, and to decide in advance what it is that you would wish to become proficient in terms of its genuine use and value and as they pertain to your actions and your deeds.

Try changing the way you walk, talk, laugh, write, or swing a golf club. And what about those things that so frequently, and predictably, press your emotional buttons! These may be the very issues that get you angry and upset, and may make you feel that you are being victimized and hard done by. On the other hand they may be those various forms of self- gratification that become a habitual component within our routine patterns of behavior. Yes, you got the general idea.

So it seems that the otherwise benign appearance of this organ, which we call the brain, can be very deceiving. So have we all come to know, and learn, through our own simple and mundane experiences of everyday life. Perhaps we would be better equipped to deal with the task and the purpose of our lives if we were to better understand what precisely can, and does, go on within the mysterious dynamics of our brain and the connivance of our mind. This is of greatest relevance as it pertains to our very own convenient little partnership of mind and of matter. Within this lump of matter there are billions of brain cells that make up trillions of connections. This maze of connections contributes to an almost infinite range of combinations, permutations and equations. Likewise, they can contribute to the formulation, and the realization of any, or all, of the real, and potential, consequences that result from their interactivity. Any one of us is capable of generating, and of implementing, an infinite spectrum of possibilities and their resultant outcomes. We can select which, if any, we may wish to apply to the fabric of our lives. We can do so from within the hidden and secretive confines of our own hardened, and well protected, craniums. Therein lies the primordial caves and the glowing embers of an awesome, yet potentially mischievous and pernicious, apprentice with unfathomable powers. He is both master and slave of his own destiny. He is a genius and a fool, a giver and a taker, a sinner and a saint. He is everything that he could ever hope to be, yet remains a mere shadow of what he really could be.

(a) EVOLUTION OF THE BRAIN

The brain has been vividly described as a 1.3 kilogram lump of unsightly wrinkled pink jelly. It is composed of a crème caramel - like mixture of fat, protein and water. Now that, by contrast to my initial description, sounds all together far more appealing, even perhaps, more appetizing. It conveys an image of something one might expect to find in the kitchen of some fine restaurant that specializes in rare and exotic delicacies. In fact, it could be a single frame taken from dear mister Hannibal Lecter's tastefully designed kitchen when he is about to prepare a gastronomic delight for some specially selected, highly intelligent, and very discriminating, guests! This delightful delicacy is driven by a myriad of electrical impulses and a host of complex chemicals. These are referred to as neurotransmitters. These are the "messenger chemicals" that convey the encoded information within the axon of the brain cell so that it can be relayed onwards through the complex interconnecting (via synapses) network to its targeted destination.

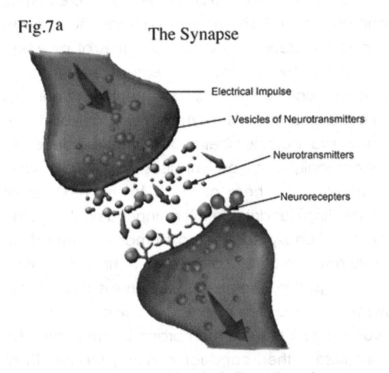

Fig.7a   The Synapse

Electrical Impulse

Vesicles of Neurotransmitters

Neurotransmitters

Neurorecepters

Fig. 7b   Neurone Circuit & Reverberation

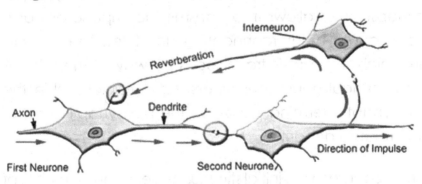

Interneuron

Reverberation

Axon

Dendrite

Direction of Impulse

First Neurone

Second Neurone

The ability of any organism to survive and maintain its internal metabolic equilibrium is largely dependent upon its ability to respond to both internal, and external, environmental stimuli. The ability to detect and respond to these stimuli depends on the activities of networks of nerve cells (neurons) and their related receptor sites. The structural unit of the brain and peripheral nervous system is the neuron. Each of these has a cell body, an axon, and a variable number of dendrites. The dendrites carry electrically charged impulses to the cell, while the axon transmits them onwards to the next set of interconnecting dendrites In this manner a single neuron may be functionally connected to many thousands of other neurons. The electrical impulse within the nerve is created in response to some form of stimulus that induces a movement of positively charged ions (e.g. sodium and potassium) across the cell membrane of the nerve. The nerve impulse is then conducted along the length of the axon to the point at which it reaches the gap (i.e. synapse) that allows it to transmit the impulse onwards to its quota of interconnecting dendrites. The manner in which this gap is traversed is by way of the release of chemical neurotransmitters from vesicles within the presynaptic terminal across to the postsynaptic end of the related dendrite.

The response to the initial stimulus depends on a number of possible variants. These include: the nature, and intensity, of the initial stimulus; the type of initial receptor site; the voltage generated within the nerve impulse; the nature, and quantity, of the neurotransmitter; the type of target receptor site; the configuration of the interconnecting neuronal circuitry; and the nature, and location, of their target destination. The response which is ultimately elicited by the individual will also depend upon a host of variables, inclusive of the historical associations that have become preconditioned in relation to the nature of any given type of stimulus. Within the substance of the brain the response is determined by the specific functional nature of the region, (i.e. the lobe, and the precise location within that lobe), that is its predetermined target destination.

It was a German pharmacologist by the name of Otto Loewi (1873-1961) who confirmed that it was through the release of these chemical transmitters across the synaptic gap that neurons were enabled to communicate with each other. Loewi is credited with discovering acetylcholine, (Ach.), the first of these transmitters. We will come across Ach. and its counterpart neurotransmitters, Adrenaline and Noradrenaline, when we discuss the Autonomic Nervous System in a later chapter. Some of the other more commonly known neurotransmitters include Gama Amino Butyric Acid (GABA), Serotonin, and Dopamine. GABA is the primary modulator of axonal excitability within the brain. It inhibits nerve excitability and is of major importance in the induction of sleep. On the other hand, suppression of GABA activity can result in seizures. We will come across some of these in our future deliberations particularly with regard to stress, anxiety, and depression.

The nervous system essentially functions like a supercomputer, taking in data, integrating it, and responding in some specified and pre-programmed manner. Electrical nerve impulses and their neurotransmitters are no more than charged particles and chemical substances. As with the material components of a computer they are devoid of any inherent properties in relation to intelligence, emotion, creativity, or morality. The responses that are elicited are a feature of the programmed content of the "software" with which they have been provided. The importance, and the relevance, of these facts will progressively emerge within the content of the coming chapters.

We have already described the evolution of the primitive nervous system in relation to the acquisition of Consciousness ("Air of Context". Part 2). We will briefly refer to these events once more, but our major focus of attention will be in respect of the more recent evolutionary history of the modern human brain and its development from infancy to adulthood. As you will recall, our brain evolved over millions of years in several distinct stages:

While jellyfish simply have an undifferentiated network of nerve cells, worms were the most simple of organisms to have a centralized nervous system with a brain represented as a single tiny swelling, and two parallel nerve cords that stretched along the length of its body. Insects were the first to have evolved to the point where the brain was subdivided into three basic segments. It was only when vertebrates emerged some 400 million years ago that the brain had developed as three distinct, and far more complex components, which we still recognize as a hindbrain (with a sprouting cerebellum),a midbrain, and a forebrain.

Fig. 8

The Developement Of The Nervous System

1. The central nervous system developes within the embryo from a simple, and primitive, tube of Ectoderm. The cells lining this tube become the nervous tissue of the brain and spinal cord. The embryo at 20 days gestation with midline depression (Neural groove) which will become the future central nervous system.

Three distinct swellings appear along the length of the tube as the innerlining of cells enlarge in number, size, and complexity. These are called the Fore, Mid, and Hind brain.

2. At 28 days gestation the forebrain has evolved cerebral hemispheres as a single midline structure called the Procencephalon. Behind it lies the early Diencephalon (in between brain)/ and the Mesencephalon portion of the Midbrain. The Metencephalon lies within the Hindbrain.

3. At 36 days paired cerebral hemispheres, and lateral ventricles have formed. These ventricles, and the central canal of the spinal cord are filled with Cerebro-Spinal Fluid (CSF).

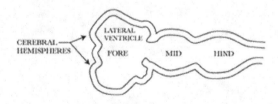

Fig. 9

The Embryonic Brain

4. **Two months gestation:**

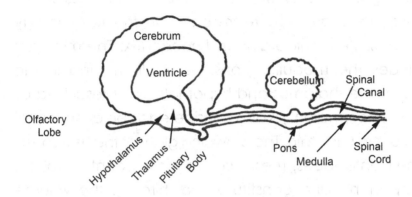

5. **Four months gestation:**

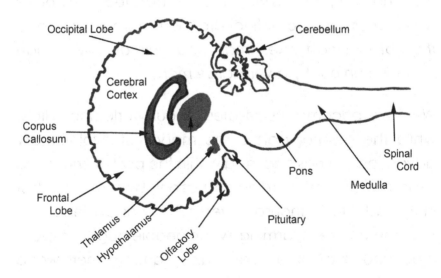

These three basic components were retained with the emergence of mammals but with two new additions:

The new cerebellum and the new cortex (neocortex) which grew out of the forebrain; as primates these components are now represented in the terminology of a brainstem, midbrain, and neocortex. The midbrain includes the medulla, pons, cerebellum, and limbic system. The thalamus and hypothalamus (described as the "*diencephalon*") is also considered to be a functional part of the midbrain. The crowning glory of the neocortex is the Frontal lobes. These are the most recently evolved components and constitute two thirds of the volume of our neocortical cerebral hemispheres. The extent to which this neocortical region grew, and developed in size, and complexity is what really separated the species of primates into two distinct groups: *The smart ones and the not so smart ones, man and animal. The human species won out by a very large margin.*

We have become the masters of our world. Incredibly, while the greater part of his marvel of evolutionary advancement has occurred within the past 35 thousand years, the more critical element has only become manifest in the last 5 to 10 thousand years. This was evidenced in the emergence of farming, when people began to plant crops and raise domestic animals. In tandem, there was a dramatic change in human behavior as reflected within the application of human intelligence. At no previous point in the history of evolution has there been such an escalation in awareness of the magnitude, scope and depth of our entire human potential. Mankind has had a greater impact upon his entire earthly environment within this brief timeframe, than had occurred in the preceding 3.8 billion years of the evolution of life upon this planet. It will be proposed that this great surge within the complexity of the human brain was instigated in response to the progressive acquisition of the facility of consciousness. This relatively recent, and significant, spiritual, and neurological, advancement would only occur within the preselected species that was to emerge as that which was uniquely human. All of these events, as they occurred within the historical timeframes of evolution, would suggest that the more relevant aspects of our evolutionary incubation as a distinctive, spiritual, and intelligent, human species on this planet earth have only just begun.

We are Homo Sapiens- sapiens, still in the process of our becoming whole and complete within the fullness of our human potential. Yet, where there are masters, there are slaves, even within the same subset, if not in fact within the one entity. There are times where the "sapiens" classification is far from obvious. It gives us all good reason to pause and wonder. Just how wisely and appropriately, have we put this great evolutionary advantage into effect for our individual and collective good and benefit? And if the existing pattern, and application, of our intellectual abilities towards life, and our universe, should continue unabated, what will the future hold for the generations yet to come?

The major evolutionary components evident within the anatomical structure of our present day brain are clearly represented in the embryonic configuration of the modern human brain. This mass of neurological tissue, which arises from a single midline structure called the "*prosencephalon*", has several distinct components that give rise to the more specialized versions of the brain as it appears at full term gestation in infancy. These embryonic regions are designated by their Latin terms as mylencephalon, metencephalon, and mesencephalon (brain stem elements); diencephalon (thalamus and hypothalamus); and telecephalon (cerebral cortex and basal ganglia). With foetal development the rudimentary midline structure differentiates, with the hemispheres being deeply divided and connected only by a wedge of tissue called the corpus callosum. The paradoxical fact concerning the functional activity of the corpus callosum is that while it facilitates the exchange of information between both cerebral hemispheres, it is also of critical importance to the independent functioning of each hemisphere. In infancy and up to preadolescence, the corpus callosum is essentially inert so that the cerebral hemispheres cannot function independently to any significant extent. By the same token, within this age group, the children respond as mature split brain subjects have been shown to act. Their right and left hemispheres are unable to share common access, nor exchange information. They may give opposing accounts of events, or contradict themselves in a variety of ways, without having any insight into the paradoxical nature of their perceptions. There is a basic inability to place ideas and thoughts within their relevant, and related, contexts. It is only as they grow into their adolescence, and beyond, that connectivity between the hemispheres becomes progressively established to permit their independent functioning on the one hand, and their cooperative integration and synergy on the other. The relevance and the importance of these facts will become evident as we proceed to describe the functional interrelationships that exist, and are essential, for the normal operative processes of a healthy, well balanced, and mature mind.

BRAIN PLASTICITY, CIRCUIT WIRING, AND LEARNING

The overall trend of cerebral evolution, and of the development of our brain from infancy, is towards that of achieving higher levels of perception and control in relation to our environmental interaction. Our genes have neurologically adapted us, through a process of natural selection, so as to provide for our survival needs and requirements. This is what we mean by "evolutionary adaptation". Yet, we have the additional cerebral capacity to acquire further knowledge, and skills, through the learned experience. The transformation of genetically determined structures and functions to those that can become involved in another, and possibly unrelated function, has been termed "Exaptation" by Stephen J. Gould.

The ability of the brain to modify itself in response to experience, so that memories and learning of new perceptual and motor skills are possible, is called "Plasticity". The general interconnecting template of neurons, and their axons, is genetically determined and controlled so that our motor and sensory nerves can predictably connect to their corresponding target sites for processing within the brain. However, it is the continued fine tuning of our complex neuronal circuitry in response to sensory and perceptual experiences that subsequently establishes the intricate pattern and efficiency of our wired highways and their connecting exchanges.

We are not born into the world with a prefixed "plug and go" brain circuitry. Perhaps even prior to birth this fine tuning in response to sensory and perceptual stimulation is occurring. This occurs through the growth of waves of synapse buds at the terminals of the axons, and the subsequent removal of unnecessary axons and synapses which are not incorporated into that rewired section of the circuitry. It has been aptly described as a process of synaptic "blooming", and "pruning". In this manner highly efficient and selective circuits of neurons that fire together, are wired together to achieve a specific and newly acquired function.

The increase in synaptic density after birth, particularly within the Frontal lobes, reaches its maximum at two years of age. The other components within the cerebral cortex also cease growing about this time so that total brain weight approximates that of the mature adult. Thereafter, synaptic density declines, so that by adolescence it is only 60% of its original maximum. This explains why we are more adaptive to new experiences, knowledge, and skills, within the first few years of life.

It is no coincidence that human beings have effected greater change on earth in the past 10,000 years than all other living things have done in the preceding 3 billion years. It is only within that time frame that consciousness had finally begun to fully engage with the conscious, and cognitive, realms of the human mind. This is the juncture at which human enlightenment was to become manifest through access to the collective unconscious and the Wisdom of the Soul. Such an engagement is mirrored within the biologically explosive growth of the neocortex, and its predominant frontal lobes.

The paradox of man is the paradox of his intellect, and his mind. Who amongst us could rightly claim to be either wise or sane? Who, if anyone, can we trust and to whom precisely should we listen? I hope that the contents of this book will eventually help provide you with a plausible, honest, and truthful, answer. It is my contention that it will prove to be an accessible, personal, and not altogether strange, or unfamiliar, answer. The resolution of our problems will undoubtedly depend on the extent to which each of us engages in a meaningful form of communication with, and remains continually responsive to, that very special source. Perhaps some of the answers lie within the extent to which there is cooperation or conflict, synergy or discord, within the content of the brain, and within the realm of the human mind. Why is there such a degree of polarization? How can we account for this, apparently counter-productive anomaly? Can it be addressed, and if so, how can we appropriatly address it in our own individual interests and those of our fellow man?

(b) THE BIPOLAR BRAIN

In order to try and explain or understand anything with respect to the factors that underlie the nature of the polarity that exists within the mind of man, it is useful to try and comprehend those that pertain to the anatomical and functional configuration of the brain. The essential clues lie within the ancient separation, and subsequent asymmetrical enlargement, of the two cerebral hemispheres. Further clues are evident within the more recent, dramatic, and explosive growth in the frontal lobes. It is the latter that is distinctly unique to the modern species of mankind as we now know and recognize it. The fundamental relevance regarding the fact that our brain, or cognitive portion of it, is separated into a right and a left cerebral hemisphere is critical to our understanding of the matter.

We have long been aware that from a motor and sensory perspective each hemisphere is representative of the opposite side of the body. That is to say that our muscular movements and sensations (touch, pain, vibration, and temperature) on one side of the body are controlled by the opposite side of our brain. This is simply due to the fact that the nervous tracts that convey the relevant messages regarding these functions down from the cerebral cortex cross over to the opposite side at a specific location within the midbrain. From there the tracts eventually emerge as bundles of nerves that supply that side of both the body and the corresponding arm and leg. It is also an established fact that while both hemispheres play important roles with regard to language and images, that they do so in quite different ways. The left hemisphere appears to have the greater "say" when it comes to handling words and speech while the right side appears to be better equipped to handle visual images. In many respects this greater role delegation that we tend to apply is more apparent than it is precisely accurate. However, much of this anatomical and functional information is anecdotal from our particular point of view and with regards to what, and where precisely, we plan to focus our attention. Suffice it to say, that both our cerebral hemispheres contribute in some, yet invariably different, ways to all of the highly specialized functions that occur within the entirety of our brain.

Within the following description, the functional dynamics of the brain are personified as the agent of the mind. As you are by now aware, this is because the mind has, for the greater part, direct primacy over the activities of the biological brain. From our perspective, it is the fact that each hemisphere presents us with a different version of reality that is of major relevance. Each hemisphere, by virtue of its functional and structural difference, has its own unique way of providing us with its own particular version of the experience that we encounter and apply to our world. It is the extent to which these two realities are integrated, and shared, that determines the perceptual paradigm that we create of ourselves, and the world, as we exist, and interact with, and within, it. Furthermore, there are a host of variables within each of the two cerebral systems that influence the degree, to which their individual versions either collaborate, or contest and conflict, with each other. This is what defines the precise shape and configuration of the unified and synergistic whole that we interpret as representative of the facts, and the truths, that constitute our reality.

We are all too aware that there are significant conflicts at work within the dynamics of this interaction. They vary in their degree and intensity depending on the nature and relevance of the issue at any given moment. There are often hostile, deterministic, and pragmatic factors at work. Indeed it is frequently unclear to our conscious mind what the agenda, the hidden motives, and the strategy, might be for such persuasive, or abjectly hostile stances. These are the kind of obstacles that can potentially threaten the collective, and reconciliatory, effort to formulate a synergistic whole.

At one time or another we all experience such moments, when we are surprised at the nature and intensity of our responses to certain individuals, or circumstances that arise within the content of our routine interactions.

We might pause and wonder as to what came over us, and perhaps even apologize for our unscripted, and intemperate, out- burst. It is precisely for these very reasons that these two opposing forces need to be kept apart at the interface that precedes the path towards resolution. The cerebral hemispheres are like sibling rivals that cannot be left together in the same room for any length of time, or all hell will surely break loose. However, there is a point where the family's agenda cannot proceed without having the rivals come to terms and settle their differences and disputes. Then they can contribute as a collaborative pair to the essential household activities and domestic chores.

This meeting of minds comes about within the brain through the interconnected pathways that are contained within the corpus callosum. This is the wedge of tissue that anatomically connects the hemispheres at the midline within our skull. The importance of these connections has far more to do with how they function as distinct from the complexity, and the density, of their nervous wiring across this chiasm. This region of the brain exerts its influence mostly by way of either facilitating or, more importantly, by inhibiting the transfer, and exchange of information that occurs between the two hemispheres at this particular site. We will revert to this aspect of our considerations when we are discussing the role that the frontal lobes play in helping us to formulate a strategy, or mandate, that can be applied within the framework of the contributions that each of the hemispheres make to the synergistic version of our reality.

How can we account for this disparity in the two perceptual versions of our reality? It has been suggested that it is due to the fundamental difference in the type of attention, or the disposition, which each hemisphere gives to the world and to those with whom we are obliged to share it. It is primarily the function of the frontal lobe region of our cerebral hemispheres that influences the type of attention we pay to the world that we engage in with our minds. The attention of the left hemisphere could be described as "up close and personal". It is a tight focus, shallow depth of field, and a high resolution frame. The attention of the right hemisphere, by contrast, is more "distant and discrete". It is global in its nature, with a wider focus, greater depth of field, and a more panoramic type of frame. This right hemispheric view has both distance and elevation. It encompasses the full field of vision, and does so with an excellent perspective of the subject matter. This is what provides us with the facility of objectivity and insight. It also provides us with the "head space" that is required so that we can stand back, and view each situation from a safe distance. It gives us the opportunity to consider a variety of options, and a range of alternative choices and responses to any given issue. This allows us to be flexible, engage in frame shifts, and apply a field of creativity to our thought processes. Most importantly, it facilitates the application of sound judgment, which is enriched within a metaphorical milieu, and which, in turn, first permeates and diffuses into our right cerebral hemispheres. It is this objective form of judgment, and its attendant implications, inclusive of any moral dimension, that is indispensably relevant to our behavior and our deeds. In terms of truth, it may be said that objectivity is a relative term, as is truth itself. The validity of any truth is dependent upon the validity and the accuracy of the interpretation applied to the metaphor upon which that facet of truth is based.

The left hemisphere is more preoccupied with fine detail, and separate pieces of information that can be viewed in isolation. By contrast, the right side is more concerned with the entire subject matter as a whole. Its role is to convey an experience within a given context and a specific setting of time and place.

On the one hand (left hemisphere)there is a need for the closed, or narrowly focused attention that provides precision and detail .On the other hand (right hemisphere) there is a need for the open, broad based, and more inclusive type of attention. The essential function and task of the brain is to forge a connection between ourselves and the outside world, inclusive of others, who are out there, and with whom we need, and desire, to interact. So, different elements and experiences of the world, and those with whom we share it, are incorporated into our perception of our reality through the interaction of our brain with what exists "out there", beyond ourselves.

The essential point is this: it is the nature of our attention that determines what precisely it is that contributes to our perception of the reality of what it is that exists within the world, and what exists beyond the confines of our individual selves. Consequently, we can appreciate that we engage within an activity that is comprised of two distinctly different types of exercise. When the outcomes are merged into some unified entity, they complement each other, so as to contribute to the totality of our perceived reality. Each of these exercises is delegated to separate hemispheres. By extrapolation, they are designed to address two different sets of needs. With regard to the left hemisphere, the agenda has everything to do with "me" and "my" needs. The right hemisphere is more concerned with me within the bigger picture, and in the context of the world at large, including others. Thus, there exists not only a conflict of needs, but a difference in the priority, and the values, that determine, and define, the precise content of this duality of needs.

All thoughts and ideas, first germinate as basic metaphorical concepts within the unlived memory of our subconscious minds (i.e. the collective unconscious). Since these precognitive precursors of thought are fundamentally intuitive and universal would indicate that they are derived from an authentic representation of our human nature. That is to say that all our concepts are initially conceived within the medium, of our spiritual mind set, or subconscious soul. These conceptual precursors are then "imported" from the soul to permeate the psyche.

This process is reflected at a neurological level by the primacy of the right cerebral hemisphere which presents and underwrites the primary content of the knowledge that is subsequently acquired, analyzed, and processed, by the left hemisphere. This initial intuitive wisdom is archetypical in the sense that it is a common prototype that is potentially available to all mankind.

Just as one may consider all human life to be sacred, so also might we consider all concepts, since they are derived from the soul, to be inherently sacred. There is a tendency to only consider those concepts and ideas that can be placed within an exclusively spiritual or religious context to be sacred and have a moral value. Yet, it is apparent that all activity, be it cerebral, emotional, or physical in its nature, provides us with opportunity to strive towards the ideal that optimally reflects a valid rendition and expression of our authentic human nature. It is from that authentic nature, which is mirrored by the soul of man, that our concepts are initially derived. In this context every human endeavor, no matter how mundane it may appear to be, has a spiritual dimension. Saint Therese of Lisieux (1875 – 1897) provides us with a perfect example of this concept as applied to the most mundane and menial of tasks of daily life. When asked shortly before her death what was the "Little Way" she was so eager to teach others, she replied that it was the way of "spiritual childhood, the way of trust and absolute surrender". She would offer every little chore, the irritations and frustrations, every word or glance, to

177

her Lord as "flowers of little sacrifices". She believed such a disposition was the means of our gaining access to the Kingdom of Heaven.

The left cerebral hemisphere simply renders the implicit explicit so that it may become the object of our will. In this manner we can exercise our judgment and our freedom of choice. What is of critical importance is that it is the right hemisphere that underwrites the knowledge that the left hemisphere formulates and that the primary source of all human conceptualization is derived from the realm of the spirit within the mind of man. It is only the right hemisphere that is able to synthesize the contributions made by both hemispheres into a functional and comprehensive whole. It is the degree of disparity, and the nature and extent to which the left cerebral hemisphere reconfigures the primary content of the right hemisphere that is of vital importance. It is within this context that the functioning of the frontal lobes plays a pivotal role. The frontal lobes, as you can now appreciate, provide us with the crucial facility of objectivity. It is this specific facility, and all that it entails, particularly with regard to the assimilation of metaphor within a milieu of cognitive fluidity, that ultimately defines humanity from all other primates. So, what is the reason for this dual presentation of reality and in what ways are they so diverse?

(c) DUAL REALITIES AND DUAL AGENDAS

Let us recapitulate and further expand on the essential features that clearly differentiate the functional aspect of both cerebral hemispheres, and their implications with regard to our perspective on life and how we relate to it.

The left hemisphere considers the world in mechanistic terms as the sum of its parts. As you know it does this as the biological emissary of the psyche – ego mind .It demands and insists on certainty, familiarity, isolation, and fixation.Its fundamental task is to bring things into focus, to render what is implicitly vague to a level of explicit clarity so that it can become the object of our will. This is the reason why it must restrain and dismantle them, ascertain their component parts, and extract whatever information can be yielded up. The products can then be formulated into language and applied to a specific task. It needs to draw the world into the immediate proximity of its grasp. It is within that lair that it can be controlled, dismembered, and manipulated to the extent that it becomes the object of our will. In effect, the left hemisphere reduces everything within its controlling grasp to mere subordination so that it can be reconfigured for its own selfish purposes. It is clinically precise, surgically detached, obsessive – compulsive in its branding and categorization, and ego centric in the extreme. It only engages in doing more of what it is already doing since it is totally reliant on the right hemisphere for its raw material. The left hemisphere is convinced of its own correctness, self- righteousness, intelligence, and authority. It is above criticism, fault, or blame, blatant denial being its specialty. It is totally oblivious to its limitations and dependency on its right cerebral counterpart. Above all, it is devoid of self- awareness, morality, justice, and empathy. Within this realm we are at the mercy of the machine, its authoritarian bureaucracy, its pride, and its selfish aspirations.

The right cerebral hemisphere,(as cerebral correlate to the soul), in stark contrast, functions in relation to all that is implicitly felt as an intuitive, unqualified, and unspoken experience. It considers the world as a living and interconnected whole so as to provide us with a disposition of empathy and compassion towards all that is "other", and beyond self. It is both, self- aware and cognizant, of others. The attention it pays to the world is broad and vigilant rather than narrowly focused. It readily acknowledges the flux, fluidity, uncertainty, and ambiguity of this ever changing and vibrant domain. The right prefrontal cortex is particularly important to our sense of justice, self- control, and morality. The right hemisphere is aware of its limitations, is able to espouse another view point, and remains reliably, yet perhaps cautiously, realistic. Most importantly, the right cerebral hemisphere has Primacy with regard to what is implicit in the context of metaphor and to what is experienced, and known, in the context of the acquisition of knowledge. It is where primordial emotions are grounded, depth of perception and affect are integrated within its fundamental matrix so as to provide us with a holistic, and caring, disposition towards all things within our world.

The right hemisphere is also closely aligned with the unconscious mind. Since over 95 - 99 % of all brain activity occurs within the realm of the unconscious this is of major significance. Most of what transpires within the apparently spontaneous context of social rapport occurs at the unconscious level. We process preconscious material to make judgments, discriminate, reason, solve problems, and experience feelings, outside of the left hemispheric focus of attention and conscious awareness. Given the gross disparity of the functional roles of both hemispheres, it is abundantly clear that in the absence of the contribution of our left hemisphere, while we would witness a holistic, living, and compassionate experience of our world, very little would ever be accomplished or come to fruition. There would be no art, science, or religion. Likewise, in the absence of our right hemispheric contribution to the workings of the left hemisphere, our reality would be denatured, disembodied from the living world of fellow feeling, and reduced to a mechanical, utilitarian, and virtual existence.

The right hemisphere needs the left to unpack the contents of experience. The left hemisphere in turn, depends upon the right so that these constituent pieces can be reintegrated into life. In that way it can live again, reincarnated and expressed as a newly created form, within the context of life. This critical process of retrieval must be performed under very specific conditions in order to create an environment that can contribute towards an appropriately balanced and harmonious reintegration of both hemispheres contributions. The goal is to create something that is acceptable, and of value, to the whole. Both the corpus callosum and the frontal lobes play significant roles in this regard.

The corpus callosum acts as a pre-editorial filter on the transmission between hemispheres. It serves an important function in shaping the content as it presented, particularly by the left hemisphere, and does so predominantly through an inhibitory mechanism. The frontal lobes also exhibit an inhibitory effect in order to prevent an inappropriate response while they also provide a critical lag- phase of objectivity. What is returned by the left hemisphere, and retrieved by the right, contributes to the reformed and unified entity. This integration of both hemispheric versions of the world is what contributes to the processes of imagination and creativity. These are the specific qualities that define the triumphs and the measure of the human spirit.

The nature of the tasks that are allocated to each hemisphere are so radically different because they are representative of responses to different sets of values, priorities, and needs. It is hardly any wonder that they are best addressed within individually separate, private, and conflict- free zones. The right hemisphere is the indirect primary inspirational author. The left is the clever logical mechanic with the essential tools. The author must surrender his fundamental wisdom and talents, and entrust them to the task master with humility and hope. That hope is that they will be returned inherently intact, true to their intended design, and purpose, and clearly embellished and configured for their appropriate application to the living world. So, it is quite clear that we require the contributions of both hemispheres to create an integrated, functionally effective, just and compassionate, composite of reality in which we can live and contribute to the world within the experience of our lives. It is also evident that the greater the degree of disparity, (and by extension of conflict), that exists between each hemisphere's effort and contribution, the greater the potential outcome of their synthesis. However, that greater potential is only realistically possible where there is reconciliation of needs and priorities to the extent that it is conducive to cooperative harmony and can lead to the realization of a higher order. Thus, a new and elevated unity can emerge through this joint collaboration of effort.

(d) THE SHAPE AND PATHS OF MIND AND SPIRIT

If you plot the course of these conceptualizing processes you will appreciate that they are not only circular but, more correctly, move within a figure of eight pattern. This neurological pathway is illustrated in the first page of Chapter Three (Figure 11).

Since precognition begins at a subconscious level the process must be initiated primarily in the region of the right prefrontal lobe. It then moves from the right hemisphere across the corpus callosum to the left cerebral hemisphere. Then the process loops back again, via the corpus callosum and frontal lobes, to the right hemisphere. We can take it that the fundamental movement of the mind occurs in a similar pattern: *From soul, across the portal gateway, to the psyche, and returning to be integrated into our lives as thoughts, words, and deeds.*

The manner by which the brain and mind interact, and reciprocate, contribute to each other's functional "networking", and reflect the manner in which they contribute to the totality of our perceived reality, provides us with a clue regarding the workings of the Spiritual Self. Thoughts that originate from preformed allegorical / metaphorical concepts do not arise from some primary antecedent nothingness. The metaphorical content of concepts must be derived from a source of raw material. This primary "seed", or "first principle", is sown within the spiritual mind of all mankind. It is imported, via the collective unconscious, to enter our biological brain within the right cerebral hemisphere. Its transfer, across the corpus callosum, to the left hemisphere is mirrored by its transport through the Gateway of the Soul into the psyche. Its representation and integration into the right hemisphere to render it meaningful to life as a new entity is analogous to the sowing of the seed, and the fruits of that seed within the context of our lives.

That process is well illustrated within the parable of the seed and the soil:

Mat. 13: 1-9, 18-23.

The surrendering by the right hemisphere, (and Soul), of the fundamental intuitive knowledge, and the wisdom contained therein, to the left hemisphere, (and Psyche), represents the scattering of the seed and the hope that it will fall on good soil rather than on rocks.

The freedom and independence which can be affected by the left hemisphere (and Psyche) in the processing of this seed, and its contribution towards the fruit of our imaginative creativity, is analogous to the parable of the wheat and the weeds:

Mat. 13: 24 – 30, 36-43.

We have the freedom to choose, to toil and nurture the primary seed so that it will yield a fruitful harvest, or yield only weeds that will be discarded at the harvest. Furthermore, we can prepare the soil, the configuration of our intellect and of our psyche, by striving to identify, and incorporate, the primary metaphorical wisdom contained within what we may refer to as sources of Divine Revelation.

CHAPTER THREE: MODULE OF COGNITIVE THOUGHT PROCESS

LOCATION	ACTIVITY	FACILITY

1. TRANSCENDENTAL / **SPIRIT**

"Wisdom of the Spirit":   Consciousness.

The Primary substrate & source (i.e. First principle) Intuitive wisdom of being / Authentic self.

2. **MIND** / SUBCONSCIOUS, FACILITY OF THE SOUL:

"Wisdom of the Soul":

: "First Principles" derived from the "unlived memory".

Archetypes within the Collective Unconscious.

The Primary metaphor derived from" Unlived memory".

3. **BRAIN (RIGHT HEMISPHERE)** RECIPROCITY:

The Primary metaphor as Archetypical Imagery.

Intuitive conscious awareness of   KNOWER.
self & other.
Implicit belief ; human intuition ; faith.
             First Moral Principle

4. **BRAIN (LEFT HEMISPHERE)** – MIND (PSYCHE) **RECIPROCITY**

GRASPED. ANALYSED & CATEGORIZED.

CROSS-REFERENCED WITH CATEGORIES WITHIN "LIVING MEMORY".

PROPOSITION.

INTELLECTUAL COGNITIVE AWARENESS.

LINGUISTIC PROCESSING (WERNICKE'S & BROCA'S AREAS).

SECONDARY METAPHOR.

Explicit proposition.

5. MIND (SOUL) - **BRAIN (RIGHT HEMISPHERE) RECIPROCITY & SYNERGY:**

REPRESENTED ACROSS CORPUS CALLOSUM .
"YES" OR "NOT YES" EDITING BY CORPUS CALLOSUM.
SECONDARY METAPHOR CONTEXTUALIZED WITHIN CONTEXT OF PRIMARY METAPHOR.

RECONCILIATION & SYNERGY
EXPLICIT FACT   KNOWN.
First logic principle

6. LIFE CONTEXT.

THE APPLICATION & EXPRESSION OF FACT IN RELATED & BROADER CONTEXT
PERCEPTION OF REALITY.EXPRESSED AS TERTIARY METAPHORS. LANGUAGE.

Fig. 11 Horizontal Section Through Brain
Module of Thought (Cognition) Process

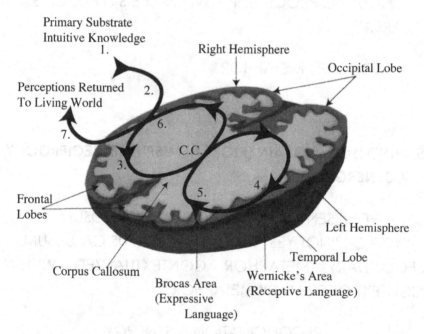

1. Wisdom of The Spirit / Primary Substrate
2. Collective Unconscious
3. Right Prefrontal Cortex
C.C.   Corpus Callosum
4. Left Temporal Lobe & Wernicke's Area (Receptive Language)
5. Left Frontal Lobe & Brocca's Area (Expressive Language)
C.C. Corpus Collosum
6. Right Prefrontal Lobe
7. Expression of Concept Within Context of Life

The schematic flow chart (Fig.10 "Module of Thought Process") provides a brief summary of the manner and means by which we acquire intuitive knowledge, and formulate concepts in regard to intellectual knowledge.

Both of the paths to the acquisition of these distinct forms of knowledge are in fact mind- brain processes. (The visual content of Figure 11 pertains only to the neurological pathway). Each pathway requires that contributions are made from a combination of different aspects of our mind, and of our brain. In the instance of the acquisition of intuitive knowledge this necessitates engagement of the soul and the right cerebral hemisphere. The left cerebral hemisphere and the psyche are the two additional participants involved in the formulation of conceptual knowledge.

1. The process is initiated by the provision of a primary substrate to our soul through the agency of our consciousness. This substrate is derived from the essence of our Spirit as initially provided by the Holy Spirit. We describe this substrate as the "Wisdom of the Spirit". Within our soul we now refer to the content of this primary substrate as "Wisdom of the Soul".

2. Within the subconscious realm of our soul this Wisdom of the Soul presents as metaphysical units within an unending stream of "first principles". These are archived and released in a continuous stream of "unlived memories" within that domain

of our subconscious mind which we refer to as our "collective unconscious."

3. The content of the collective unconscious is presented to the Right Cerebral Hemisphere in the location of our Right frontal lobe. At that location the "first principles" are neurologically categorized into types These are what we refer to as "Archetypes". Within this process they are rendered within the format of symbolic imagery to which we can cognitively relate. We refer to these as Primary metaphors. These provide us with a conscious awareness of what is inherently valid and authentic. Acknowledgement, and trust within the implicit content of their validity is what constitutes intuitive belief. This is what we more commonly refer to as "spiritual enlightenment", "human intuition", or simply "faith".

Within another context this consciously apprehended intuitive awareness is what we frequently describe as the "creative spirit" of what is ultimately expressed within the intellectual, or artistic, content of our inspirational endeavors. Moreover, we may also consider these preliminary insights as constituting the fundamentals upon which our "first moral principles" are based.

4. These Primary metaphors are transferred across the Corpus Callosum to be presented to the Left cerebral Hemisphere. Therein the categorized

content is analysed as individual units. These are cross referenced with the content of categories that reside within the subconscious "living memory" of our psyche. In this manner they are formulated as conceptual propositions which we term Secondary metaphors. These may be processed within Wernicke's area of the temporal lobe, and that of Broca's area within the frontal temporal region of the brain. Processing within these areas provide a neurological format that can be linguistically apprehended and verbally expressed.

5. These Secondary metaphors are represented back across the Corpus Callosum to the Right Cerebral Hemisphere. In so doing, the content is edited within the corpus callosum within a facilitative, or inhibitory manner which we have referred to as a "Yes, or not yes" binary format. This mechanism is representative of a specific aspect of a quality control system in respect of the neurological formulation, and construction, of the conceptual content of the Secondary metaphor. Evidently some particular criteria of acceptance must be satisfied prior to the transmission of this data back to the original domain of the Right Cerebral Hemisphere.

The mental correlate of this audit mechanism is what contributes to the application of our judgment, as a facet of our "conscience", in regard to the content of our Secondary metaphors. The content of the Secondary metaphor, as representative of the intellectually integrated and conceptualized version of the primary substrate, must undergo a process of synergy and contextualization. This reconciliatory process occurs within the region of the Right frontal lobe.

A further, and final, audit process in regard to the propositional content, as is now presented to the right frontal lobe, is an inherent feature of this synergistic process. As we noted in Chapter 2, in regard to the functions of each brain lobe, the Frontal lobe exercises control over our judgment and decision making, in addition to that of our emotional, social, and sexual control (Fig 6 in text). Once again, this feature is also represented within the mental jurisdiction of the soul as a moral conscience.

This synergy of effort, and contextualization, provides a source of knowledge, which we now refer to as "known facts". These are what constitute our "first logic principles".

6. These facts may then be integrated within the content of related, and preexisting concepts, and within the broader context. This is what contributes to the fundamental composition of our perceptions in regard to the nature of our reality. It also provides a means, and a mechanism, by which this knowledge may be expressed as Tertiary metaphors within the context of the living world.

It is evident from the configuration of the module of thought, as presented, that if the content of the Primary metaphor is altered, modified, or disregarded in any manner, that the content of the intellectual proposition that is represented to the Right hemisphere will be inherently misrepresented. It would be a distortion or corruption in respect of its original, and intended, interpretation and expression.

Any reluctance, or refusal, to submit one's trust to the validity of the Primary metaphor is seen as an exercise wherein the precedence of the Spirit is subjugated to pride of intellect and of reason. What is finally acknowledged to be factual and authentic is what ultimately determines the configuration of our paradigm. This in turn is what is reflected in our attitudes and behavior in regard to ourselves, our fellow man, and the world in which we live.

It is proposed that the authenticity of our concepts, and of our perception of reality, is a measure of the extent to which they are in compliance with the spiritual content, and "first principles", of our Primary metaphors.

CHAP 3B. THE PIXEL THEORY OF THOUGHT & PERCEPTION & THE EVENT OF THE INITIAL PRIMARY METAPHORICAL INFUSION

Most of us have some idea as to the optical principles that apply to our ability to see (i.e. visual perception). Photons of light are focused upon our retina which is composed of light sensitive cells called rods and cones. The human eye contains about 125 million rods and 6.5 million cones.

Rods function best in dim light, and are not sensitive to colour. They help us to detect shape, and movement. Cones respond to light at higher levels of intensity, allowing us to see fine detail, and are responsible for colour vision. There are three types of cones, each named after the wavelengths to which they are most sensitive. They are described as blue, green, and red cones as these are the three main types of rhodopsin- related photo-pigment which they contain. Light induces a chemical change within these pigments which activates nerve impulses that are subsequently transmitted via our optic nerves to our primary visual cortex in the brain. The rods and cones synapse with a number of different types of neurons that receive and transmit different aspects of the visual stimulus along the length of the optic nerve.

Axons of the optic nerve end in the lateral geniculate nuclei of the thalamus. These thalamic nuclei, together with neurons of the Reticular Activating System, control which information is sent to the primary visual cortex within our Occipital lobes. This information is relayed to other areas of the cortex for further detailed integration, and processing.

From a functional perspective, the human eye is described as a "complex" eye of the camera variety which is common to all vertebrates.The content of the retinal image, as it first appears within the eye, is relayed through this photoreceptor system of interconnected nerves within the fundamental electrochemical format that pertains to all nerve conduction. In all probability this format also involves a system that is comparable to that of computer graphics and the digital camera. This mode of image reproduction involves the encoding, and transfer of individual units of graphic information within the format of picture elements, or "pixels". The reintegration of these pixels reproduces the composite of the original image.

Computer graphics are commonly used in the media (e.g. television, films, weather reports), and in business and financial graphs and related visual data. They are also widely used a in a variety of medical and surgical types of equipment. Computer science studies methods of digitally synthetizing and manipulating visual content. One of the first computer systems to advance man-machine interfaces in interactive graphics was developed in 1959 at M.I.T. This involved the use of a light pen with a tiny photo-electric cell at its tip. This cell emitted electrical impulses when it was placed in front of a computer screen and the screen's electron gun fired directly at it. By timing the electronic pulse with the precise location of the electron gun it became possible to pinpoint the exact location of pen on the screen. The computer could then draw a cursor at that location so as to generate a visual rendition of the image as inscribed by the pen. Since then far more powerful tools have been developed to visualize data. These include two dimensional, three dimensional, and animated graphics.

A pixel is a single sample point of an original image. These are usually represented on a two dimensional grid using dots or squares. The intensity of each pixel is variable and is reproduced in colour using the same three components, (i.e. red, green, and blue), as do the photo sensitive cones in the eye. However, a highly complex system, analogous to that used in the generation of computer vision, would be required to reproduce all of the elements that are an integral feature of our visual perception. These would include shape, texture, three dimensional depth of field, and motion. Such a system of image reproduction was developed by David Lowe at the University of British Columbia (1999-2004). Technically it is described as the Scale Invariant Feature Transform, or .S.I.F.T. Basically it is a means of matching key points within any cluster of visual material with those of a preestablished data base. In Chapter Two we made reference to the critical role which Hubel and Wiesel described in regard to the inherent ability of neurons within the visual cortex to encode and interpret our optical input data. However, this input data must be presented to the visual cortex within the first few weeks of infancy . This ensures the procurement of the critical data base of primary optical elements and the source of reference material upon which the visual cortical neurons are ultimately dependent.

There is every probability that a similar process is applicable to the manner in which mental imagery, and archetypical symbols, are constructed and conveyed within the substance of the brain. This provides us with a means by which we can identify, interpret, and relate, to the content of our Primary, and Secondary metaphors.

Ii is quite likely that you may have heard someone say to another person to "connect the dots" so as to provide the answer to some query, or question. What they are saying is, by our having recourse to some key elements of data, we are provided with a means towards their being analyzed, and converted, into essential pieces of information. This can then be assimilated so as to generate knowledge. Perhaps it is curious that we may also refer to someone who finds difficulty in the completion of this intellectual task, as "going dotty". Evidently, they are unable to analyze, and categorize, the haze of dots within which the key content of their substrate has been encoded. This is because their Left cerebral hemisphere has been compromised in some fashion (e.g. congenital, traumatic, or acquired process). Some of the more common examples in which this may arise in otherwise healthy individuals would be in a case of fatigue, a hangover, a slow learner, attention deficit disorders, (ADD/ADHD), or Savant syndrome, and pre-senile dementia. However, it may also be the consequence of one's refusal, or inability, to acknowledge the primacy, and authenticity, of the substrate of their Primary metaphors. They cannot see the picture for the pixels.

The facility of consciousness conveys a constant stream of primary substrate to the collective unconscious as a means of animating, and empowering the human mind, and of our acquisition of enlightenment in regard to authentic knowledge. In order that we may apprehend this authentic Wisdom within our mind, it must be reformatted, within a symbolic form of imagery, or Primary metaphor. This is necessitated owing to the fact that we must retain the freedom of choice as to the manner, and extent, that we may choose to incorporate the content of this Wisdom within the construct of our own Secondary metaphorical concepts. It is also an inevitable consequence of the fact that the content of what is being conveyed has yet to be "transcribed" within the construct of a human concept. In this sense it is pre-conceptual, implicit, and intuitive. That is to say that the Wisdom of the Spirit, as key elements of data, cannot be conveyed directly within the explicit format of information. It is our job, and our responsibility, to decide upon the precise manner, and the means, by which this process of transcription, and conceptual reconfiguration, is to be performed.

Precisely how we construct the content of our concepts is very much dependent upon the nature of the Secondary metaphorical concepts which we have pre-configured, and allocated to memory in the past. It is from these Secondary metaphors that we must selectively retrieve suitable allegories in order to formulate our current concepts and our thoughts. Besides, we are not slaves, or robots, who are pre-programmed to automatically respond to the intonations of the Spirit within a fixed manner, and in the absence of free will. However, it is appropriate that we are provided with guidance, and direction, so as to assist us in our discernment as to what is authentic, relevant, and appropriate to our needs and purposes as human beings. Such essential guidance is provided by the provision of the content of the Wisdom of the Spirit through the agency of consciousness.

Reciprocation of the mental content of this wisdom and guidance, as represented by the Wisdom of the Soul, with the neurochemistry of our brain necessitates that it is transmuted into units within which the modus operandi of our brain functions. All sensory,(and motor), information that is transmitted within the network of nerve axons, and conveyed to their specified target regions within the various lobes, depends upon the transmission of an electrical impulse within each nerve fibre. These impulses must be relayed onwards within the interconnecting synapse that can convey the impulses to their target destinations. Selectivity of the nature, and content, of this data is probably a function of the specific type of neurotransmitter that transfers the data across these synapses. This data must then be retranslated into an information format that can be read, and encrypted, within their delegated cerebral locations.

It is proposed that in the instance of the cerebral correlate of the content of our collective unconscious that this encryption task is performed within the location of the Right prefrontal lobe, and within a binary mode analogous to that of a super computer system. Furthermore it is proposed that the conveyance of the content of the substrate is facilitated within a pixel format similar to that of computer graphics. In short, an archetypical symbol, (that is representative of the content of the primary substrate of the Wisdom of the Spirit), is formatted within the prefrontal cortex in the same manner as is a computer graphic. This encrypting process occurs within a binary, sonic, and electrochemical digital type format within the material substance of our Right frontal lobe. (Chap.1. Air of Clarity, Part Two: Explicit definition of Consciousness). In this manner it may also be subsequently decoded so that we may acquire a conscious awareness of its implicit content.

The resultant visual symbols most likely resemble Salvador Dali style art (Spanish artist 1904-1989) in computer animation format. This would not be too surprising given that such art forms are expressions, and conceptual renditions, of the content of our collective unconscious. In this manner the Wisdom of the Soul is registered within the domain of our cognition within a recognizable, and familiar, format of conscious awareness. We have alluded to this event as "ensoulment" since it provides us with a means towards achieving a conscious, and cognitive, awareness of all that pertains to authentic knowledge.

A similar mechanism probably accounts for the manner in which spiritual visions, and the related content of ecstasies, are experienced. However, it is also acknowledged that the symbolic content may be conveyed through any one of our special senses, (e.g. auditory), besides that of the visual mode. There are many well documented examples of these types of transcendental experiences contained within Scriptures, and many more within our more recent history. The Marian apparitions at Fatima, and Lourdes, are typical examples within our more modern times. Drug induced, and epileptic hallucinations, (particularly those of the Temporal lobe variety), are probably the result of the spontaneous release of random, and disassociated, secondary metaphorical concepts which had been previously constructed, and allocated to memory, within this computerized pixel format.

The application of this cerebral binary system is also well illustrated in the manner by which the Corpus Callosum responds to the representation of the conceptual contribution of the Left cerebral hemisphere to that of the Right hemisphere. It may only do so within the format of "Yes" or "Not Yes".

(Chap.2b The Bipolar Brain). As you may recall we have alluded to the manner in which the corpus callosum exerts a major influence on the transfer of information between the Left and Right hemispheres. It performs this task primarily be way of inhibition of inter-hemispheric exchange, as opposed to one of facilitation. The mental correlate of this inter-hemispheric audit, as reflected within the representation of the conceptualized content of the psyche to the primacy of the soul, is manifest in the manner in which our conscience and free-will operate.

Conscience may be considered as a means by which moral judgment is mentally applied in respect of any specified proposition. It is proposed that the soul will be receptive, (i.e. respond in "Yes" mode), to the content of the psyche in so far as it satisfies some fundamental terms, and specified, criteria. These are conditions that apply to compliance with the implicit nature of the Primary metaphorical content of which the psyche was initially in receipt. Failure to comply will result in a "Not Yes" mode of acceptability.

However, should the decision-making process been inappropriately relegated to the psyche over that of the soul, then the conceptual content of the psyche may forcefully intrude so as to become functionally contextualized within the content of our thoughts and our perceptions. In other words, the facility of human conscience is over-ridden as an expression of willful motive and intent. In fact, the modus operandi of our entire biological system throughout our body functions within a framework of inhibition versus facilitation. Homeostasis, or equilibrium, is maintained through a reciprocal feedback loop which controls these opposing mechanisms. This is well illustrated within the operative dynamics of the sympathetic, and parasympathetic nervous system elements of our Autonomic System (Chap.7b). It is also a feature of our hormonal systems as evident within the Hypothalamic- Pituitary-Adrenal Axis which controls the menstrual cycle, ovulation, fertilization, pregnancy, and breast milk flow, amongst a host of other vital hormonally dependent functions.

The Right cerebral hemisphere is in receipt of the quota of primary substrate through the process of reciprocity that exists between mind and brain. This substrate, which initially is presented as metaphysical units, is encrypted, sorted, and reconfigured, by the Right hemisphere within the format of a consciously apprehended image or felt experience. This is what we now term a Primary metaphor or archetype. Thus it is encoded as the primary, and intuitive, content of our knowledge. As it now exists within the Right cerebral hemisphere, this knowledge is still within a pre-conceptual, and implicit, format since it has not yet been surrendered to the Left hemisphere for intellectual analysis. However, it may be registered as a conscious awareness, and subsequently acknowledged, as it currently presents, within the context of intuitive belief, or trust (faith).

This pre-conceptual "cloud" of pixels is presented to the Left hemisphere to be separated, and sorted, into self-contained packages, or small units (analyzed). These are classified, and categorized, so as to locate, and identify, some related, and familiar categories of information that had been previously archived within our living memory. In this manner we begin to construct a proposition through the integration of the content of our Primary metaphors with that of the pre-existing Secondary metaphors that had been consigned to memory. It is within this format that it is reciprocated directly with the content of the psyche.

It is proposed that it was the consequence of a massive influx of Primary metaphors that the dramatic evolutionary stimulus was provided so as to instigate a spectacular series of changes within the primitive brain and the instinctual mind of our biological hominid host. This event is described as the Initial Primary Metaphorical Infusion, or simply IPMI. The outcome of this event is now evident within the configuration of the human brain, and spiritual nature of the mind,(within the context of soul), which is unique to our species.

What resides within the psyche is very much a reflection of the primordial, and genetically inherited, construct of our Hypothalamus and selective neurological components of our Limbic System and brain stem. These are largely representative of our "selfish genes" wherein self-survival, and self-preservation, is an absolute priority. The psyche has its origins, as instinctive awareness, (in stark contrast to that of conscious awareness), from within this primitive region of our brain. In addition, what is contained within the psyche is also a mental composite of the Secondary metaphors which we ourselves have accrued throughout the duration of our conceptualizing lives at any given point in time.

The psyche now has the opportunity to impose its own construct upon the manner in which our Primary metaphors may best be interpreted, and applied, within the construct of our concepts, and within the context of its own particular priorities, values, needs, and desires. The ego invariably reigns supreme within this discerning domain of our human mind.

It is within this rationalized format that these constructs are represented to the primacy of the soul, and thus finally reciprocated within the encrypting, and synergistic system of the Right hemisphere. At the cerebral level we have alluded to the critical "editing" function that occurs within the corpus callosum when the content of the Left cerebral hemisphere is represented to the Right hemisphere. We also noted that this process occurs within a simple binary mode of "yes", or "not yes". Furthermore, as we shall discuss in a later chapter, (Chap. 8 "Confabulation & Memory"), there is also an editing, or audit mode affiliated within the process of memory retrieval. This is a critical factor in ensuring that a confabulatory form of bias is not integrated within the content of the memory so as to corrupt its inherent validity.

The process of reconciliation of the content is undertaken within the Right hemisphere. In this manner a new thought comes into being from the synergy of Right and

Left hemispheric contributions of effort, purpose, and intent. The outcome as finally configured, will be largely dependent upon the perceived hierarchy of needs, and the relative strengths of the roles that we have, as individuals, delegated to the psyche, and the soul, in that regard. Ultimately, these concepts will be expressed within the world, and within the format of our Tertiary metaphors, as our thoughts, and words, and invariably as our actions and our deeds.

We will examine the manner in which these processes may become disrupted, or distorted, within that of the acquisition of knowledge, the construction of our concepts, and the subsequent configuration of our perception of reality. These events will then be considered within the framework of both Left, and Right Hemispheric Shifts (Chapter 8).

IMPLICATIONS AND SUMMARY OF THE PIXEL THEORY OF THOUGHT.

The critical importance of what has been proposed here cannot be underestimated. The core content of what has been stated is in regard to these four most fundamental facts:

a) The human Mind is the primary source of our consciousness and of our inspirational creativity. It is the unified composite of the psyche and the soul.

b) The Brain is the location of our biological Awareness, Alertness, and of our inherent Primordial Instinctive responses. In addition it is the source of our Autonomic–reflexive responses. It provides the means by which the content of the psyche and soul can "speak" so as to communicate, direct, and guide the specific nature of any of these human responses. These activities include those of the spiritual, emotive, artistic and intellectual types. The intellectual component refers to that of the data processing variety. These include computational analysis, and the categorization and cross referencing of metaphorical data(i.e. Conceptualization).

c) While A and B are co-dependent, and function within a system of bilateral reciprocity, the mind, as soul, has preconceptual primacy, and epistemological precedence, over that of the brain.

ARTISTIC CREATIVITY

She writes her music in the night,
In the dim and smoky candlelight.
The voices in her head call out
From their archaic vaults and caves.
The catacombs of lime-burnt bones,
Sing out a sweet refrain.

They sing to her in ancient tongues,
They speak to her through fire.
Upon their lips are burning coals,
In their hearts dwell pure desire.

From "The Songwriter", by the author.

Most individuals are familiar with this module of trust, belief, and imagery as it applies to artistic creativity. Many artists, whether they are musicians, poets and writers, painters or sculptures are well aware of the apparent spontaneity by which creative imagery emerges, and is experienced. These are the moments in which the artist becomes aware that the substrate of the spirit *"has entered the room"*. It may suddenly explode out of the darkness as a solar flare, or an incandescent firework bursting violently into the stillness of the night. In turn, this seed of thought will impregnate, and ultimately be astutely propositioned by the opportunistic and clever human mind (i.e. psyche). The artist will also be acutely aware that any premature effort to impose intellect upon the primary substrate, in an attempt to shape and reconfigure it, it may seriously distort and disfigure the pristine nature of the original presentation. Yet, at some appropriate point this becomes necessary and inevitable.

The content of the primary substrate must be surrendered into the manipulating hands of intellect and reason. Occasionally, this transfer can be affected almost instantaneously as a spontaneous stream of consciousness that is authentically and accurately reconfigured by the rationalizing psyche. Far more often it is necessary that the initial inspirational debut continues to revert to its source prior to its eventual presentation for cognitive processing and the application of artistic skill. (We will be describing the manner in which this form of continuous feedback, or reverberation, occurs in greater detail within the context of "Reciprocity" in the next chapter). The goal of such a retrograde referral is to patiently unveil, and clarify, the content of that which had been divulged within the substrate. Even then, it is often necessary to continue reverting to the source in order to achieve the most valid rendition of the primary imagery as can be accomplished through the application of intellectual or artistic skill.

The manner in which this process is facilitated is by averting our propensity to engage within the realm of our cognitive thinking. This is achieved by way of our unique human ability to inwardly reflect. Alternatively, we may choose to consign this creative substrate to our memory. Therein, it may slowly ferment beyond our conscious gaze. At some later time it may reemerge as something that has evolved, and crystalized, into a more vivid and malleable form of imagery. In either instance, this creative interlude is one in which there is a requirement to listen out, patiently and unconditionally, rather than to speak in haste. In this manner we facilitate the unfolding of our intuitive wisdom so that it may guide and direct the creative process. In effect, this is an evolving process of incubation and metamorphosis of a primary substrate, or embryonic seed, to one that is mentally readapted for its survival and expression within an alternative environment. This is the closest encounter that most of us will ever experience of a visitation from an extra-terrestrial life form within the context of our human and earthly domain. In reality, such a phenomenon is constantly and relentlessly occurring at a subliminal level.

An unending stream of allegorical inspiration from the collective unconscious permeates our mind incessantly. This occurs in a similar manner as that which we have already described in relation to the formulation of concepts and their linguistic expression. Indeed, if you have been alert and observant you may now begin to appreciate the manner and the means by which intuition is conveyed to the cognitive mind in order that it may be conceptualized and expressed within the world. The intuitive precepts are unfolded, or unpacked, upon their eventual relegation to the left cerebral hemisphere, by the process of retrieval of secondary metaphors that reside within our "living" memory. In this manner these intuitions are formulated as concepts that can now be expressed as rationalized thoughts and ideas. The same fundamental process is applicable to both the expression of our spiritual beliefs (i.e. faith), and to other forms of human creativity (i.e. intellectual or artistic).This process is that which we commonly describe as one of "enlightenment", or of our "source of inspiration". Thus, enlightened by the Spirit, we may freely choose to contribute to, and participate in, the means by which "flesh and blood" is conferred upon the Word through our human thoughts, words, actions, and deeds.

It is clearly evident that propositional concepts, as a product of our intellect, are no more than an imperfect reproduction of our facility of enlightenment as we have defined it. Intellectual concepts can convey, at best, partial and transient truths. On the other hand, intuitive beliefs, as human enlightenment, provide us with the facility by which we may strive to communicate elements of the implicit, authentic, and enduring truth. As well we know, when these are expressed artistically, they may achieve the recognition and well deserved status of a universal appeal that endures for all time. Regrettably, we are generally over preoccupied at a cognitive level within each passing moment that we personally fail to register, or acknowledge, these intuitive insights within the routine activities of our day. Our episodes of enlightenment sadly fade, undetected, and unnoticed, into the darkness of our human intellect. This then is a descriptive account of what we most commonly term the "creative process". In reality, these are representative of what we usually describe as either inspiration or enlightenment. Oftentimes it may be experienced as a painstakingly tedious and laborious process. Within the context of artistic expression this is simply a reflection of the intensity of effort and the desire to strive towards the achievement of perfection through human endeavor.

Mankind does not actually create anything. We have yet to acquire such an awesome ability. We can however, reconfigure or adapt a primary spiritual substrate within another context, and another form, which we can express and apply to the living world. The most important variable within this entire process is the extent to which our rendition of this substrate is accurate and authentic. Ultimately, it is this level of authenticity that defines the real value of our human endeavors. When this work is conducted in a manner that is a valid rendition of its source, then it may be described as a "labor of love", and not yet another vain expression of our human pride.

CHAPTER FOUR: MIND – BRAIN-BODY RECIPROCITY

(a) RECIPROCITY

In order to even begin to comprehend the manner in which the mind, brain, and body interrelate, or communicate, we first need to grasp the fundamentals concerning the nature of our mental activities within the broadest sense of the term "human mind". We will trace the origin and source of all our mental perceptions from the first instance of their initial conception, through their assimilation within the neuronal complexity of their cerebral correlates, and their eventual expression within the context of our existence within the world. It is through such a mental – cerebral process that the aggregate of our perceptions contribute to the formulation of our paradigm. This is what constitutes the specific parameters that define the matrix of our reality within the lived experience. This may be considered as a process that requires a primary substrate, is initiated at some particular site or location, undergoes some form of cognitive assimilation and transformation, and finally emerges as a perceptible entity with which we may freely choose to interact or apply within the experience of our existence. We have already alluded to various aspects of this complex process within Chapter 1 ("Air of context" and "Language & Beliefs"), and again in the previous chapter. There is general agreement among neuroscientists concerning the "primacy of affect" as it pertains to the right cerebral hemisphere. Coincidentally, there is also a widely held, and fundamentally flawed, scientific consensus that the human mind is the outcome, or product, of the physiological activities of the brain.

Primacy of affect is the term that is applied to the precedence which the right hemisphere has over that of the left hemisphere in respect of the basic substrate of all that is fundamentally implicit. It is implicit because it has not yet been subjected to the processes of abstraction and explicitness of the left hemisphere. The right hemisphere underwrites the knowledge that the left side initially acquires as its unprocessed material. The right hemisphere simply needs the left to unpack its treasured cargo so that it can then integrate, and synthetize, what both know into a usable whole. Inevitably, the truth about our world, in respect of our perceptions, is grounded within the nature of the attention that is provided by the right cerebral hemisphere.

What is of particular interest to us at this precise juncture is that the processes of cognition and conceptualization of thoughts ultimately revert back to the primacy of the right cerebral hemisphere. Furthermore, even while the inter-hemispheric traffic proceeds onwards upon its journey, these neural signals are continually reverting to their site of origin. This reverberating feedback mechanism occurs at multiple interconnecting cell stations within the circuitry of each cerebral hemisphere. It is very suggestive of a quality control and audit mechanism, to reaffirm authenticity, and compliance, with the intrinsic content of its primary source. In some respects it might well be visualized as occurring in a pixelated type of mode as each individual unit of the cognitive image begins to coalesce so as to provide an integrated, and validly reconstructed, rendition of its original prototype. Within a far broader and cosmic context, these neural signals flash across the hemispheres like a comet descending to earth, its trail of luminous dust streaming back along the path of its trajectory. In like fashion the Spirit of the Word descended to this planet to disperse the primary essence of its authentic Wisdom within the entire content of our human atmosphere.

This form of bidirectional neural reciprocity is particularly intense within the region of our frontal lobes. As you may recall, it is the frontal lobes that provide us with the unique facility of objectivity so that we can engage within the world in a considered and reflective manner. The entire cognitive process is one of a reverberating, and bidirectional, reciprocity through its starting point. At a cerebral and right hemispheric level, it is this type of reciprocity that brings the world into being as a perceptual reality. When the process is fully grounded within its primacy of context it acquires the property of authenticity, and relevance, as it applies to our vision of life, and the experience of our living, within such a reality.

However, despite lack of neuro-scientific consensus, we have already proposed that the mind, within the specific limitations of the soul, (and human Spirit), has primacy of affect as it pertains to the source of our cerebral substrate.

Consequently, the Wisdom of the Soul holds precedence over the implicit substrate to which the right hemisphere is in receipt. The physiological activities within the neural circuitry of the right and left hemispheres of the brain are cerebral correlates of what initially transpires within the soul, and subsequently within the domain of the psyche. The product of this unique, and collaborative, reciprocity is what constitutes the totality of our mental processes. These include our intellectual thoughts and inspirational ideas, our concepts and beliefs, our feelings, and emotions.

(b) THE "SPHERE OF THOUGHT"

An analogy of Mind- Brain Reciprocity

Fig.12

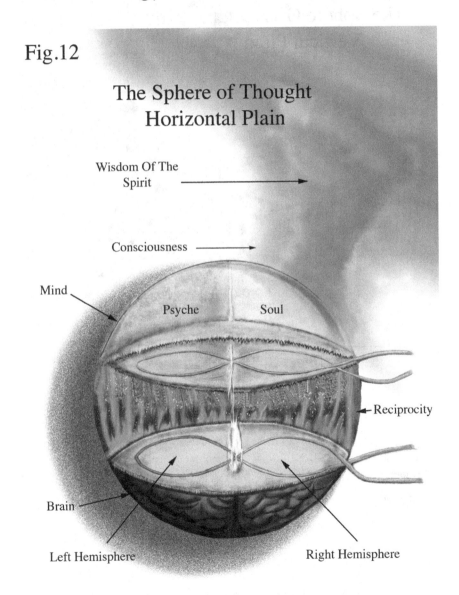

The Sphere of Thought
Horizontal Plain

Wisdom Of The
Spirit

Consciousness

Mind

Psyche   Soul

Reciprocity

Brain

Left Hemisphere   Right Hemisphere

Fig. 13

The Sphere Of Thought
Vertical Plain

The Spirit of Wisdom
The Primary Substrate

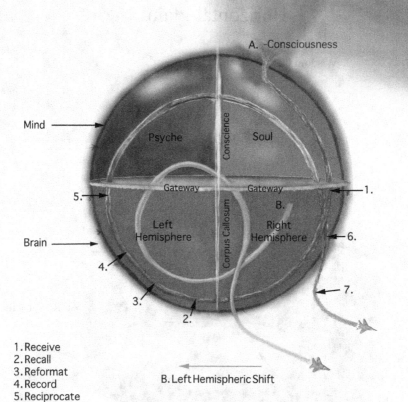

A. –Consciousness

Mind

Psyche

Conscience

Soul

Gateway

Gateway

1.

5.

B.

Left
Hemisphere

Corpus Callosum

Right
Hemisphere

6.

Brain

4.

7.

3.

2.

1. Receive
2. Recall
3. Reformat
4. Record
5. Reciprocate
6. Reconcile
7. Respond

B. Left Hemispheric Shift

The best analogy that I can provide is to consider mind and brain as represented by a single, and solitary, glass sphere (see Fig. 12 & 13).

In order to describe this sphere more precisely, we will apply the more extended version of the term: *"The Sphere of Consciousness – Inspired Thought"*. The upper half of the sphere represents the mind, and the lower half, the brain. The right upper quadrant of the sphere represents the soul, and the right cerebral hemisphere lies directly below it. The left upper quadrant of the sphere is the psyche, and left hemisphere directly below it. The visual imagery of the mind as a dual agent, (psyche and soul), is for illustrative purposes only. As will be explained in Chapter 6, the mind is considered to be a "trans-symbiotic" unity. It will be subsequently defined as the "Ensouled Psyche". This trans-symbiotic process is also applicable to the unitary nature,(mortal and spiritual), of our humanity.

As you follow both the text and the graphic *"Sphere of Thought"*, pay particular attention to the four most critical capital *"R's"*: These are:

Receive (as from, and within, the Primacy of context); *Reciprocate; Reconcile; and Respond.*

A lazer light source, (representing consciousness), directs a perfectly formed beam of light, (as the wisdom of the soul), onto the right upper quadrant of the sphere to activate the collective unconscious, and simultaneously penetrate into the right lower quadrant (i.e. the right cerebral hemisphere). The light source is moved from right to left, in a figure of eight pattern, so as to finally return to its original position on the right side of the sphere (at location of soul and right cerebral hemisphere). As the beam travels in time from right to left, on the upper part of the sphere (mind, it simultaneously presents the light from above to penetrate the lower half of the sphere (brain) and is reflected (represented) back again to its source of origin. At any given instant within this process of movement, the light constantly reverberates (reflects) between its source and internal glass structure of the sphere. The accompanying theoretical graphics that describe this process makes it a little easier to visualize. They are depicted within a horizontal plane, as the light moves within the figure of eight pattern, (Fig.12), and simultaneously within a vertical plane,(Fig.13), in a reflected, or circular type of motion. It is acknowledged that this analogy could not be replicated by experimental demonstration since the curvature of the sphere would deflect the light at right angles to its source and so distort the imagery as visually represented within this spherical module.

This reciprocal and bilateral, exchange of content between mind and brain describes the dynamics of the operation that takes place when we transform an archetypical primary metaphor into a thought that may be applied within the context of our perceived reality. It is also mirrored in the bidirectional movement of the neural traffic within our brain. That is to say, that the signals reverberate through their starting point. We have already identified the right cerebral hemisphere as the provider of the primary metaphor (i.e. as having primacy of affect) in respect of the left hemisphere. In addition, the collective unconscious was identified as the repository from which the wisdom of the soul is retrieved by the right hemisphere. This transcendental form of wisdom / knowledge is representative of the archetypical substrate that is enfolded within the content of the primary metaphor. That authentic substrate has, in turn, been delivered through the medium of human consciousness as the wisdom of the Spirit

"In the beginning was the Word", and the Spirit is the "standard-bearer" of the Word.

"Through him all things came into being-- - -What had come into being in him was life, and the life was the light of all people. The light shines in the darkness, and the darkness did not overcome it". John 1: 3-5.

It is precisely in this unified form of transcendental- cerebral reciprocity, reverberating through its point of origin that the world is brought into being as an experiential phenomenon. What comes into being in this manner is authentic life. It is life within a meaningful context that pertains to our human existence. The light of spiritual wisdom is conveyed to the right cerebral hemisphere through the facility of our consciousness. The darkness of the psyche is grounded in the intellectual ignorance of the left hemisphere in respect of our spiritual nature. Ultimately, the inherently flawed nature of our intellectual concepts will not overcome the truths contained within the content of our spiritual wisdom. The composition, and the eventual synergy, of these two sources of knowledge is what constitute what we have simply termed our "sphere of thought".

Now, you may also begin to appreciate the manner in which this reciprocity serves as a means through which repetition of thought and deed reinforces the "traffic pattern" of that activity. This in turn contributes to our establishing personalized patterns of behavior. In time, these may become semi-autonomous, reflexive, and habitual traits. We become what we think, even in what we might casually dismiss as harmless fantasy. Given opportunity, self- reinforced cerebral responses, and inflated self-confidence, the content of our thoughts will invariably emerge within the pattern of our behavior. As with the insightful, and foreboding, statement which Oscar Wilde attributed to himself, most of us can resist anything, except temptation. Yet, it is ourselves who ultimately determine the nature and magnitude of our temptations and our leverage to resist them.

(c) A THEORY OF CEREBRAL PRIMACY AND LEFT HEMISPHERIC SHIFT

For those of us who believe that mankind has a spiritual nature and a soul, the concept of cerebral primacy over mind poses as a source of serious contradiction that cannot be easily reconciled. Mind and brain are represented as "The Sphere of Consciousness – Inspired Thought" that may be applied within the context of the world. Since mind (psyche and soul) and brain (right and left hemispheres) are functionally bipolar each exists within a state of inner conflict. This is a reflection of the disparity inherent within their nature (psyche and soul) and mode of attention (right and left hemispheres). Reconciliation through synthesis and synergy are required in order that a thought or decision can be reached.

For a person of faith, the process begins at 12 0 clock and moves clockwise to inscribe the full circle (Fig.13. Green circle) An atheist, acknowledged and professed or otherwise, would conceptualize the process as beginning at 3 0 clock and inscribing a smaller circular type of movement. (Fig.13. Red circle) The sequence of activities that constitute our thought processes, within the context of mind- brain reciprocity, are listed from 1 to 7 depending on your terms of reference:

1. Receives the primary substrate from the Spirit. (encodes).
2. Recalls and Relives information and emotions from memory.

3. Reformats and reconfigures the information within the left Hemisphere (and ultimately represents it to right hemisphere whence it was derived.)
4. Records data as memory storage.
5. Reciprocates these activities with the mind.
6. Recreates a new entity (a concept) through the reconciliation of the contributions from both left and right hemispheres.
7. Responds with the application of this process as reflected within attitudes, values, and beliefs.

It may be no coincidence that all of the terms that can be applied to describe these cerebral activities are prefixed by "re" which indicates a return to a previous condition or source. This is to imply that the brain does not have primacy with regard to what it is that initiates the process of thought (i.e. inspiration).

If the process was to begin within the brain then the soul is excluded from the equation at both the initiation and the termination of the process. The brain, specifically in respect of the left hemisphere, and psyche would then mastermind the entire cognitive process. This is what we refer to as a "left hemispheric shift". In effect, it also describes the fundamental nature of the process that may become manifest as that of a confabulatory mode of thinking. Moreover, within this spurious scenario it is the brain that is identified as the creator and provider of the substrate of thought, and it is the motives and objectives of the psyche that dictate the nature and the range of applications in respect of the outcome.

If the process of cognition was to be initiated within the right cerebral hemisphere then the cognitive activities of the left hemisphere (and the psyche) would proceed in the absence of a spiritual substrate. Beyond this point any reference or allusion to spirituality or the Divine would be post cognitive. That is to say that it would be nothing more than a meaningless and hollow "after thought". Since a spiritual principle had not been factored into the cognitive process it would have been excluded from the reconciliatory process of synergy upon its representation within the right hemisphere. Likewise, spirituality is absent from the mind- set that is now subject to the unrestrained dictates of the ego. A thought, an idea, or belief, has been created within a spiritual void. Authentic self has been excluded from the negotiating table and has been locked out of the conference room. To infer otherwise is flagrant insincerity. It is more than an error, a misjudgment, or a lie. It is hypocritical and deceptive in the extreme. Perhaps one might better describe it as a form of intellectual and spiritual autism since it fails to relate to the reality of what could be said to be either implicit or intuitive. It is a total and misleading misrepresentation of self and of our human nature.

The application of the theory of cerebral primacy produces an extreme version of left hemispheric shift and self- delusion. While this theory is inherently flawed and invalid, regrettably it has become the popular modus operandi for a great number of people .Many of these are highly acclaimed, responsible, and persuasive academics. The inevitable result is the loss of respect for the sanctity and dignity of mankind. We are all too well aware of the consequences of such a loss for our world and of the manner in which it is mirrored within society as man's inhumanity, prejudices, discrimination, and injustices, to his fellow man.

CHAPTER FIVE: CREATION AND THE EVOLUTION OF HUMANITY

> What is this thing called Time,
> Time bound to the human race?
> 'Tis but an undeserved measure
> Of God's Love and His saving grace.
> Yet it's melting down and burning out,
> It's falling back in place.

> From "In Time-Out of
> Time", by the author.

(a) CREATION IN THE SECOND GENESIS

Let us leave the current domain within which we now exist, and revert back through time to the beginning of our story. This will provide us with some insight as to how we, and the world in which we live, evolved to their present status. First of all, we will briefly reflect upon the events described within the opening passages of the Forward. This will help us to maintain everything within its proper context. It will also contribute to the retention of continuity within the sequence of events as we now proceed to describe them in further detail:

In the aftermath of the loss of perfection, and the de-contextualization of the first creation, man was to be granted a Devine reprieve. All that had formerly existed within the context of the first creation would be newly reconstituted within the construct of a material domain. Love, mercy, and compassion would prevail on our behalf, despite our Fall from Grace. The potential content of the entire universe, of every created thing, constrained within an infinitesimal singularity, precipitously burst forth through a portal from within the eternal domain. The substrate of all that was to materialize as matter within the universe was contained within this minuscule point.

There is a wide diversity of opinion within the scientific community at large with respect to many of the issues relating to the creation of the universe and the emergence of life upon our planet. By and large, that which is presented here as scientific knowledge is representative of a broadly accepted, and currently popular, set of proposals. Inevitably these will change with the advancement of science and of our intellectual comprehension of these phenomenal events.

The entire cosmos, and its multitude of galaxies, stars, and planets, and the unfolding events relating to the emergence and purpose of life within the universe, were mysteriously encoded and concealed within some primary miniscule point (i.e. a singularity). This singularity was a material expression of the spiritual substrate of the first creation. It had been reconstituted in the wake of mankind's ignominious separation from perfection. In biblical terminology it is representative of the downfall, and ejection, of mankind from paradise, and his subsequent re-emergence within the imperfection of a material, and earthly, domain. The arrow of time for each and all of these events was set in motion. All of this was constrained within the confines of a solitary dense and superheated point no larger than a billionth of the size of a single nuclear particle.

The emergence of this singularity represented the most profound spark of creative inspiration, love, and mercy, that mankind could ever hope for, or seek to understand. It was the spark that would ultimately ignite as the light of the Holy Spirit within the heart and mind of a sacred living species. This species was to be that of the human race. It would inevitably emerge as a mortal being within the content, and the context, of a material universe. Many within that select and indigenous fold would accept and absorb that Light with profound thanks and gratitude, while others would reject and refute it. Unannounced this singularity spontaneously arose as a mere glimmer of hope and reconciliation into the dark void of nothingness. The intensity of its heat and energy foreshadowed the magnitude of its power, and the extraordinary consequences that would arise from its imminent and astronomical expansion. The majesty and mystery of all of these events are what we now commonly, and perhaps all too casually, refer to as the "Big Bang".

The essence of the "Big Bang Theory" was originally proposed by Georges Lemaitre in 1927. The term was later coined by the British astronomer Sir Fred Hoyle in 1950 during the course of a television interview. This was in fact a silent event without a bang, since this massive nuclear-like episode occurred within a vacuum and without the air that would be necessary to convey any audible sound.

Many of us may be inspired to contemplate upon the idea of "Intelligent Design" by an omnipotent creator when we gaze up at the night sky, or view the planets through a telescope. A little knowledge with regard to some of the scientific theory that has been proposed in an effort to explain how the universe began adds yet another dimension to our level of wonder and awe. However, we must be cautious in our choice, and our interpretation, of some of these scientific theories as they have been extrapolated, and applied, to our understanding of creation, the evolution of life, and the emergence of humanity.

In recent times it has become popular to advocate that the universe, earth, and all life forms came into existence because the laws of chance, and probability, made this inevitable. This has been summarized within the statement "we exist because we had to exist". In tandem with this statement, it has also been proposed that there is no good reason to assume that these laws would not have led to the creation of multiple universes, and multiple variations of the human condition. The idea of "purpose" has never been considered within these scientific proposals. It would appear that the idea of there being a requirement or a need of a purpose in respect of creation within any form, context, or domain, is an irrelevancy within the scientific mind-set. The fact of the matter is that the creation of our universe, of the planet earth, and of life, was executed on behalf of the humanity that was to emerge from the midst of this great and magnificent act of creative inspiration. In the absence of humanity upon the earth this creative event would have been entirely meaningless. It would have been a non-event.

There is no good reason to entertain the possibility of there being multiple alternative universes. Humanity alone suffices as the purpose for which the creation of all that exists, and all that might ever yet come into being. That is the measure of the importance, and the value, that is attached to each, and every one of us. Such an attitude is not a measure of human arrogance or of an over inflated sense of self-importance. That is the true measure of god's love, and the importance which he attaches to all of us. For this we must reciprocate within our praise, and our humble offerings of thanks, and gratitude. *"Love is reciprocity. Reciprocity is Love"*.

Despite all that however, for those of you who have an interest in things scientific, and cosmological, we will briefly consider some of the fundamentals regarding the theory of the Big Bang. Even then we must exercise our intuitive and intellectual discernment in regard to the scientific interpretation that may be applied to this module of creation.

According to the theory of general relativity the concept of a singularity implies the existence of a point that is infinitely small and under infinite pressure. Consequently, it only exists in theory since infinity can only ever be approached but never reached. The Big Bang theory does not provide any explanation for the initial conditions of the universe. It is limited to efforts to describe and explain the general evolution of the universe going forward beyond the reference point of its primacy of context. Perhaps not surprisingly, a theory has been proposed (the "Hartle- Hawking state") which suggests that if you were to travel back towards the beginning, time would give way to space, since time, or space-time, did not exist prior to the Big Bang. Consequently, since the concept of a "beginning" is bound up with time, James Hartle and Stephen Hawking concluded that the universe had no beginning within the classical sense of the term. Where the term "eternity" describes a realm beyond time, space, and matter, we may extrapolate this idea to propose that the substrate of the universe was conceived from, or since, eternity. The application of the word "eternity" provides us with an appropriate term within which to describe the original life setting, (i.e. Sitz im Leben), of creation. Eternity places the universe within its proper conceptual location in respect of its primacy of context.

The Big Bang theory depends on two major assumptions: the universality of physical laws (e.g. the general theory of relativity and quantum theory) and the cosmological principle. The latter principle states that on large scales the universe is homogenous and isotropic. The four primary forces within the universe are gravity, electromagnetic, and strong and weak nuclear forces that pertain to the atomic and sub-atomic level. In brief, the general theory of relativity explains all the physical phenomena controlled by the force of gravity.

Quantum physics, on the other hand, provides a unifying theory to explain the behavior of the other three forces. However, these laws of physics appear to break down when applied to the initial conditions at the onset of the Big Bang. One must assume that the content of the singularity was derived from some primary source of energy. Yet, energy cannot exist within an eternal void. Indeed, even the concept of an infinite void having an existence independent of a universe yet to be created, is highly questionable. The property of energy is dependent upon a source, and its containment within some specific spatial parameters. As a consequence, within the scientific module of the creation of the universe, no provision has been made in respect of specifying, or defining, its contextual primacy. Any scientific theory concerning these primary events must therefore be based on pure speculation. In so far as intellectual deduction is concerned, intuitive beliefs based on the "first principles" that are encoded within our "primary metaphors" are equally, if not more, deserving of our rational consideration.

The first period immediately following the Big Bang is known as the Planck Epoch. This is the time from 0 to 10-43 sec. which is the smallest theoretical time that can be measured (a Planck Time) That describes the time taken for light (a photon) to travel one Planck length. The Planck Epoch is an era in traditional Big Bang cosmology wherein temperatures were so high that the four fundamental forces of gravity, electromagnetism, and strong and weak nuclear forces were one fundamental force.

The next epoch is the Grand unification Epoch (GUE) which began when gravity separated from the other forces of nature. It lasted from 10- 43 sec. to 10-36 sec. As the universe expanded and cooled, it crossed transition temperatures at which forces separate from each other. The non- gravitational physics in this epoch are described by the Grand Unification Theory (GUT). The GUE ended when the GUT forces further separate into strong and electroweak forces. The Electroweak Epoch began 10-36 sec. after the Big Bang. At this point the temperature of the universe was low enough to separate the strong from the electroweak force.

The Inflationary Epoch began at 10-32 sec. This phase of cosmic inflation was one of accelerating expansion. It was produced by a hypothesized field called "Inflation" and would evidently last long enough to account for the high degree of homogeneity which is observed in the universe at the present time.

After the Inflationary Epoch the universe is filled with quark- gluon plasma. Plasma is one of four fundamental states of matter. The others are solid, liquid, and gas. This form of plasma occurs when a gas is ionized. Since stars are in this state it is the most common form of matter in the universe. Quarks and gluons are some of the basic building blocks of matter. Protons and neutrons are composed of quarks while gluons act as exchange particles between the strong forces of quarks. It is from this point onwards that the laws of physics are more applicable to our theoretical comprehension of the early universe.

As the universe expanded, its energy density decreased and it became cooler. As it cooled down the elementary particles of matter could associate more stably into larger combinations. Consequently, in this early part of the matter- dominated era, stable protons and neutrons formed within a second after the Big Bang. Three minutes later it was cool enough for these to combine to form atomic nuclei. However, even at this stage the universe was composed mostly of hot dense plasma containing negative electrons, electrically neutral neutrinos, and positively charged nuclei.

It took 380,000 years of further expansion and cooling of the universe before electrons became trapped in orbits around nuclei, and so forming the first atoms. These were predominantly hydrogen and helium, and which are still the most abundant elements in the universe. Progressively heavier atoms and molecules are formed as further particles undergo stellar nucleosynthesis (a form of nuclear fusion). These provided us with the vast array of chemical elements that constitute Mendelev's entire Periodic Table of metals, non- metals, and metalloids. Elements 1 -98 occur naturally, while the remainder, up to 118, has since been synthesized in laboratories. Most of these later elements probably existed naturally at the beginning of the universe but would have rapidly decayed due to their inherent instability.

At this point the radiation decoupled from the matter to form the ubiquitous isotropic background of microwave radiation which we can observe to this very day. The dense fog of particles slowly cleared over the ensuing 380,000 years to reveal the first light of our universe. For the next 300 million years this cosmic background radiation is the only visible light. A few hundred million years after the Big Bang, thick clouds of gas and dust coalesce and collapse under the force of gravity to form stars and galaxies. Nuclear fusion lights up the stars as heavier atoms such as carbon, oxygen, and iron are continuously produced. These are catapulted from within the centre of the stars, and throughout the universe, in spectacular stellar explosions called supernova within the firmament. Gravity, as exerted by matter (inclusive of "dark matter") slows down the cosmic expansion for the next 10 billion years. Finally dark energy, leads to an accelerated phase of expansion which persists until the present time. It appears that this will continue for billions of years yet to come. Yet, even stars and galaxies do not tell the whole story. Astronomical and physical calculations suggest that the visible universe is only a tiny fraction (5%) of what the universe is actually made of. A massive 26% is composed of an unknown type of matter which we call "dark matter". An even more mysterious form of energy called "dark energy" accounts for about 70% of the mass-energy content of the universe. It was to take about another ten billion years before the earth was formed, and thirteen billion before humanity would emerge upon our planet.

There are over a hundred billion galaxies in our universe, each with hundreds of billions of stars. Our Milky Way is but one, and thus far it appears that it is the only galaxy that contains a planet such as earth which can sustain life as we know it. Some 4.6 billion years ago a star exploded as a supernova which caused a massive gravitational collapse that would form the Sun. Immense clusters of particles clumped as silicon to boulder size which were held together by the force of gravity. Multiple collisions of this boulder debris formed the planet Earth. Repeated impacts from asteroids covered the surface with craters, some over 300 miles in diameter. These events produced an intense heat of molten Iron and Nickel (the Great Iron Catastrophe) within the earth's core. This molten core created a magnetic field which would prevent erosion of our solar atmosphere and protect the Earth to this day from solar radiation. The atmosphere at the planet's surface for the first 3.8 billion years was a Hell on Earth throughout this Hadean eon of our geological history.

The surface temperatures were in the range of 230 C (446 F) due to intense asteroid bombardment and extreme volcanic activity.

The oxygen deficient atmosphere was filled with clouds of noxious and toxic gases. In the early history of the earth one major impact from a planet the size of Mars, called Theia, tilted the planet on a 23.5 degree axis from the vertical, while also sending it spinning in its current elliptical orbit around the Sun. It is this axis tilt, which the gravitational pull of the Moon stabilizes, that accounts for the variability of orbital distance from the sun and gives rise to our seasons.

This Great Impact Theory was proposed by William Hartman and Don Davis in 1972 as an explanation for the origin of the Moon from the resultant earthly debris. Finally the Late heavy Bombardment period would cease and the next geological eon, called the Archaean period, would begin within a more tranquil environment. When the earth cooled some 3.9 billion years ago it formed a silicon crust with an Iron – Nickel core. Our early atmosphere contained hydrogen sulphide, ammonia, methane, carbon dioxide, phosphate, and water, but no oxygen. Water arose from the cooling of volcanic steam which was ejected from the core as a consequence of the shifting of tectonic plates on the surface of the planet. Some may also have been delivered as ice from asteroids in outer space. By this time water covered most of the planet's mantel. Most recently however, scientists have reported locating massive volumes of water some four hundred miles below the earth's surface. This water has been calculated to be three times the capacity of all our oceans combined and may transform our understanding of how our planet was formed. Some of our carbon compounds, including amino acids, may also have been delivered from space while others were formed from inorganic elements and carbon reacting within a high voltage climate of electrical storms within our primordial pools. The formation of amino acids from the basic contents of the early atmosphere (as described in the Hadean eon), and the catalytic activity of electricity, was demonstrated in the laboratory by Miller and Urey in 1953. Ultimately, either gravity or anti- gravity will prevail. If gravity were to halt, or reverse, the expansion the universe would collapse with a big crunch. Should dark matter prevail, it will all end in a big rip.

Regardless of the precise manner, means, or time frames, the universe, and all contained therein, will ultimately revert, to the primacy of its context, to its Sitz im Leben. Ultimately the cycle of life will turn full circle to where it had all begun within the first celestial Genesis. Time and space, and the material content of the universe, will be finally "re-contextualized" within the domain of its celestial primacy. Humanity, then fully redeemed to its former glory, will revert to "man ", the eternal Spiritual essence of which he was first created in the image, and likeness, of his creator.

Yet, there is far more to these instigating creative events of our universe than the eye can see or the intellect can scientifically deduce. There are many accounts within ancient mythology and modern science that likened these first great historical phenomena to a birthing process, or the hatching of a cosmic egg e.g. the Orphic egg of Greek mythology and Georges Lemaitre's similar descriptive of analogy. As we have previously stated elsewhere in the text, all genuine artistic expression, inclusive of allegory, metaphor, imagery, and symbolism,(inclusive of rites and ritual), is initially derived from the archives of the collective unconscious. These are what constitute the primary metaphors contained within the unlived memory of all mankind. They are pre-conceptual recollections of the lived experience within an eternal domain. They are reflections of man's (as this term was defined in Chap.1 "The Air of Clarity", Part One) knowledge and experience as recalled from the memories of a previous life within a realm of eternal perfection. Consequently they are representative of the universal truths with regard to our human nature and our universe. Such art forms have not been expunged of their primacy of context nor over-written by intellectual and linguistic misrepresentation.

With regard to the Cosmic Egg analogy of the creation of the universe, the scientific module is an apt description of the dense yoke that chemically and biologically evolves and matures to become a living creature within a sustainable environment. The egg-white is the nutrient of the Spirit that fills the perceptual void of the cosmos. The Holy Spirit will breathe life into the elemental chemistry of the universe. It will spiritually ensoul, and thus animate, (from the Latin word "anima", meaning life force / soul) that which will finally emerge as the human species upon this earthly planet. It is the Spirit that creates the light within the darkness, a Light that will illuminate the mind of man throughout all ages. So it was with the hatching of the Orphic egg and the birth of Phanes –Dionysus. A deified Light of all lights would emanate, and would glow incessantly within the darkness and the ignorance of the world of human kind.

THE EMERGENCE OF LIFE.

The snowdrops have all but faded now,
And daffodils are bending down.
Small buds appear on every tree,
And noisy crows fly cheekily
To capture the highest crown.

Life reawakens at this hour
To push our spirits high,
And rise as a cloud of morning mist
Floating upward from the ground.

From "In a Wicklow
Light", by the author.

By the end of the Hadean period 3.8 billion years ago the earth's mantle is almost entirely covered by the primordial oceans within an oxygen depleted, and sterile environment. These oceans were rich in a vast array of inorganic elements that were exposed to the dynamic activity induced by highly charged electrical storms. It may have been some hundreds of millions of years after the transition from the inorganic to the organic form of chemicals that the necessary atmospheric and environmental conditions would be sufficiently established so that sustainable life could finally emerge upon the planet.

All life forms are organic compositions. That is to say they all contain a carbon base. The fundamental unit of all living things is the cell. Protein molecules are the critical component of every cell. These are composed of folded strings of amino acids of varying lengths and configurations. Every living thing is composed of some or other combination of just twenty such acids, which we describe as "essential amino acids". Some of the major quandaries with regard to the origin of life include the precise time, location, and under what specific conditions, did the first inorganic elements become organized into complex organic compounds. Additionally, we would ask as to how these were to become intricately, and mysteriously, organized into viable self-contained units which we call cells. Furthermore, we would ask how these cells acquired the ability to generate energy to survive, grow, repair, and to ingest and excrete food products so to control their homeostasis. We would seek to ascertain the manner in which they would multiply, divide, replicate, and propagate so as to endure for future generations. We would also try to understand the manner in which the massive variability within cells would occur so as to account for the progressive evolutionary diversity of the species within the Tree of Life. In effect the answers to all of these questions as to how life emerged from inert chemicals relate to self- organization and self- replication, to metabolism, and to external cell membranes. We will not necessarily consider each and every one of these issues in great detail. However, finally, and most importantly from our particular standpoint, we will ponder on the question as to the why, where, when, and the how of the matter, did the unique species of which we are all members, emerge within this apparent ancestral chain of life.

At the very root of all of these complex issues lies a single and undeniable fact: the very existence of the basic "stuff" of matter, and the laws that govern the behavior of its inherent energy, wave, or subatomic particle within any possible environmental context, has been determined, established, and selectively appropriated from the first instance of its emergence within the cosmos. The fundamental nature, and specific properties, of all primary components of matter that emerged from the Singularity were appropriated in such a manner that they possessed the natural potential to act, and interact, in the manner in which they can, and in which they have done, since the moment of their first existence. Such a pre-ordained and intelligent design would ensure that the unfolding sequence of events would ultimately result in the materialization of the world as it has evolved, and as we have come to know and experience it.

The range of interactive possibilities may have been infinite, and the laws of chance, chaos, or quantum theory, may well have resulted in any number of alternative outcomes. Yet, there has been but one particular outcome that did materialize as the world, as this great symphony of life, and as that ubiquitous and amazing species which we have come to know as human. This is what we believe to be the Creative plan that was preordained before the world began. These inherent primary properties of matter are what constitute, and contribute to, what we term the "self-ness" of their nature. They are the "the true substances", or "monads", to which we will be shortly referring. The attributes of their apparent natural, and oftentimes predictable, spontaneity of behavior have been appropriated, or programmed, within the creative singularity from which they first emerged. These primary properties are what subsequently govern, and apply to the determination of the relevant mass, charge, and orbital patterns of atomic particles and their interactive behavior with other atoms at the molecular level. They are also applicable to every natural scientific phenomenon, inclusive of gravity and anti-gravity, time and entropy, but to mention a few. These are not physical properties that have spontaneously arisen in response to some scientifically autonomous laws that govern their behavior. Whatever the magnitude and diversity of such primary properties, we might well conclude that they arose from a single, and universal, common source that gave "birth" to the Singularity in the first instance.

Within the language of philosophy, such a source is that to which Gottfried Leibniz (German philosopher.1646-1716) was alluding within the terminology of "monads". Leibniz perceived these as singular, universal, irreducible, and indestructible elementary constituents from which every material substance had first arisen. He described monads as metaphysical "true substances" that are both "exact and real" and are representative of the constituent units of our reality. Consequently monads would effectively constitute the metaphysical essence from which emerged the material content of the singularity that signaled the creative event of the universe. Regardless of this philosophical construct we have no immediate requirement to explain the creative event beyond that of the realization of the "conceptual" power of the Word.

What is of immediate relevance to us is that the authenticity of the primary content of our concepts, and a share in this same animating power, is imbued within the content of our archetypes as the Wisdom of the Spirit. Regardless of the type, quantity, or mix, of any chemical matter, or the infinite variety of environmental conditions within which any chemicals could possibly exist, chemistry alone does not constitute life. As yet, no one has ever created a "self-organizing", or "self-replicating", cell or organism. Of far greater import is the fact that chemistry alone does not constitute a human life as a unique and distinct entity within the Tree of Life. Additionally, the ancestral chain of evolution to which we most commonly allude, only describes the biological aspect of the events that were to culminate within the mysterious, and distinctly unique, emergence of the human species on our planet. It resolutely fails to incorporate the essential ancestral heritage that refers us back to the fundamental primacy of context within the celestial domain of the first creative event to have ever been conceived.

The traditional and commonly held theory concerning the emergence of life on earth is based upon the biochemical laboratory analogy. The fundamental essence of this theory is that the pervading turbulent and unstable atmospheric and environmental conditions provided a suitable type of incubation unit and nutrient medium within which living forms would inevitably and predictably arise. This formulaic "cook-book" theory emphasizes the pivotal role of the information centered perspective that underpins Darwinian fundamentalism, evolution, and modern day genetics. However, in more recent times this has been challenged, particularly by the biochemist Nick Lane with a more teleological type of theory. Lane suggests that the origin of life forms on our planet is fundamentally based on the direction of water flow and the production of energy particles. He proposes that life originated within deep sea alkaline vents owing to the specified and predictable patterns of water flow that emerged from these vents. These were to create a proton gradient that would yield quanta of energy. This energy is what provided the initial and vital animating stimulus. ("The Vital Question" by Nick Lane. Pub. Profile. 2015/ ebook). Finally we see some new evidence that science has the potential to move ever closer towards the primacy of context as it pertains to life and our humanity.

This concept is supportive of the idea that natural processes express purpose within a specified meaning and direction as they unfold on earth and within the cosmos. The movement of water as an energizing, life giving and life sustaining event is reminiscent of several biblical stories, particularly that of the pool at Bethsaida.

This describes how people were healed upon entering the pool at the first instance at which the water stirred in some mysterious and numinous pattern by the energy and power of the Almighty Spirit.

However, as it currently stands there is as yet no firmly established consensus of opinion, nor any standardized theory, as to the origin of life upon our planet. At the present time it is generally accepted that at first there were monomers of inorganic chemicals some 5 billion years ago (5Ga) then polymers of organic compounds were formed and primitive life forms emerged (3.5 Ga). These were simple microscopic cells called prokaryotes, the most dominant forms of which evolved as bacteria and Archaea. These do not have a true nucleus, mitochondria, chloroplasts, nor other complex organelles within their cytoplasm. Like all living organisms bacteria do contain Ribosomes for the production of proteins, and particularly that of the genetic RNA molecules. The structure of their ribosomes differs from that of Archaea and eukaryotes. Some antibiotics bind specifically with these bacterial ribosomes to inhibit their protein synthesis. Consequently the bacteria die while the ribosomes of the host eukaryote cells remain unharmed.

The pivotal role of photosynthesis and production of oxygen were significant factors in the organization of the cell, the formation of the cell nucleus and its complement of nucleic acids (RNA / DNA), and the subsequent emergence of more complex organisms (2 Ga). This second phase of great evolutionary divergence occurred when bacteria entered into endosymbiotic association with archaea to form mitochondria and establish the conditions necessary for the emergence of eukaryotes. Mitochondria are the site of ATP production, which is oxygen dependent, and is the common source of fuel for all cells. They have their own DNA (derived from their ancestral bacteria) as opposed to the type that is contained within the nuclei of their host cell.

The main source of oxygen in the atmosphere is oxygenic photosynthesis and this oxygenation of a previously O2 depleted atmosphere is called the Oxygen Catastrophe since it rid us of most anaerobes, accelerated the ATP production of mitochondria, and thus the overall metabolism of eukaryotes. This led to the greater "complexification", and efficiency, of these cells and to the emergence of multicellular life about 1 Ga.

Photosynthesis is the process used by most plants, algae, and cyanobacteria to convert light energy into chemical energy. This chemical energy is stored in carbohydrate molecules, which are produced by a series of light – independent reactions involving carbon fixation of carbon dioxide (usually via the Calvin cycle), that can be later released to fuel the organism's activities. Proteins located at sites called reaction centres in plants and cyanobacteria absorb light using the green pigment chlorophyll. In plants these proteins are located within specific organelles called chloroplasts (mostly in the leaf cells). It appears that some eukaryotes that already contained mitochondria also engulfed cyanobacteria type organisms which lead to the formation of chloroplasts in algae and plant species. In bacteria these proteins are simply embedded in the plasma membrane. Chlorophyll is a chlorine pigment which is similar to other porphyrin ring pigments (with the addition of a Magnesium ion at its centre) such as haeme. This is the haeme of the haemoglobin contained within our red blood cells and which transports oxygen from our lungs to all our bodily tissues. It also accounts for the familiar purple to yellow-green stain that arises within the skin following a bruising injury. Furthermore, the rich content of Magnesium within plant leaves is often used as the source of this element, alone or in combination with other trace minerals and vitamins, in the manufacture of many commonly used health supplements. Our biological ancestral relationships are rarely out of sight, and never too far away.

Oxygenic photosynthesis uses water as the electron donor within the light- depended reaction phase of the process and this is then oxidized to molecular oxygen (O_2) at the photosynthetic reaction centre. The biochemical capacity to use water as a source of electrons in photosynthesis evolved from an ancestor of cyanobacteria. Prior to this event the first photosynthetic organisms used reducing agents such as Hydrogen or Hydrogen Sulfide as sources of electrons. This anoxygenic photosynthesis consumes CO_2 but does not release oxygen. It is likely that some of these very primitive prokaryotes were extremophiles; particularly those that thrive in hot temperatures such as would have existed near the end of the Hadean eon.

These are called thermophiles. It has been proposed that these may have evolved within hydrothermal vents below the sea and most likely represent our closest relative to LUCA.

Simple multicellular organisms evolved along with meiosis and sexual reproduction about 1 Ga. From here we will skip forward to the emergence of Primates 50 to 60 million years ago (60 Ma), and immediately onwards to the hominids 6.5 Ma since it is about this juncture that we intend to focus our greatest interest and attention.

(b) THE EMERGENCE OF HUMANITY

A symphony of Spirit,
An odyssey of Life.
This symphony of Love
Plays in harmony with Light.

The symphony of Spirit,
Transfigured as a dove,
Flies onwards and forever,
O'er the sea of eternal love.

From "Symphony of
Life ", by the author.

The main topic of our deliberations concerns the issue of the precise nature of humanity, and the meaning and purpose of human existence. Our immediate concern is in regard to manner in which the human species emerged upon the earth as a fundamentally unique creature from within the midst of a bipedal subgroup of primates which we call hominids. It is believed that the answers to these questions cannot be fully discerned through the sole medium of the biological sciences, physical anthropology palaeoanthropology, genetics, linguistics, or evolutionary psychology (as this discipline is currently defined). A far more radical approach to manner, and the means, by which we attempt to acquire knowledge and insight is required. This necessitates both a shift in our explicit intellectual perspectives, and one of a right hemispheric shift that is aligned to that which is far more implicit and intuitive.

One of the most important biological advances ever made with regard to the evolution of life on earth was made by Alfred Russel Wallace, and Charles Darwin. (in 1858 and 1859, respectively). As well we know, Darwin received the historic accolades since he was the first to hastily publish the theory of evolution in his book "On the Origin of Species". This theory firmly established that all living organisms that ever lived are situated somewhere within the intricate architecture of the Tree of Life.

Ancestry is the term that applies to a direct line of biological inheritance that ultimately connects at a common root. Consequently, the extinct organisms on all the branches that connect us to the root are described as "our ancestors". The remainder, even while they are directly connected with our own branch, are only close relatives, but they are not our ancestors. The location at which each of these direct ancestral domains occurs, and at which a new species emerges (and its branching subdivisions), identifies the site of its most recent common ancestor (MRCA). Richard Dawkins refers to these as "Concestors" as they have been aptly described, and neatly categorized, in his book "An Ancestor's Tale". There are approximately forty such common ancestors between modern humans and our last common ancestor (LUCA).

Fig. 14a

MRCA & The Biological Clock

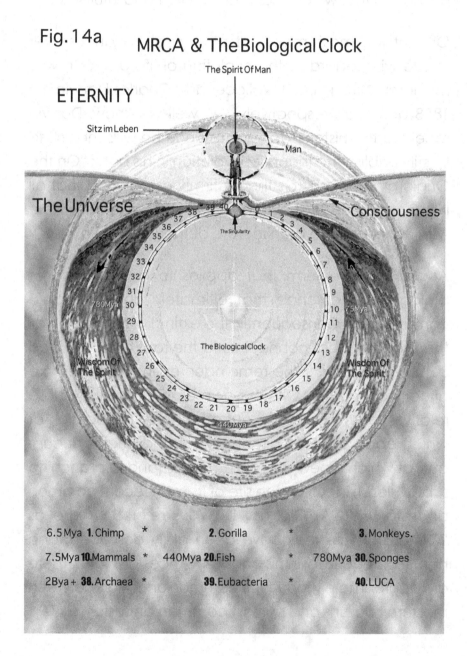

ETERNITY

The Spirit Of Man

Sitz im Leben

Man

The Universe

Consciousness

The Singularity

The Biological Clock

780Mya

75Mya

Wisdom Of The Spirit

Wisdom Of The Spirit

440Mya

6.5 Mya	**1.** Chimp	*		**2.** Gorilla	*		**3.** Monkeys.
7.5 Mya	**10.** Mammals	*	440Mya	**20.** Fish	*	780Mya	**30.** Sponges
2 Bya +	**38.** Archaea	*		**39.** Eubacteria	*		**40.** LUCA

Fig. 14b

MRCA & Biological Clock

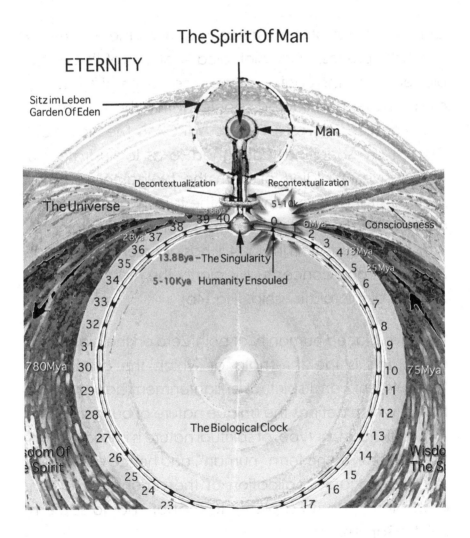

Figure 14a illustrates the evolutionary sequence of our MRCA's from Luca (3.8 Gya) to Sponges (800Mya); Fish (400 Mya); Rodents and rabbits (75 Mya); and Monkeys (6 Mya). On the clock face of the graphic the numbers 1, 2, and 3 indicate Chimps, Gorillas, and other monkeys. The number 38 and 39 are Archaea and Eubacteria respectively, and 40 is LUCA.

Our main focus of interest has to do with the manner in which the process of the biological evolution of life can be placed within the context of the emergence of humanity as a unique, and sacred species within the tree of life. The graphics (Fig.14a & Fig.14b "MRCA & The Biological Clock") are specifically designed so as to illustrate the progressive unfolding of both the biological and the spiritual strands that constitute the totality of our human nature. The most critical element contained within the graphic, as illustrated in Fig.14a, has been enlarged so as to visually, and conceptually, clarify the most important aspects of this relationship. (Fig.14b).

We have placed humanity at point Zero on the biological clock. This is the threshold at which the process of "ensoulment" and spiritual enlightenment had evolved to that which defines the unique nature of our humanity. A specific form, or type, of spiritual nature is implicit within the definition of the term "human", and hence also within the appropriate application of the amended version of the term "Homo sapiens" to that of "Homo sapiens Spiritus Sapiens".

The process of the acquisition of consciousness, which was to be a prerequisite to that of ensoulment, predates the final emergence of humanity upon the earth. The discoveries at the cave sites at Altamira, Lascaux, Chauvet, among others, indicate that consciousness had emerged at least 40 to 60 thousand years ago. Indeed the findings at the South African sites of Blombos and Klipdrift Shelter suggest that this event may have occurred more than a 165 thousand years ago.

The emergence of consciousness is a prerequisite to the instigation of the process of enlightenment and ensoulment. Consciousness would foreshadow that which was yet to come, and was yet to be imbued within the mind of the primate "Homo". The arrival of consciousness would prefigure ensoulment, and indicate within which lineage of the species "Homo" that humanity would emerge.

The taxonomic term "Homo" is an inadequate definition in which to describe the essence and the nature of the human species. The term is only applicable as an identifying reference within a category of primates who, in varying measure, share similar biological features and behavioral traits. This evolutionary classification unequivocally fails to include the essential essence, and the primary substrate, of our humanity within the relevant context of its terms of reference.

Allegorically, as with "John the Baptist," the arrival of consciousness would prepare the unenlightened mind for the coming of that which is most sacred upon the earth. Ultimately, and providentially, "Homo sapiens Spiritus Sapiens"would set foot upon this earth. The primate "Homo" would be utterly transfigured so as to emerge within a human form. Mankind was thus conceivedby the power of the Holy Spirit. Humanity, as in the instance of the Messiah, would "pitch his tent" as a unique and sacred life form on this planet.

The process of ensoulment is what provided the essential impetus necessary for the spiritual, mental, and neurological evolution and subsequent emergence of the species which we define as "human". The aggregate of these particular characteristics, as reflected within the integrated artistic, intellectual, and spiritual expressions of our human nature, only become fully manifest within the past ten thousand years. In point of fact, this process of ensoulment and of enlightenment was only completed through the mission of Christ upon his institution of the Eucharist at the Last Supper. That was the point in time at which humanity had sufficiently matured in mind and spirit so as to begin to comprehend the nature and the meaning of the "Blood of the New and Everlasting Covenant" that was to be poured out by Christ on behalf of all of us. This is in fulfillment of the Old Testament prophesy of Jeremiah (Jer, 31: 31-34).

Henceforth, mankind would come to know the fullness of the reality with respect to his spiritual nature and the true purpose of his existence. That great moment of revelation was firmly copper fastened by the Holy Spirit after the resurrection and on the day of Pentecost ("Shavuot" in Judaism). From this point onwards within the history and the mind-set of our species, the relevance and the significance of the biological clock and the "Origin of the Species" as an isolated biological and historical event fades by comparison.

What are often referred to in text books as "Homo", "Hominid", or "Archaic Homo sapiens", all reside between point zero (point of emergence of humanity) and number 1 (6Mya) on the biological clock(chimpanzees and bonobos). None of these are considered as being fully representative of the species "Homo sapiens Spiritus Sapiens" as this terminology defines the nature of our humanity within a holistic spiritual and biological context. In that regard Figures 14A, and 14B, are amongst two of the most important graphics within this book.

When we use the term "ancestry" in common parlance we are usually referring to our genetic inheritance as defined by our genome. The genome is the total aggregate of all DNA contained within both parental strands of our chromosomes. I acknowledge that within such a limited context this implied definition would only take us back to the third last evolutionary domain within which we still exist. This, the Eukaryotes, is that phase when cell division, or meiosis, and the emergence of complex life became established. Either way, this great evolutionary leap forward is but a stone's throw from LUCA, the penultimate Last Universal Common Ancestor. It does not really matter, within the context of our deliberations, that this throw may be a mere few billion years ago. However, the lineage does continue back beyond the Eukaryotes and meiosis. Within these domains, identified as Archaea and Eubacteria (2 billion, and 3.8 billion years ago respectively), the precursors of our complex genome existed as simple pieces of DNA, or chains of amino acids, and its original antecedent, RNA. These primitive unicellular organisms increased in number through a process of cellular multiplication, or mitosis, since they had yet to acquire the facility, and related energy resources, to undergo cell division. As you will recall, it was only when bacteria entered into a symbiotic relationship within Archaea, so as to function as the organelle which we describe as the mitochondria, that this simple cell was empowered, and elevated, to its higher life status as the multicellular Eukaryote. The term "symbiosis" refers to the cohabitation of two organisms of different species for their mutual benefit.

The terms of reference which are applied to the immense contributions made by Wallace and Darwin, (in 1858 and 1859 respectively), with regard to the evolution of life, relate solely to the biological aspects of this process. These biological advances provided us with a unique insight into the manner in which life emerged on earth in all its beauty, complexity, and diversity. However, mankind has both a biological, and a spiritual ancestry, and a related inheritance. The spiritual aspect of our humanity was not factored into the Darwinian equation. The introduction of a spiritual element within the terms of reference that apply to evolution, and the emergence of the human species, does not necessarily imply the existence of a duality of natures within the human person. Neither is duality of nature implicit within the context of the phenomenon of mind and brain, our dual cerebral hemispheres, nor the existence of two strands within the double helix of our DNA. We will remind ourselves of the fact that the unity of soul and body are so profound that the soul is considered to be the "form" of the body. Spirit and matter, in man, within their union, forms a single nature.

This profound form of unity has been redefined within this text as being one wherein Spirit and primordial mind become mystically united within a process of symbiotic fusion. Within the manner, and analogy, by which cyanobacteria contributed to the empowerment of Archaea, and the emergence of a higher life form,(i.e. a symbiotic process), so also did the induction of the spiritual principle empower, and elevate, the biological hominid. The emergence of a new, distinctly unique, and sacred species, which we describe as "human", was the resultant outcome of this transcendental event. This may be described as a "trans-symbiotic" unity of Spirit and matter as it applies to the nature of humanity. This unique from of unity is manifest within the transcendental and synergistic type of relationship that exists between the psyche, and the soul, as the functional agents that comprise the unified composition of the human mind. Consequently, we may define the human mind as the "ensouled psyche". This type of unity is also evident within the nature of the transcendental synergism, and of the reciprocity, that exists between mind and brain. At the purely biological level, this synergy and reciprocity is also mirrored within the bi-hemispheric operative dynamics that apply to the right and left cerebral hemispheres of the brain. It is in this manner that both aspects of the mind, (psyche and soul), and of the brain, (right and left hemispheres), can function as an integrated unit within the modus operandi of this relationship.

Consciousness describes the means by which this symbiotic unity of matter and Spirit was conveyed, and implemented, through the power of the Holy Spirit. The outcome of this process was to spiritually animate humanity with the "life force", or "breath of life". It was in this manner that humanity was to be progressively raised up to his sacred, and ultimately unique status within the Tree of Life.

The definition of "trans-symbiosis", as with the term "endosymbiosis", implies that each of the life forms that contribute towards the synergistic process still retain a fundamental degree of individual autonomy. As it applies to the cell, this is reflected in the retention of the mitochondrial DNA as distinct from the nuclear DNA of its resident host cell. Likewise, Spirit and psyche retain their individual autonomy within the synergism of the unified human mind. This form of synergism, and reciprocity, also applies to the unitary relationship that applies to the functionality of the mind and brain. The soul does not become the right cerebral hemisphere, nor does the psyche become the left hemisphere. Trans-symbiosis therefore must not be confused with the term "Consubstantial", nor with that of "Transubstantiation". These are related terms that are used to describe a mystical process wherein one substance coexists within the substance of another as a single, real, autonomous and indivisible living entity. The former term is applied in the instance wherein Christ is as "One being with the Father", while the latter is reserved to describe the mystical process wherein the bread and wine of the Eucharist become the body and blood of Christ at the consecration of the Mass.

We may consider the psyche as being derived from, or as representative of, the substance and biological activity, of the brain. The psyche, as initially represented, and defined, (i.e. prior to the ensoulment of the biological host), was described as an "instinctual awareness" of the biological self. The soul is representative of the Spiritual, and authentic, nature of our humanity. The process of ensoulment describes the acquisition of a cognitive awareness in regard to our authentic spiritual identity.

The psyche will expire with brain death. The soul will live on, eternally. The ultimate disposition of the soul is determined by the extent to which it retains its primacy within the authenticity of its content, and as the substrate, (i.e. first principles), of that content is finally expressed through the agency of the individual mind-set. These are issues that pertain to the individual exercise of a person's conscience and free will.

This mystical process of spiritual awakening reached some critical status of enlightenment at which time the "ensoulment" of mankind was functionally completed. Thus ensouled, mankind emerged within the biological content, and the living context, of an evolving genetic pool. The evolution of mankind as a specific species within the tree of life can only be considered within the context of the concurrent, and synchronous, history of his biological and spiritual unfolding and awakening. Indeed, as you can obviously predict, we are emphatically stating that our spiritual "evolution" predates, and in turn will inevitably postdate, that of our biological history here on earth.

The primate, within the category of hominids, had evolved biologically to some critical threshold of physical, neurological, and instinctual mental complexity that could accommodate the specific needs, and requirements, of the process of ensoulment. However, the acquisition of consciousness was an absolute prerequisite in order that such a biological threshold could be exceeded. Consciousness provided the primary, and critical, impetus that was required in order to instigate the enigmatic, and spiritual process of humanization.

Humanity is more of a transcendental process of "becoming", than it is one of a biological state of "being". It is a process of spiritual animation, and of enlightenment, through the power and the Wisdom of the Spirit. We refer to these processes as "Ensoulment",(spiritual animation and spiritual awareness), and "Revelation", (enlightenment), in respect to the manner in which the authentic spiritual nature of our being, and the mystery of an omnipotent Creator, are revealed to us. The mystery refers to something hidden which one cannot know or understand unless it is revealed to us. This is an intuitive knowledge as opposed to one that is explicitly conceptualized by way of intellectual deduction. The paradox in relation to the manner in which this knowledge is acquired is that it is only through our willingness to acknowledge its validity that it can be known and understood. "Believing is seeing". The essence of humanity is man – "man" as a spiritual being created in the image and likeness of god in eternity. The phenomenon in regard to the existence of humanity as a unique and sentient being pertains to the primacy of becoming over being. It conforms to the principle of the primacy of process over structure and form. The process is fundamentally one of a spiritual and transcendental nature which is reflected within the evolutionary history of our species. The spiritual process of becoming human has precedence over the biological expression that defines the unique nature and characteristic traits of our human identity.

The application of the human intellect cannot disclose the authenticity of these truths as something that is known. Just as the process of Revelation was instigated through the prophets of the Old Testament and continued to unfold until it was finally realized in the Word made flesh as Christ, so also has the process of our becoming human proceeded through these centuries. It is only as we seek to embrace, and respond, to this continuous process of revelation that we have the potential to become more fully human. The realization of our full human potential in that regard would be to become like Christ in the expression and actualization of his humanity.

The process of ensoulment, and the acquisition of the intuitive knowledge that accompanied this spiritualizing phenomenon, initiated a dramatic sequence of events within the neurological growth and complexity of the Neocortex . In turn, these neurological adaptations would be mirrored within the physical, intellectual, artistic, and spiritual expressions of our human nature. As a consequence of these events it is evident that the nature of humanity is intimately related to the nature of the human mind. It is through the process of spiritual symbiosis (i.e. "trans-symbiosis") of our instinctive mental capacities, through the agency of the Holy Spirit, that the emergence of a new form of life upon our planet was to occur. That new life is life "ensouled", and man reborn, as the species which we describe as "human".

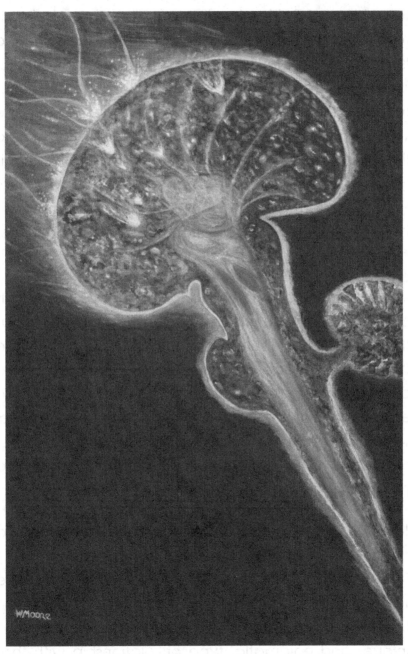

Enlightenment

The mind of the chosen hominid was raised up to a new status of Spiritual enlightenment. The mind was transfigured as a synergistic composite of Soul and Psyche. Therein they would remain in constant conflict as is reflected within the reciprocal bipolarity of our cerebral hemispheres. Free will would determine which of these, as master and as emissary, would ultimately hold sway in our decision making. Within this context, ensoulment, more than any other physical, or biological acquisition, is the ultimate defining factor that differentiates humanity from hominids, or any other life forms.

Within the various scientific disciplines that pertain to the study of evolution, the identification of various characteristic attributes are helpful indicators in the classification of each species. Those which are specific to the human clad include a variety of anatomic features, brain size and configuration, gait, manual dexterity, speech and language, and evidence of higher intellectual capacity,(inclusive of abstract thought and the use of allegory / metaphor).

However, most, if not all, of these indicators are a manifestation of the acquisition of specific primary mental attributes. These particular attributes, are derived from a source that is extrinsic to the human organism. This metaphysical source has entered into a unique, and enigmatic, type of relationship with that organism which we have described as one of "trans symbiosis". The acquisition of this spiritual form of mental empowerment provides the human organism with the prospect of realizing its true potential as expressed within its environment, and within the wider context of its entire evolutionary history.

It is absolutely imperative that we address the nature of the human mind within the context of the primacy of its substrate. It is also essential that we make every human effort possible to address the core issues that pertain to the nature, source, and content of this substrate. In effect, this demands that we revert to the domain of the subconscious, the collective unconscious, and finally, to search beyond the mystery of the instigating singularity of the cosmos and the material universe. This is a journey beyond the limitations, and the conceptual framework, of our human intellect. It is an odyssey of faith, a quest in search of the Omega, the Word that has spoken, and yet still speaks through the Holy Spirit, to all of us. We must be prepared to listen, so that we may hear, and reciprocate with gratitude and thanksgiving.

For our stated purpose we will confine our discussions to within the evolutionary domains of the last six or seven million years. This is the period at which the bipedal hominids started to emerge following the divergence of the gorilla, and then that of the chimpanzee, from the biological architecture of our tree of life.

FROM HOMINID TO HUMAN

We have fallen as mere particles,
Particles of stardust, and particles of light.
We have fallen from the centre,
From the source of our perfection,
God's mercy, and God's might.
This separation would forever prove
To be our sad, and sorry plight.

We have been transmuted
In the alchemy of atoms,
That will burn in the naked flame.
As earthly creatures we would evolve,
Our true essence to reclaim.
The message of redemption
We would incessantly proclaim.

From "Stardust to Earthly
Clay ", by the author.

Primates diverged from other mammals approximately 85 million years ago. The earliest fossil evidence of this event dates to 55 – 60 Mya. Hominidae, as Great Apes diverged from the Gibbon family 20 Mya. The Ponginae (Orangutans) diverged from Hominids 12-15 Mya, then the Gorillas 9 Mya, and lastly the Chimpanzees 4-6 Mya.

The earliest bipedal Hominid is now considered to be Sahelanthropus which is our last shared ancestor to the Chimpanzee, with Ardipithecus emerging later. It was only in 1967 that the divergence time of humans and apes was estimated to have occurred as recently as 4-6 Mya. These conclusions were arrived at by Vincent Sarich and Allan Wilson through the application of genetic technology which functions as a "molecular clock". The infamous discovery of "Lucy" soon afterwards was to support these innovative technological findings. Lucy was determined to be a member of the species Australopithecus aferensis, and was discovered in N.Ethiopia in the 1980's.

These early bipedals eventually evolved into the australopithicines, and subsequently into the genus Homo.

The earliest documented members of the genus which we presently refer to as "Homo" are Homo Habilis 2.3Mya. However, you will appreciate that this title is a scientific misnomer. It is a misappropriation of terminology in so far as an authentic definition can be applied to the genus Homo. Nevertheless, it is about this time (2.3-1.3 Mya) when Habilis emerged that the process of "encephalization" took place with the arrival of the much larger brained species "Homo" Erectus. The cranial capacity of H. Erectus doubled to that of 850 cm. over the subsequent one million years. Homo Erectus and H. Ergaster are considered to have been the first of several subsequent migrations out of Africa. They spread through Africa, Asia, and Europe between 1.3 and 1.8 Mya. The second line of migration, 50 – 100 Thousand years ago, was by Homo Hedelberggenis and H. Rhodesicasus. It is possibly from these that modern humans have biologically emerged. These were to replace the earlier populations of the first immigrants, including those of Neanderthal.

Various hominids anatomically reminiscent of the modern human form started to emerge 200 thousand years ago. Yet it has only been within the past 50 thousand years that we start to see evidence of behavioral modernity which is consistent with the activities of the genus Homo. These are reflected in such parameters as those of symbolic culture, language, and technology. This has been described as the "Great leap Forward". However, the most dramatic biological acceleration within this evolutionary phase has only occurred within the past 10 thousand years.

From a scientific perspective, human evolution is characterized by a number of morphological, developmental, physiological, and behavioral changes that have taken place since the split between the last common ancestor of humans and chimpanzees. The most significant of these adaptations are bipedalism, increased brain size and complexity (particularly of the Frontal Lobes), lengthened period of gestation and of infancy, and decreased sexual dimorphism.

Examples of behavioral changes characteristic of modern humans include specialization of tools and hunting techniques,, use of jewelry, creation of artistic images, organization of living space, rites and rituals, and the use of barter trade networks. Given the relatively brief period of time within which these various features emerged, and especially those which explosively arose within the past 10, 000 years, there is strong support for the contention that modern human evolution occurred as a relatively abrupt, and dramatic, form of "revolution". This hypothesis is aligned with the concept that a precipitous escalation within the domain of human consciousness, and the related acquisition of an authentic spiritual awareness, came to an ultimate fruition in a rather explosive manner. These events are those that define the process of "ensoulment". The spark of spiritual enlightenment had finally reached the threshold at which it would ignite as a fire within the mind of our human nature.

It is the nature and the source of consciousness, and the manner in which it was acquired (regardless of whether this occurred abruptly or gradually) that is of core relevance to our inquiry. From our perspective it was the acquisition of consciousness that was the ultimate defining factor that separated the human species from all other primates. We have proposed a definition of the term "consciousness", within both an implicit and explicit context, in the first chapter ("The air of Clarity", Part 2.). We might now ask as to why one particular subset of hominids, rather than any another one, or several, was to be in receipt of this remarkable facility. Did consciousness emerge as a biological facility that arose as a consequence of natural selection, variation, and the modification of our

DNA ? Are we human because we exhibit a number of human specific biological features, are in procession of a species-specific genome, and demonstrate a pattern of genetically acquired behavioral traits that are indicative of consciousness? Alternatively, did the acquisition of consciousness as a prerequisite to spiritual enlightenment render us human, and thus instigate the evolutionary changes within our genes that would become species specific to our kind? The question then is whether we became human through the acquisition of consciousness, or was it the ultimate modification of the primate's genome that determined the means by which we achieved the facility of consciousness.

It is proposed herein that the human species did not arise as a consequence of some process of natural biological selection and variation within a primary evolutionary, and genetic context. Humanity did not evolve from a Hominid ancestor. Rather our humanity "evolved" into a specifically appropriated primate precursor. All other strands of hominids, including Neanderthal, would become extinct since their biological purpose, and their contribution to this process, within the context of evolution, had been fulfilled. The essential essence of our humanity arose from a source that was extrinsic to the primate creature that was to become its biological host. In this manner the authentic nature of humanity would enter into a synergistic form of relationship with its recipient.

This is a unique form of synergy that transcends that of biological endosymbiosis. It is a form of synergy of spirit and of matter, which we have termed "trans-symbiosis", such that this biological organism would become spiritually animated, empowered, and ensouled, as a new and sacred entity upon the Earth. This trans-symbiosis, of the mortal and the spiritual, is what raised up the primate to a new and sanctified status. It was to instigate a dramatic, and progressive series of events within the mind and body of its host. Of critical importance was the fact that these would be reflected within the context of its physical, mental, spiritual, and cerebral makeup, and in the manner in which they would be conveyed, and expressed, within the world in which we as humans now exist. Henceforth, the master of the human mind would be the Soul, and the Psyche its mere emissary. Humankind, as the species "Homo sapiens" would finally evolve within this second Genesis to emerge upon the Earth as the unique, and sacred species, "Homo sapiens Spiritus Sapiens " .

Since no life form was ever endowed with the precise spiritual principle that is specific to mankind, then none of his biological predecessors can be rightfully described as being representative of his ancestral heritage. All other descendants are but biological precursors to mankind. All life forms that preceded mankind were a prelude to someone yet unborn. They would foreshadow a species that was yet to come within the enfolding mystery of the world. They would prefigure, and herald, the arrival of another, and far more important living entity. That sacred entity, which had been spiritually awakening,(or "evolving "), in parallel with the biological component within the Tree of Life, would finally emerge. This new life form would issue from within its previous, biologically unexpressed and hitherto encapsulated, temple and domain. A magnificent and unique species, at once unified biologically and spiritually, was to emerge triumphantly within the existing context of the genetic pool of life.

Mankind is now reborn. Humankind has been spiritually resurrected from the clay of the earth within which he had been re-sown since the time of his prior demise in eternity. The human species finally arises to claim his rightful place within the world and all that lives therein. Those life forms, which we describe as hominids, that had emerged from the biological gene pool had served their essential purpose. They had toiled as living and organic workers, or labor hands, within the pasture lands of biology. They had worked selflessly in order to construct the genetic footprint that would be the firm, and highly complex, foundation of our human genome. And they would sacrifice their lives so that such an unprecedented and sacred cause would be fulfilled within its preordained time.

Ultimately, and not so very long ago, the breath of consciousness would animate this evolving genome to ensoul a creature now reborn upon this earth. This human creature would rise up above all living forms and claim mastery of his earthly kingdom. This is the one whom we have called Homo Sapiens – the "knowledgeable man". Yet, this human is the "man" of both intellectual knowledge and of Spiritual Wisdom. This is you and I. We are "Homo sapiens Spiritus Sapiens". We are one in purpose and in vocation. We are one in Spirit and in kind. We are sacred, and we are blessed to have been amongst the chosen members of this divinely inspired and creative plan.

Mankind emerged from a Tree of Life that had evolved from a seed within which resided both a spiritual and a material embryo. This is a seed, or enigmatic ovule, that had been sown at the dawn of the creation of the universe. Its central location within this world mirrors that of the Tree of Life, of good and evil, within the Garden of Eden. Yet, mankind is strictly neither the Tree nor any of its branches. Rather, mankind is the fruit that issued forth from that defined and singular branch. Man had blossomed from the bud upon the branches of "the Vine". A portion of the essence of that fruit would sustain his life eternally. A breath, as the breath of consciousness, one that glows in a sacred light, would rekindle life within a new-formed human seed. Life would be imparted as a soul so as to resuscitate a mortal being with the potential to be reinstated with its Spirit. Therein it could regain the life of immortality for all eternity. In clear and easy hindsight, the biological metaphor of the Tree of Life had been long foretold in the book of Genesis. It had also been foretold within the context of a spiritual metaphor as represented by the Tree of Life upon which Christ was crucified so as to gain our salvation for a life eternal. Therein, both of these metaphors had been long written by the ancient scribes within words, and vivid imagery, of the Old Testament.

Wallace and Darwin have only managed to observe, and partially reconstruct, the imagery of the Tree of Life as portrayed in the Old Testament. They failed utterly to perceive, acknowledge, or respond to the essential essence contained within the substance of that living tree. They failed to identify its root, the source that gave it life, and the nature of the fruit it bore.

Consequently, the biological theory of life, as an isolated phenomenon, is fundamentally flawed and incomplete. It is denatured within its material fabric and at its very core. That tree is made of wood, the dead wood of our biological ancestors. It is sterile and devoid of enduring life. No fruit could it ever bear.

Sometimes we must revert, follow the long trail back, to try and get our proper bearings. We hope to identify some familiar point of reference so that we may constructively move forward once again. Anyone who likes to go walking off the beaten track, along lone trails through woodland or over mountainous terrain will be quite familiar with such incidents. Regardless of all the modern navigational gadgetry, it is often something simple and easily identifiable within the immediate landscape that guides us to safety and points us in the right direction.

It may be a bush, a tree, or some familiar rock that is firmly embedded in the earth. Perhaps our evolutionary theorists ought have turned around and sought to find their bearings in the far distant past. Both the landmark tree, and guiding rock, had been in evidence long before themortal quest had ever been initiated or begun.

A simple glance into the night sky, the twinkling of a star, the chance vision of a hail of meteorites, or perhaps a lone comet, was all that was required to set the compass right. The three wise men from the East were guided by a star, or perhaps by a comet falling through the earth's atmosphere. These noble kings may be thought of as representative of Earth, Fire, and Water. These are the essential elements that would nurture the seed of our humanity so that it would survive and grow to its full maturity. So also, and in a similar manner, would our scientific brethren have been given right judgement and right guidance. Enlightenment is only found by those who seek to find the sacred origin and the spiritual truth regarding our human heritage.

We too had fallen from the infinite heights back at the beginning of time and the creation of our vast universe. We fell as grains of stardust enveloped within the Light of the Spirit. These grains, a mere collection of five groups of inorganic elements constitute the totality of our original basic chemistry and of anything ever known to exist on our planet earth. These fundamental building blocks of all material matter, both animate and inanimate, were first charted as then known, by Ivor Mendeleyev (1834-1907).

Some of these are incorporated in trace amounts within our bodies. Yet, for the greater part we are composed of only three basic constituents: carbon, hydrogen, and oxygen, and the greatest proportion of these is present simply as water.

We were immersed within earth's primordial pools as seeds carried upon the winds of time. These were seeds borne from a far and distant shore. That "dust" would chemically evolve, from the simple and inorganic, to the more complex and organic. Together they would constitute the biological template that was to provide the mortal temple of our physical bodies. That glowing, and sacred light of the spirit was destined to become enshrined within that temple. It would be slowly kindled to a flame that would ignite the spirit of humanity. That synergy of dust and of metaphysical light, would emerge in time as mankind upon the earth. This living entity would be endowed with Spirit, and with the Wisdom of an intuitive knowledge. Human kind would be a unique life form upon this planet. He would be Homo sapiens Spiritus Sapiens, in nature and in kind. We have been brought back to life, resuscitated, and reborn, through the kiss of the breath of life of consciousness.

The biblical account of the birth of Christ is a re-enactment of our own arrival, and our subsequent evolution, upon this earth. Christ would follow the path that had been laid out for us since creation. The star of Bethlehem prefigured this great moment. The Star of David shines out in its brilliance, and in its glory, at the apex of our symbolic, and perennial, Tree of Life. It is right that we should remember that joyous day and rejoice with reverence. We should always, and everywhere, give thanks for His great glory.

Through the life, death, and resurrection of Christ we were redeemed:

> "Dying, He destroyed our death
> Rising, He restored our life"

All humanity would have the facility to come to know the truth concerning their authentic nature through the acquisition of consciousness. It is consciousness that provides humanity with the means whereby he may gain access to the Wisdom of the Spirit. It is the means by which we may hear the Word should we but listen out in the silent humility of the soul.

The Spirit speaks, we are called to listen, to reciprocate and respond. This, and this alone, ultimately defines the authentic nature of our humanity. This is the second most critical statement contained within the entire content of this book, and to which reference was made within the Forward:

> The Word has spoken,
> Now the Spirit speaks,
> And it is heard.
> Therefore, "I am".

CHAPTER SIX: THE EVOLUTION OF THE MIND

Helplessly hoping to open doors of perception
To the mysteries and the quandaries of mankind;
The secrets of the universe are all we wish to find.
Yet, we only hear the echoes resounding in
our mind.

Helplessly groping through fine particles of dust
And dried bones that lie scattered in the sand
Endlessly searching in this sterile, barren, land
We find only what can wither, die, and rust.

From "The Doors of
Perception" by the author.

(a) THEORIES OF MIND & COGNITIVE FLUIDITY

There are several schools of thought concerning the manner and means by which our human minds historically evolved and currently develop from infancy to maturity. I will attempt to briefly summarize two of the most widely quoted versions concerning these illusive and dramatic events. One is a utilitarian and technological concept which is grounded in Darwinian fundamentalism. The other is more of a humanistic and intuitive version.

Suffice to say that both are highly allegorical in their expression and that despite their obvious differences in principle and in their implications, by and large; there is a general consensus of opinion with respect to the outcome that renders the species of mankind distinctly human compared to other primates. For all, or the greater part, this evidence is confined to the biological, and by implication to the human expression of these biological distinctions. We, on the other hand, and in due course, will extend our terms of reference to a far more comprehensive and holistic account of the human condition.

Since the early nineteen eighties, there has been a major resurgence of academic interest in the phenomenon of the mind. A multitude of varied scientific disciplines have undertaken the challenge to be the first to unlock the mysteries of the human mind, the manner in which it evolved, the means by which it interacts within the functional and reciprocal dynamics of our brain, and why it is a uniquely human property. The resurrection of Ernest Haeckel's biogenetic law (1866) appears to have prompted much of this current research. What began as a biological, and Darwinian inspired, theory of evolutionary and genetic racism, has been catapulted into the modern domain of the neurosciences. This in turn has spawned the emergence of evolutionary psychology as a subspecialty within the discipline of cognitive science. The new age scientific language speaks of the mind within a structural, architectural, and modular format. It appears that Homo sapiens is unique among primates because we have selectively acquired the cognitive facility of biological super-computerization. The status of our higher intellectual function is what characterizes & defines the human species as unique among primates. It is this specific attribute that identifies us as distinctly human, or so we are informed by the cognitive scientists and their related cohort of academic colleagues.

Haeckel's Law proposes that the sequence of developmental stages that is traversed by the juvenile within a species reflects the same sequence of evolutionary changes that was experienced by the adult forms of its ancestors. In scientific jargon this is expressed as "Ontogeny reflects Phylogeny". The term "ontogeny" refers to the history of the embryo, while that of "phylogeny" refer to the history of race. In effect this theorem describes a process of accelerated recapitulation by children of previously established genetic traits acquired by adults throughout the ages.

Haeckel's Law was to subsequently suggest that in the case of human beings, the entire ancestral file of our adult fore bearers over millions of years is recapitulated, or "down loaded" within the first two years of infancy. Additionally, this process is completed in the same order and sequence as it evolved ("Ontogeny and Phylogeny" by Stephen Jay Gould. Pub.1977). The concept of recapitulation has long since been discredited. Biological and morphological research has demonstrated that there is not a one-to –one correspondence between phylogeny and ontogeny. However, some form of "recapitulating interrelationship" does appear to exist between these two domains. The precise basis for this correlation is as yet not fully understood. Nevertheless, recognition of the potential wealth of information that could be derived from the extrapolation of this Law to the study of the developing mind in childhood was finally recognized in the nineteen eighties. To a large extent this recapitulation phenomenon appears to explain the speed, and scope, of the acquisition of highly complex skill sets of intelligence manifest by children within their first few years of life.

At the fore front of this research was Jerry Fodor (The Modularity of the Mind) in 1983 and Howard Gardner (Frames of the Mind: The Theory of Multiple Intelligences, 1983).Their work was expanded and further advanced by a number of other great academics including Leda Cosmides and John Tooby (The Adapted Mind 1992) and Karmiloff- Smith (Beyond Modularity 1992). These studies were to suggest that from a primitive architectural template of general social intelligence, the mind progressively evolved in magnitude and complexity to its current status. It was proposed that this occurred as information - rich modules of intelligence were inherited in advancing order over the centuries. As a result of this acquisition the fundamental primary template expanded as a pre- primed data base of knowledge. The final outcome is what is described as the evolution and development of a state of "Cognitive Fluidity".

However, when you trace the trajectory of these mental concepts all the way back to Haeckel's tombstone, you will discern that what is being described is no more than the evolutionary history of the human brain cloaked within the language of the evolutionary psychologist. It is no more than an allegorical representation of mental events as they are deemed to have progressively evolved within the primitive brainstem, and subsequently proceeded onwards to the midbrain, the cortex and the neo-cortex .This might be an acceptable means of attempting to portray these evolutionary (i.e. phylogeny) events, but only with the precondition that (a) It was clearly acknowledged to be no more than a biological analogy that has been superimposed upon a series of evolutionary cerebral events, and (b) that the analogy was only applicable within the limited context of the human psyche, but not to the heterogeneous composite of the entire human mind.

The conceptualized sequence of events, as they are applied to the mind, simply describe the genetically encoded modules within the brain that have been "mapped out" so that they could establish a template upon which the complex circuitry of the brain could be constructed, and "fine- tuned", in response to the nature of the pervading environment. At a developmental level (i.e. ontogeny), this process is reflected in the manner in which the millions of neurons, and their multiple synaptic connections, within the cerebral cortex of the new born, become progressively ordered and configured into identifiable circuit patterns. Initially these neurons, and their complement of axons, exist as a relatively undifferentiated mesh of interconnecting fibres. Those neurons and their array of ganglia which are not incorporated within these circuits are absorbed (dissolve) in their millions throughout infancy. In fact, as much as 40% of the original total cortical content of axons vanish like snowflakes, or unused pieces of Lego, by the early teens.

On the other hand, the circuit patterns that do become established are partially guided by genetic factors, but also, and most importantly, in response to the nature of the presenting mental substrate which the brain has acquired from the workings of the mind. Much of this early childhood substrate is retrieved from memory as metaphorical concepts that are being continuously generated in response to the constant observational influx and the related felt experience. It is only within the specific context of the human psyche that these mental events could be expressed within a language that is clearly grounded within the biological context of the evolving brain. The "modularity – mapping" theories of Fodor and Gardner, and their more recent contemporaries, might have some validity within this limited mental context. This is because the primitive psyche appears to have evolved as a mental expression that was derived from neurological elements within the primate's brain stem. This would serve to explain the means by which the primate originally acquired what we have alluded to as a self- protective, and life preserving "instinctual awareness".

It was only following the acquisition of consciousness that the status of the primordial psyche was elevated to that which is now in evidence within the mind of humanity. These evolutionary events occurred in parallel with the massive surge in the biological complexity, and functional capacity, of the human brain. They were also accompanied by a process of transfiguration in mind, and spirit, that lead to the final emergence of the human species upon this earth. The curious fact of the matter is that despite the misappropriated analogy that has been scientifically constructed in respect of the human mind, paradoxically, it retains a fundamental truth, albeit for all the wrong reasons. The transfiguration of the human mind occurred through a transcendental process of ensoulment which instigated a reciprocal, and parallel, biological process within the neurological configuration and functional complexity that is unique to the human species. The spiritual process of becoming human has total precedence over the biological existence and structural form of being.

The alternative concept, as represented and expressed by Mc Gilchrist, is far less technologically constructed. He suggests that this analogy is largely a product of deduction that has all the classic logistical hallmarks of the left brain firmly and quite clearly inscribed within its signature. Implicit within the more Darwinian and Haeckel based view is the belief that the driving force is purely utilitarian and functional and that it is fuelled by a process of ruthless competitive advantage. Mc Gilchrist believes that this model is grounded within the excesses of hard core natural selection theory. It is based upon an ideology that is fundamentally divisive rather than inclusive, concerned more with self -survival than collective survival. It is presented as a gladiatorial arena of conflict, pitting one individual against the next and all others so as to gain the greater advantage in our quest for personal survival and success in our individual aspirations and goals.

Mc Gilchrist suggests that we need not resort to a concept of inherited pre- enriched "modules of intelligence" since a process that involves our intuitive natural tendency to imitate, that is to inhabit the emotional world of others, suffices as a valid explanation. This concept, or belief, identifies the motivational drive as being fuelled by our intuitive empathy, and is adapted for the collective use and benefit of the group, as opposed to the individual and the ego. This concept acknowledges the fundamental role of the right brain, of our natural affinity towards synergy, collaboration, cooperation, and cohesion. Indeed, the recent identification of the so called "mirror neuron" could in theory support Mc Gilchrist's concept. It has been suggested that this specialized mirror neuron provides us with the facility of mimicry. It also enables us to read another's thoughts and feelings and to experience empathy. Likewise, the module which we propose in respect of the evolution of the mind is founded upon the primacy of our human intuition and the corresponding activities of the right cerebral hemisphere. However, this module will be expressed within a different form of language, an alternative context, and imagery.

From a functional cognitive perspective, what clearly distinguishes the human from the animal is the acquisition and use of this Cognitive Fluidity. If we reapply a purely cerebral, and biological, adaptation of the "modularity of mind" to our understanding of the events as they are described within this conceptual model, in effect it simply refers to the integration of previously isolated neurological circuits, and their intermediary cell stations, that had existed prior to the emergence of language. Obviously, Mc Gilchrist conceptualizes and verbalizes the process quite differently. In the final analysis, it is the procurement and the application of this integrated and homogenous data base of cognitive intelligence that defines the critical transition point in this biological aspect of the humanizing process. What is of the utmost importance is that any theory of Cognitive Fluidity must be interpreted as a process that is instigated within the human mind and is subsequently mirrored within the neurological sequence of events as they are conveyed and orchestrated in response to the directives of the evolving mind. In summary, this is to state quite clearly, and unequivocally, that the mind, (as represented by the soul), has Primacy of Affect in relation to the cognitive activities of the human brain.

Through a process which Carey and Spelke describe as "mapping", language was a major triggering agent that permitted communication and exchange of knowledge that had previously been inaccessible to each other. Advanced intelligence is the consequence of this open accessibility and fluid like interchange. It provides us with a highly complex and integrated global data base. Regardless of which model you may choose either one simply describes an evolutionary process that is reflected within the genetically determined neurological configuration and electrochemical activities of the human brain. In actuality, the process is instigated within an entirely different location and milieu which is unique to the mind of man. The sequence of evolutionary events, as they pertain to the brain, are but a mirror image of what first transpires and unfolds within the mystery of our human minds.

The most important of these cerebral events is that of the critical degree of separation, and independence of functioning, that was to occur between our right and left cerebral hemispheres. This biological phenomenon was to occur in tandem with, and in response to, the creative and mystical process that would culminate in the majestic inauguration and investiture of the soul within the hallowed cloister of the mind. Therein it was conceived that the soul would reign supreme, as lord and master, in relation to its mortal emissary – the now highly honored, and much exalted, human psyche.

As a consequence of this process, the intuitive knowledge acquired by the right cerebral hemisphere could now be separated and presented to the left hemisphere so that it can be apprehended, processed, and finally, represented back to the right hemisphere. The concurrent participation of the more recent and explosive evolutionary development of our frontal lobes contributes greatly to the process of reintegration and cooperative inter hemispheric synergy by imbuing it with a sense of objectivity and a conscious awareness, or perception, of knowing and understanding. This is the process by which metaphorical concepts are reconstructed as thoughts and ideas. They are then translated into language and reintegrated back into the fabric of life. It has now been reconfigured into a useful and functional commodity that can be productively applied to manipulate our world and assist in the pursuit of our chosen objectives.

Since the biological evolution of the brain occurs in parallel with the evolution of the mind we must also conclude that it was some aspect of the mind that was a major contributor towards the provision of the template upon which the substance of the brain was to evolve in complexity and functionality. From such a perspective it is clearly evident that it was the acquisition of intuitive awareness, or ensoulment, that provided the primary impetus for the emergence of advanced intelligence or of "cognitive fluidity". Indeed, when we acknowledge that it is the spiritual principle within mankind that renders him uniquely human, it is clearly evident that it was this specific evolutionary event that instigated the mental, and hence the biological cerebral adaptations, that are distinctive features of the human species.

Steven Mithen likens the evolutionary process of the human mind to a phased architectural program. It begins with the construction of a single nave of general intelligence. A series of "chapels" of specialized intelligences which are isolated from each other and from the central nave are built next. Finally, direct access routes are created that provide a means of movement and exchange between all elements of what by now would be seen as an open "Cathedral of the Mind". (The Prehistory of the Mind. 1996). I find this analogy both intriguing and provocative.It is clearly evident that Mithen, as with most of his quoted contemporaries, has failed to identify the critical relevance of his metaphorical imagery. He, like many of his learned colleagues, has been mesmerized by the architectural elegance of the building while being blind and oblivious to the spiritual presence for which this majestic cathedral was originally designed to accommodate. Such an attitude is akin to being smitten with admiration for the genius of Michelangelo while gazing in a catatonic state upon the "Pieta". Therein, one stares utterly detached and unmoved by the historical event that inspired its creation. There stands a mortal creature without empathy, one who cannot fathom the magnitude of the pain and suffering that was endured.. Such is the one who would fail to consider the implications that this great moment was to have for all mankind. Who among us could possibly fail to ponder the nature of the mind that was so filled with compassion that he was inspired to apply his artistic skill in the creation of this magnificent masterpiece? Yet, many a hardened heart has wept bitter tears in the silence of their souls as they dwelt within the presence of this cold and indifferent chunk of hand carved marble.

The conceptual representation of the mind as a cathedral, or any fixed and solid physical structure, is an accurate reflection of the denatured, mechanical, and frenetic constructs of left brained cognition. If any appropriate analogy could be applied to the human mind it would be that of something liquid and fluid. The specific term "cognitive fluidity", that was employed to convey a concept of mind, evokes such analogy. Yes, it would be an image of two streams that meet to form a river that cascades into a great lake. From there it empties and flows onwards to the sea.

This image, when viewed within a more holistic framework is depicted within a dual context, *one celestial* (the mind as soul and psyche), *and one earthly* (the brain as right and left hemispheres). This double imagery conforms with that which has been traditionally applied to the Holy City of Jerusalem. Within the descriptive terminology of Scriptures, the celestial streams are interpreted as representing the Pishon and the Gihon; those of the earthly domain being the Tigris and the Euphrates. As depicted in Genesis, one celestial stream arises as: *"a stream would rise from the earth, and water the whole face of the ground" Gen. 2: 6).*

This stream contains the" water of life", the "living water", for which we all thirst. It is the stream of spiritual consciousness. It is that which contributes to our ensoulment so as to provide a source of spiritual nurture for the human mind. It is the primary source of wisdom that is representative of our soul. It is that which enriches the cold and sterile waters of its sister stream, the human psych. These two sources of water will inevitably merge together to contribute to the great lake of "Cognitive Fluidity" that describes our mental reservoir. Finally, as with all other rivers that course throughout the landscape of our planet, these waters will flow onwards into the vast ocean of our universal mind and memory. Its nurturing waters will contribute to the collective cosmic consciousness of mankind. All of these images that relate to the mind are reflected within a similar form of imagery that applies to the concurrent events as they transpire within the right and left cerebral hemispheres of the human brain. These enriched waters will be applied within the context of the world, of our lives and of our living, for all time.

The evolutionary sequence that culminated with the emergence of cognitive fluidity was instigated by the developing mind and its spiritual content. Yet, it is the influence of the specific genetic endowment and the variability of the life experience within its personal geographic, social, and cultural environments that uniquely shape each individual human mind. Of critical importance is that cognitive fluidity enables us to actively engage in conceptual thought in the form of metaphor and allegory. These, together with our human intuition, are in fact the fundamental tools of creative thought and are what distinguishes the mind of man from that of his primate ancestors. They provide us with the means necessary to consider and comprehend beyond the basic core of historical and genetically encoded internal data and the external hard data that is continuously delivered by way of our sensory perceptions.

Metaphor and analogy, as they are presented to the primacy of the right hemisphere, are derived from our collective unconscious. This is a precognitive intuitive knowledge concerning self and other as being in the world. Cognitive fluidity simply provides us with a means of acquiring a conscious and intellectual awareness regarding this fundamental wisdom so that we can focus, and choose to interact and engage with it in a purposeful manner. Metaphors pervade every aspect of our thought and lie at the heart of all our advanced cognitive, creative, and abstract facilities. These include all of our Scientific, Artistic, and Spiritual / Religious attributes. ("Metaphors we Live By": Mark Johnson / George Lakoff pub. 2009).

Implicit to this process is the emergence of the facility to choose and to discriminate between the perceived choices. We also have the capacity to project the likely outcome of our choices in terms of our action. However, most of this current research focuses solely upon the biological aspect of human nature as it pertains to the mind. It is fundamentally exclusive of the spiritual principle that reflects the authentic image of man and renders him uniquely human. The fact of the matter is that cognitive fluidity simply provides us with a means of applying a cognitive intellectual process to a primary intuitive assessment of our paradigm of life and our perception of reality with regard to our being in the world. In other words the intuitive assessment comes first, the cognitive assessment follows suit. This principle, wherein the implicit grounds the explicit, has been described as the "Primacy of Affect". Cognitive fluidity permits the superimposition of conscious intellectual awareness upon an intuitive disposition regarding the nature and existence of self within the world. This intuition is a product of our right brain as reflected within the spiritual aspect of our mind. In this regard, such intuitive feeling, or belief, could well be described as being a creation, or an image, of our mind, or of our imagination. That being the case, it must be also acknowledged that this creation fundamentally differs from what we might refer to as a "figment of the imagination". Such a figment simply reflects the imposition of the workings of our cognitive left brain to reconfigure what had being delivered to it from our right brain. The distinguishing feature regarding the intuitive image that is acquired by our right cerebral hemisphere is that it is an inherent truth, a fundamental "fact of our imagination".

It is not a reconfigured version of fantasy, wishful thinking, self -delusion, or a manifestation of confabulation.

Intuitive faith is a reflection of an authentic image of self within the mind of man. Faith is an expression of trust in the fundamental truth concerning self. This is a truth that is derived from the soul (and hence the spirit) and delivered to the gateway of our collective unconscious. It is abundantly evident that at this threshold it may be either acknowledged, or remain disregarded, refuted, and rejected. The mind influences the evolutionary anatomy, neurophysiology, and the expansion of the brain. Likewise, it is continuously molding and reconfiguring the neurological networking of interconnected axons and their related complement of multiple synapses throughout the entire brain. Repetitive activity along these particular pathways serves to strengthen and reinforce these initial prototypes. In this manner well established routes of communication are imprinted upon the brains circuitry that will determine the manner in which the many specialized regions within our brain will respond to the directions of our mind's will and command. This is what contributes, to a large extent, to our familiar personal traits, including our body language, habits, emotional responses, and other learned and memorized activities. In a similar manner the brain serves to configure the manner in which our minds perceive and respond to the patterned activities of our brains circuitry. No doubt there is a considerable genetic contribution underlying the manner in which both mind and brain respond within any given experiential context. However, as most of us well know the resultant outcomes have far more to with how we use our mental and cerebral faculties as opposed to the content and configuration of what resides therein. That is where free will, a moral and social conscience, judgment, and our ability to choose come into effect.

It is clearly evident that there is some form of continuous feedback- loop, or reciprocal relationship that is operational between mind and brain. (We have described the nature of this reciprocity in the previous chapter). To this extent we are the unwitting masters of our own destinies. We direct and dictate how we are going to evolve biologically. We also mastermind, from the stand point of our evolving perception, or paradigm, of life, precisely how we are likely to think, interact and relate to each other. In effect it is what we identify, and promulgate, as representative of our priorities, attitudes, values, and beliefs that are the architectural agents of the human mind and brain. These are the instruments through which we ultimately design and plan the future configuration and the content of the Cathedral of our Mind. These architectural renovations and innovations are what ultimately influence our perception of life and the purpose of our living. It serves to shape the purpose and the path of our endeavors, and do so within the context of the world in which we continue to evolve and must continue to share between us. There could be no greater onus of responsibility placed upon any living organism. Homo Sapiens is endowed with the unique facility of being able to exercise *Free Will*. He has the capacity to make decisions based on his ability to choose. The critical choices include those that are relevant to his personal self- survival and those that are relevant to his sense of justice and morality as they pertain to self and to others. With regard to issues of justice and morality such a level of self- awareness requires that he has the capacity to discern the nature of these things. In effect, it requires that he has a conscience.

(b) CONSCIENCE

Conscience has been described by Thomas Aquinas as the "mind of man passing moral judgments". A prerequisite to moral judgment is the capacity to access some code of reference with respect to what is right and what is wrong. This is a code that provides us with a reference as to what is good and what is evil. Such a code is beyond the primitive, self- preserving, instinctual, and purely biological realm of living organisms. It is imprinted within the non- biological spirit of all mankind. Scientists have recently discovered that infants can start to make moral judgments by six months of age and may be born with the ability to discriminate good from evil hard- wired into their brains. This research is being led by Professor Paul Bloom at the infant cognition centre at Yale University in Connecticut. The results of this fascinating study contradict the theories of Freud and many other noted scholars who believed that humans begin life with a moral "blank slate". No doubt, but as we intellectually mature, access to, and application of such a code within the progressive complexities of our decision making, requires that there is the capacity and the fundamental ability to evaluate process, analyze, and project possible outcomes of response. This level of consideration also necessitates access to an integrated and complex memory bank so that comparisons can be made based on previous experience and acquired data bases of knowledge.

TRANSFIGURATION AND TRANS-SYMBIOSIS

Rejoice, be glad, and have no fear,
Surrender to the Light.
The Word has spoken and proclaimed,
It beckons and it calls.
So listen as it speaks to you,
And answer, as did Saul.

From this very moment
You will see and understand,
Yourself, and life, all living things,
As never seen before.
Awaken from your silent sleep,
And enter through this door.

From "Sunrise at Dusk", by the author.

We can appreciate that both the brain and psyche would have to have evolved beyond some critical threshold in order that a sense of conscience could be integrated into the mind of any life form. In all probability this could only have become possible when a primitive architectural template of neurological circuitry, and their corresponding cell stations, became sufficiently established to enable an explosive, and highly complex, integration of inter-hemispheric activity to occur. These evolutionary progressions within the matrix of the neurological system would also facilitate the emergence of a more advanced and complex psyche from the primitive content of the Limbic system (i.e. instinctual awareness of self and other). It is at this juncture that a pre-primed Hominid had evolved that had the potential to acquire both a mental and a neurological state of "Cognitive Fluidity" .These neurological advancements would be accompanied by the acquisition of a corresponding intuitive awareness that is indicative of highly integrated mind. Such a mind is reflected within the integrative process of the psyche and the soul. These neurological priming events would only have begun some 60 thousand years ago. In this instance it could only be said that mankind, as a morally responsible human being, was then set on a course that would ultimately lead to the emergence of such a unique species as that which we classify and define as representative of the modern human species.

Homo Sapiens, as a unique and distinct species, reflects the chosen Hominid that was to become human: The body and blood that had once constituted the primordial prefiguration of mankind had been selectively prepared throughout the millennia to undergo a most remarkable and dramatic transformation. This was far beyond the realms of a mere biological event. It was a process of transfiguration involving mind, brain, and body. The facility of consciousness was to ensoul the mind of man within his collective unconscious. In tandem with this event, what had once constituted the primitive and instinctual Limbic "psyche", was to enter into a unique, and symbiotic, form of relationship with the soul. Henceforth, this newly elevated psyche, and the spiritual nature of the soul, would constitute the functional content of the human mind. Likewise, the brain, as the animating biological principle of the body would become the reciprocating ambassador, and the "host", to the true essence of humanity.

Through a process of transformation, and transfiguration, the brain would become the material correlate of the human mind. The consciousness of mind, which contains the substrate of the Spirit, enters into a profound and transcendental form of symbiotic, and reciprocal, relationship with the material matter of the brain. By extension, this unique form of trans-symbiosis is then shared with the physical body which the brain neurologically animates. Consciousness, as provider of the primary substrate of all intuitive knowledge to the human mind, encrypts the content of its Wisdom within the neurochemical circuitry of the living brain .This intuitive knowledge is encoded within our collective unconscious. It is this Spirit of Wisdom which has the Primacy of Affect in respect of the content of all human thought and human inspiration. Consciousness, as the source of the Spirit of Wisdom, is the penultimate provider of our Primary metaphors.

By the sacred consecration of the living and biological substance of the prefigured primate, this lowly creature was transfigured, and reborn, as humankind by the power of the Holy Spirit. The physical body of a preordained primate becomes the biological form of its authentic, and fundamental, spiritual essence. Through a process of trans-symbiosis, the Spirit becomes substantially present, and real, within the mental, and material substance of what had been a mere biological entity. In effect humanity, as a unique and sacred species within the Tree of Life, was conceived by the power of the Holy Spirit and thus emerged upon the earth.

It is because of this trans- symbiotic event, and the related acquisition of consciousness, that we can now describe this transfigured, and reborn, being as "human". A living and a permanent testimony to this miraculous event would ensue, as evidenced and witnessed by all mankind through the miracle of consciousness. It is this consciousness, which we as humans can all access, and which in turn animates the mind of man with the universal presence of the Spirit, that defines us as uniquely human. This extraordinary evolutionary event mirrors, and foreshadows, that of the mystery of the Incarnation. This describes the "Word made flesh" wherein the divinity of Christ was to be embodied within that of our humanity. Christ, as the "son of man" had so humbled himself that he would come in the flesh to dwell among us.

It was only when an awareness of this authentic spiritual nature had been accomplished that the process of our becoming human was instigated upon this earth. The biological primate was then transfigured to a higher order that transcends nature and mortality. The spiritual principle within him would endow him with the prospect of a true vision of his authentic nature and of his immortality. In actual fact, all the available evidence suggests that it has only been within the past five to ten thousand years that this facility had evolved to a level of critical application within the context of our moral and spiritual maturity.

The second account of Adam and Eve within the book of Genesis some three to four thousand years B.C. could well be considered as the symbolic bedrock of this process of spiritual transfiguration. The "re-ensoulment" of man may be considered as an evolutionary process of infusion and enlightenment that occurred in parallel with his biological evolution since the beginning of time. The process is one of spiritual awareness, or a reawakening to the existence of the spirit within the self. It provides a means by which authentic self becomes identifiable and recognizable for what it really is. Such a level of awareness provides the stimulus that prompts mankind to seek and yearn in hope of being reunited once again with the original source of its creation.

Prior to this event there would have been no agenda for the prophets or mystics that were to help prepare the spiritual mind set of man for the message of redemption. This, in turn, would prepare the way for the Good News that was yet to come with regard to our salvation. This spiritual quest is an on- going and continuous process that occurs in tandem with our biological evolution. No doubt but that it will proceed unabated until it is fully realized and fulfilled at the end of time. In tandem with this mystical process, and as a direct consequence of it, the final evolutionary phase of mankind would ensue.

The animation of the mind of man would be reflected in a unique manner at a mental and a biological level. Biologically this would be evidenced by a simultaneous and parallel surge in the neurological growth and development that are now unique features of the human brain and of its cerebral expression. Prior to this event the chosen primate had evolved neurologically to a status wherein a primitive level of cognitive awareness of his biological self was possible. We may consider this as the initial advancement of the instinctual mind towards that of an expanding psyche. The acquisition of consciousness would greatly enhance the biological and cognitive substrate of the left cerebral hemisphere. The left cerebral hemisphere and selective regions within the Limbic system, are representative of the cerebral correlates, from which the modern human psyche had predominantly evolved.

(c) ENSOULMENT

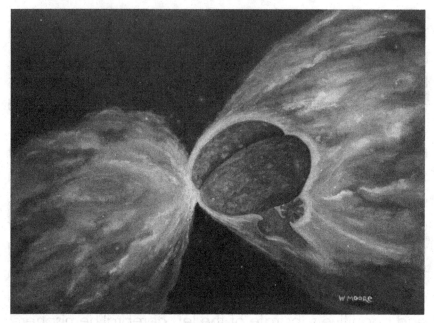

Ensoulment

"Ensoulment" is the term which refers to the gradual acquisition of a specific form of subconscious wisdom and awareness that would become evident within the mind of man as a result of his spiritual rebirth. Ensoulment is what animates the mind of man, and the totality of its embodiment within the individual, with a sense of its spiritual and authentic self. What had once been nothing more than a biological entity has now been sanctified through a process of transformation and transfiguration of both mind and body to become a single spiritual entity. What now constitutes the human mind is inclusive of both psyche and soul. Henceforth, this re-born creature, which had been no more than an instinctively aware and an

THE KEYS TO THE DOORS OF PERCEPTION

organic living substance, would become consciously aware and spiritually sacred.

Additionally, in so far as the brain is the material form, and biological expression, of the mind, both brain and mind function within a unified and reciprocating type, of mode. Mind and matter have become one in nature and essence so that their activity is contained within a single unitary process. Consequently, we have the capacity to configure, or reconfigure, the neurological circuitry within our brain through the mental induction of a reciprocal pattern of preoccupation within our own mind. Likewise, the neurological patterns within the circuitry of our brain are reflected within the configuration of our mind-set. In this sense, our thoughts, and behavioral patterns, become mutually augmented as they are represented within the reciprocating domains of the mind and of the brain. Ultimately this becomes manifest within the manner by which we perceive, relate, and respond within the context of our self- generated paradigm of life. It is in this manner that we become the purposeful, or the unwitting, architects of our own destinies and of human history. What is of paramount importance is that we acknowledge and accept that the spiritualized, and ensouled, human mind rightfully retains primacy, supremacy, and authority over that of the ego mind. This is reflected at the biological level wherein the right hemisphere has primacy over that of its left cerebral counterpart.

309

We can now finally appreciate something more definitive with regard to how mankind was to become a living host imbued with the spirit of his godly essence. None of this is to suggest that the spiritual essence of humanity did not exist prior to the emergence of our species upon the earth. On the contrary, as we have previously described within the Primary Thesis,(Chap.1. "Air of Clarity", Part 1), the Spiritual essence of man has existed since the first creative event. However, it would "lie in slumber" until such time as it would be reawakened as the Spiritual Principle that was to "ensoul" every human being since his first emergence as a unique species upon this earth. Indeed, this infusion of the Spirit is a reality that has yet to be fully realized in the mind and soul of mankind. It is a reality towards which we must groan and strive within the context of our daily lives. It is something to which all of us are called, both individually and collectively.

(d) THE MORAL LAW & CONSCIENCE

The code of reference that applies to human behavior is commonly described as the Moral Law. It has been inscribed by God and is neither a product nor creation of man himself. Free Will in the context of a guiding conscience is the critical cognitive factor that separates, defines, and distinguishes man from animal and from all other living things. Once the capacity had been established such that free will and moral judgment could be applied by the mind within the context of his life, he became a separate species that was distinct from all others. The evolutionary process that leads to the emergence of modern man has its beginning at this juncture in time. It describes a pathway where biological evolution had reached a critical threshold of awareness that would now permit and facilitate communion between a biological nature on the one hand, and an inherent spiritual principle on the other.

When we take all of this into account we can appreciate how mankind fashions the neuro- anatomy and neurophysiology of his own cerebral capacities. In turn, and of far greater importance, is that he also influences the manner in which he perceives his world and how he is likely to relate and interact with his fellow man. In effect, it can be stated that to this extent, mankind fashions and molds his own version of reality and shapes his own evolutionary development. This includes the biological development of his brain and the configuration, shape, and complexity of his mind.

(e) THE EGO & THE SOUL

The most predominant functional component of the psych is invariably the ego. The ego represents the central and domineering defender of the biological nature of mankind. It has the capacity to delude our conscious processes of rationalization. It poses as an illusionary self that has a self- centred agenda which most of us fail to accurately identify and are often consciously unaware.

Consequently, the ego is often misinterpreted as self and this is felt to be the ultimate, universal, and all pervasive form of self-deception. It exemplifies the potential for reason to be misguidedly raised to the status of God Head in denial of the true and authentic nature of man that is contained within his spirit as the image of his creator. Such is the rational basis for atheism.

There are many other elements, apart from the ego, that constitute the functional content of the psyche. These include both genetic and acquired, or learned, contributions. Some of the most critical of these are well established within the first five years of life and are stored in their specific memory banks. Other contributions are generated throughout life as we grow and develop into maturity. They reflect our individual and personal analysis and interpretation of what we learn and experience throughout our lives. These too are stored in their own particular set of memory banks.

The spiritual contribution to the mind is what we simply describe as the soul. It is seen to be the central defender of the authentic nature of man. The soul is the true and valid representative of self that is imprinted as the image of our creator within each and every individual. The inevitable consequence of this prioritization of interest is the generation of conflict between psychic ego and spiritual soul. Both will vie for the central position of authority and command. Each will be projected within, and to, the mind as the unilateral representative of the valid and living Self.

The extent to which this polarization and conflict occurs when critical choices are being considered is often reflected in the measure of inner conflict experienced by the individual. The magnitude and degree of such conflict will also depend on the extent to which each of these elements have been nurtured and empowered. In the final analysis, it is the exercise of Free Will that determines the final choice and the outcome of our actions. However, in the extended context, this also molds the collective cognitive template that shapes the evolutionary configuration of both the human mind and biological brain for future generations. As Ian Mc Gilchrist so brilliantly pointed out in his recent publication, we have reason for concern given the ascendancy to power and control of our left brain function at the expense of our right cerebral advocate. ("The Master and his Emissary". Yale University Press 2009).

We are creating a mechanistic, fragmented, material, and decontextualized paradigm of our world that is becoming progressively amoral and dehumanized. Likewise, as Karen Armstrong the writer / theologian, has pointed out in her book "The Case for God" (pub.2009 Bodley Head) "we have lost the knack for religion". It is as if the success of science in the material world has rewired our brains, made us tone -deaf to myth. We are becoming both deaf and dumb to mysticism and spirituality. Everything must be deduced and expressed within an explicit context. As Armstrong states, even the words "I believe" have changed and become

313

scientised, to mean "I assert these propositions to be empirically correct". Yet, the original Greek word Pisteuo simply means to "give your heart and loyalty". This is the essence of faith. It is to commit and surrender oneself on the basis of trust alone. Instead of applying scientific and intellectual rationalism to Spirituality, Religion, and God, Armstrong suggests that we should try "silence, reverence and awe", and a "graceful acceptance of mystery and unknowing".

The interface at which the psyche, or ego dominant aspect of it, and the soul interact within the context of the mind may be described as a portal that controls and facilitates the process of interchange and communication between these two facets of self. In effect, such a portal between psyche and spirit would function much in the same manner as a modem that connects the software data of a computer to the Internet that is potentially available to be shared by everyone on- line. I use this analogy because authentic self, or the true spirit of man, while it is both personal and individual; it is also collective and shared by all mankind. By its very nature, it is an intrinsic part, or member, of an interconnected and all inclusive network that exists between all souls and all that is the totality of the Spirit. It is not selfish nor self -centred. Rather, it is all inclusive, all serving, ever constant, loyal, and true to the absolute essence that is representative of the authentic nature of mankind.

CHAPTER SEVEN: THE SOCIAL AND EMOTIONAL MIND

Most of us think of our minds within the context of that convenient little term "Psyche". Some will think of it as a biological product of the brain, while others may not. Many of those who have a spiritual attitude in regard to life and humanity may also consider that the soul is a separate, and unique, spiritual counterpart, or guiding principle, in relation to the activities of the imperfect human psyche. However, we consider the mind as existing within a single and holistic context, and as being composed of both the psyche and the soul. Both of these aspects of our mentality serve to inform, instruct, and instigate specific neurological responses within the brain's complex circuitry.

The word "mind", or "psyche", invariably conjures up ideas about the state of our mental health, of being sane or emotionally disturbed. We may think about the marvels of our conscious and unconscious streams of thought, of human intelligence and artistic creativity. Most importantly of all, we are only too well aware of the mental and emotional vulnerabilities that so often override our rational judgments and decision-making. Sometimes, we are fortunate enough to come to realize, and accept, that many of our errors, and misjudgments, our interpersonal conflicts, and our mental pain, have been the outcome of our misguided thinking and related responses.

Periodically, we may also have occasion to ponder upon those more mysterious aspects of our minds that have to do with dreams, near death experiences,(NDE's) visions, and ecstasies. Alternatively, some people may be more intrigued by issues pertaining to transcendental states of altered conscious awareness. These include such activities as those of day dreaming, meditation, contemplation, or even prayer within a variety of formats. Yet again, some individuals are drawn towards the various "psychic" phenomena of the mind in respect of precognition, extrasensory perception, clairvoyance, or cult phenomena such as voodoo, witchcraft, spells, or the use of natural and chemical psychedelic agents. We will endeavor to address as many of these core activities within this chapter in so far as they are deemed to be of fundamental relevance to the workings of our mind, and their outcomes, as reflected in our attitudes and behavior within the lived experience. More peripheral examples, such as NDE's, visions, and day dreaming are dealt with in other locations within the book.

We have already addressed many of the essential facts in relation to human consciousness, and the collective unconscious. We have considered the mental-cognitive processes as they apply to the formulation of our thoughts and the manner in which we may seek to express them. Within the content of the previous chapter we have also considered the more popular theories concerning the evolution, and developmental maturation, of the mind. In addition we have addressed a number of fundamental issues in relation to the nature of the psyche, the soul, the ego mind, conscience, and free will.

However, one cannot really comprehend the nature of the mind, and the manner in which it functions, in the absence of some greater depth of understanding concerning those primitive neurological structures that are buried deep within the centre of our brains. These are what influence our reflex, and emotional responses. In many instances the rational mind and its cerebral correlates, must play second fiddle to these instinctual, and for the most part subconscious, energies and forces. I am referring to the Limbic and the Autonomic nervous systems that are centrally located within our mid brain, and in close proximity to our Temporal and Prefrontal lobes. In addition there is a need to understand the nature and complexity of the interconnectivity of these structures with other specific elements within our nervous system. These include a variety of complex neurological components within the diencephalon, brainstem, special senses (via our cranial nerves), hormonal systems, and our neocortex.

If you glance at the cover design, and related graphics, you might be struck by the resemblance between that of the brain and the shape of a mushroom. This visual similarity could just as easily apply to the shape of a jellyfish. However, the mushroom best provides us with an excellent, and very simple, analogy as to the manner of our neurological evolution and the basic anatomy of our brain. We might well imagine how we incubated as spores within the compost or peat moss of our highly carbonated wetlands. The narrow stalk grew upwards over time, and finally expanded to mushroom as a marvelously domed mantle at the very apex. Yet, we remain fixed upon the stalk, and firmly rooted in the soil. Yet, as individuals within society we consider ourselves to be predominantly sane, rational, and intelligent beings. However, we are still very much creatures of our primitive emotions.

The long list of criminal sociopaths and mass murderers over the successive decades attests to this fact. The incidence of blind rage, rape, sexual deviancy, muggings, bullying, and intimidation, continues unabated. Within the home, schools, workplace, and recreational facilities there are recurrent episodes of serious relationship conflicts, and related forms of physical trauma and mental abuse. Very few of any of these individuals are known to have any underlying structural brain pathology. Consequently, we may surmise that these are manifestations of our human nature, and our basic instincts, albeit within the more extreme context. While we may exhibit varying degrees of tolerance, and restraint, it has been shown that given the opportunity to exercise power and control over other human beings, many of us will do so. This is despite the fact that we would be fully aware that we were subjecting these individuals to pain, humiliation, and violence. We might rephrase our assessment of our nature by saying that we are "sinners". That is to imply that we are fundamentally flawed in a manner that predisposes us to evil, inhumane and unjust thoughts and deeds. There is a genuine truth contained within this insightful statement. We are all anchored to the stalk, and rooted in the damp and decomposing compost.

(a) THE LIMBIC SYSTEM

FIG. 15   THE LIMBIC SYSTEM

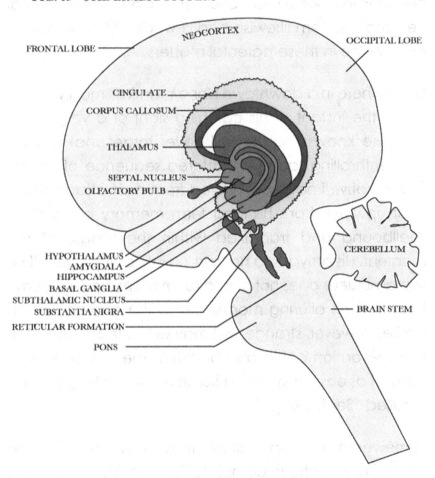

Somewhere, in the silence and the dead of night, a new born baby stirs within its cot. Soon it is frantically flaying its arms, kicking, whimpering, and then crying incessantly towards a peak sonic crescendo. A mother promptly lifts, cuddles, and feeds, the hungry infant. The baby's primitive hypothalamus had let loose. It was far more experienced in matters of survival than bambino. After all, it had been around for some 450 million years. The mother's female, and maternally orientated, cingulate had prompted her prefrontal lobe into action. That cingulate aspect of her limbic system likewise had a wealth of evolutionary experience in these parental matters.

Somewhere in a downtown bar a man falls madly in love within the instant of his catching sight of a very pretty lady. He knows that he will never forget that precise and enthralling face. A scattered sequence of distant and emotive images, rekindled from past attachments, float upwards from his long term memory bank. He is spellbound and transfixed within the magic of the moment. His amygdala has sprung into action. Now, if his septal nucleus does not dive in to save him, he may come to regret this alluring moment, and the surge of sexual desire. However, strange as it may seem, that attempted salvage action could also backfire. The septal nucleus can just as easily instigate a fierce outburst of rage which is called "Septal Rage".

Somewhere a group of students have gathered at the community centre to complete their weekly assignment. Many are members of the local rugby team or of the tennis club. The bigger guys have chopped enough timber in the past few days to fill a large truck. Those with a little culinary skill have been slaving away in the kitchen preparing meals to feed a multitude. Both groups would soon head off into the town to deliver these goods to a designated list of individuals within the community. All of these people are poor, or lonely, and living on the fringe. Some are elderly, frail, and incapacitated. Others are members of large families who had lost their source of income. All of the young volunteers are working in harmony. They are doing so within the shared and cooperative unison of their individual amygdala and their prefrontal lobes. This is the source of their motivation, empathy, and zeal. Supportive roles are played in respect of their physical stamina and endurance. This is provided by means of the complex interconnectivity that exists within their Hypothalamic Pituitary Adrenal axis (HPA), and their Autonomic nervous systems. The group activity involves far more than just adolescent brawn and an extended fitness workout.

Somewhere a mailbox rattles as a postman delivers the mail. A middle aged man rises from the breakfast table, collects the post, and then opens it out beside his plate of burnt toast. Within an instant he is in a mad rage of anger, then a flurry of intense fear and anxiety. The bank statement was in disarray. He was steeped in debt. Most of the debits related to expensive clothes that had been purchased by his wife. With a single sweep of the back of the hand, the total contents of the table went flying through the air. The amygdala and the hypothalamus had fired off like a two barreled sawn –off shotgun.

Somewhere an elderly person goes off course on his way to the local shop. Upon his delayed arrival he cannot recall the reason for his errand. Neither can he remember the name of his next door neighbour whom he meets in transit. The hippocampus is progressively malfunctioning as senile dementia (or perhaps Alzheimer's disease) sets in.

The mother and child, the Romeo, the student group, the angry man, or the unfortunate elderly gentleman, all fundamentally reflect the activities of various elements within the individually named components of the Limbic system. Depending on one's age and gender, these examples could be representative of the behavior of any one of us

On a far more sinister note, a young man takes a shotgun, shoots his parents, and then repeatedly stabs his wife to death. He then advances to the rooftop of the local school and kills dozens of innocent students. He is later discovered to have a brain tumour within his temporal lobe which has extended to the proximity of his thalamus, hypothalamus, and amygdaloid nucleus.

A schoolteacher with high moral standards, and a responsible disposition, begins to download child pornography and make advances on his young stepdaughter. He is soon diagnosed as having a tumour in his prefrontal lobe which has a close functional relationship with elements that reside deep within his midbrain. When the tumour was removed his behavior returned to normal. However when the symptoms recurred again at a later date, it was discovered that the brain lesion had returned.

These are specific examples of some of those who are misfortunate enough to have sustained pathology within the circuitry of their Limbic systems. Even now, it may have come to your attention that some individually named regions of the Limbic system appear to have contradictory modes of expression. However, it must be born in mind that most of these structures have bilateral representation (i.e. we have two, one for each side of the brain), and each one is a composite of various nuclei, or related parts. Consequently, there are a host of integrated, yet variable, activities that may be attributed to any one named structure. Some of these are often opposing, or contradictory, in their nature. In addition, some that have bilateral representation,(and may in fact be larger on one side compared to that on the opposite side), can exhibit a preferential form of activity on a given side of the brain compared to that of its counterpart on the opposite side. Those components that exist as single midline structures are also composed of a cluster of separate parts each of which have their individually delegated modes of action, and diverse circuits of interconnectivity (e.g. Thalamus and Hypothalamus). Let us take a closer look at four of these ancient Limbic structures, and their relevance to the nature of our responses, the patterns of our behavior, and the level of control which we can apply in the determination of our ultimate choices.

1. The Hypothalamus:

Within the early phases of our evolutionary development the hypothalamus reigned supreme in regard to our primitive emotional behavior. These were a reflection of our survival instincts, and our basic needs. By and large, the hypothalamus acted as an "inward eye" that monitored internal homeostasis. It could trigger an immediate, profound, and uncontrollable reaction as required to address a need, and maintain the status quo. Examples include hunger, thirst, aversion, rage, and pleasure. Most of these correspond to what we now describe as "infantile needs / demands", or in Freudian terminology, to the Id. In fact, the hypothalamus is fully functional from birth, and is the central core from which all emotions derive their motive force. Its scope is wide and diverse since it is greatly involved in a range of other functions such as hormonal, reproductive, vegetative, and autonomic (ANS) /visceral activities.

Two areas within the hypothalamus share an antagonistic relationship in respect of the ANS. In this instance one region is mostly consigned to the activities of the parasympathetic system, the other to the sympathetic system. Many of its activities are linked to its status within the Hypothalamic- Pituitary- Adrenal axis (HPA) particularly in relation to our hormonal balance and our circadian rhythms (i.e. sleep / energy / mood cycles). Many of these attributes also have a functional relationship with our olfactory (smell) and optic (visual) systems. Of critical importance is the fact that because of the existing interconnections between hypothalamus and other regions of the limbic system, in addition to those that connect with the Frontal lobes, we can now mobilize, and motivate ourselves to either cease, or persist, in our initial reflex pattern of behavior.

2. The Amygdala:

It was the later evolutionary emergence of the amygdala that was to provide the more discerning form of "inward eye" and in so doing brought the uncontested reign of the hypothalamus to a close. The external features of reality could now be scrutinized, certified, and tested. When prompted by the hypothalamus, the amygdala will scan the inflow of sensory information for the appropriate emotional / motivational stimuli until the need is more clearly identified, and more specifically addressed. The scanning process will include evaluation of input from what is seen, felt, heard, or anticipated.

The amygdala has Primacy in respect to the perception, and expression of most aspects of our emotions. Consequently, it holds the greatest sway in respect of fear, rage, sexual desire, facial recognition, other peoples stare, (even when the observer is out of our line of vision),and our long term loving attachments. It is critical in the mobilization of higher order emotional, and impulse control, and the analysis of social-emotional nuances.

The amygdala is 16% larger in the male. It enlarges, or shrinks in response to a rise or fall in testosterone levels. It also plays a significant role in sexual orientation, and the stereotypical sex differences that are characteristic of each gender. The right amygdala is also 9% larger than the left and this may be a factor in augmenting those particular attributes that are features of the right cerebral hemisphere. In addition, the right cerebral hemisphere is 4% larger than its left counterpart. As you may recall, these right hemispheric attributes have to do with the nature of the attention that it pays to the world at large, its sense of the collective, of empathy, and those such as objectivity, self-control, justice, and morality which are intimately related to the activity of our right Frontal lobe. Furthermore, the emotional discrimination and analysis of content by the amygdala would serve as an additional accessory to the primary intuitive content to which the right hemisphere is in receipt from the collective unconscious. In terms of functionality the right Amygdala, (in contrast to the left), is more aligned towards the agenda of the right cerebral hemisphere, and with that of our subconscious mind as a whole.

In addition to all of that, the amygdala is very involved in the processes of memory formation, (including facial recognition), learning, attention, and the reinforcement of patterns of behavior. However, it can also over-ride the neocortex, (i.e. Frontal lobe),to dictate the nature of any given response and its outward expression In summary, the amygdala may function as our social- emotive interface, and may do so as our advocate, and learned mentor, or as our greatest enemy and adversity.

3. The Cingulate:

The cingulate is highly involved in the expression of maternal behavior and in establishing the mother/infant bond. It is also active in speech and language tasks, particularly within regard to vocalizing how we feel within a social-emotive context. I imagine that most men reached this inevitable conclusion without resorting to neurological texts!

4. Hippocampus:

Of greatest relevance to us is the critical role that this region of the limbic system plays in regard to our short and long term memory. Almost all of its input is from the neocortex within whose five layered mesocortex it resides. In this respect alone it is unique as part of the limbic system. It is has a major role in information processing. This activity includes our spatial orientation in regard to knowing in which direction you are going so as to achieve your target destination (i.e. cognitive mapping).It also includes behavioral arousal, attention, and movement towards a defined goal. This "satnav" part of the hippocampus is selectively well developed in city taxi drivers and damage to it impairs their ability to perform their work.

Pathology excluded, it would appear that, as a species, we have not yet fully emerged from the primordial swamp of our original psychic existence. The Limbic system can hijack our rational brain within the instant. It can cause us to spontaneously exhibit an extensive range of intense reflexive reactions and emotional responses. Such forms of behavior reside beyond the specified remit of our conscious, and premeditated, decision making. By nature we are oftentimes the cooperative accomplices, or perhaps the unwilling victims, of the neurochemical and hormonal activities that arise from within the confines of our ancestral Limbic systems.

Of critical importance is the fact that these reflex, and emotionally charged, reactions are invariably brief and short lived. Most last but a few seconds, some may persist for a few minutes. It is the extent to which these momentary responses are augmented, and empowered, by the supportive action of the psyche, and the ego mind, that will determine the subsequent sequence of events as they unfold. Likewise, it is the extent to which one has reinforced the neurological circuitry through habit and repetition that will prime, or precondition, the likely nature of the cerebral response. As a consequence, perpetuation of the initial reaction by willful intent is a far more likely outcome where an individual had pre-relegated mental control and governance to his psyche over that of his soul (and their respective left and right hemispheric correlates)

At one time or another, and more often continuously, we have written and still write, the script that largely defines the configuration of our personalities. Yet, how often do we strive to rewrite it in recognition, and acceptance, of our accumulated behavioral vulnerabilities? To what extent, and over what time span, have we enthroned our ego as master of our minds?

Count to ten, (or maybe 110), and seek the insight of your human intuition, the guidance of your spirit, and the objectivity of your conscience when next you experience a sudden surge of emotional prompts, or pent up needs and desires. It is these that are seeking some form of immediate and ego-based gratification. They will do so in the absence of any concern for the welfare of others. It is these basic instincts that will set in motion a furious flurry of activities, and do so without any regard for the ultimate, and inevitable, consequences. These are the emotions that can "swamp you" in the instant. It is most unlikely that they will be the consequence of some, as yet, undiagnosed, brain tumour.

These various responses typify the primitive, the archaic, and the subconscious "undead", within the ancient caves of our instinctual self-awareness. These are what lurk as mindless zombies beneath the surface mantle of our warm, and intellectually vibrant, neocortex. Yet, be aware that they, as the evolved neurological expressions of our "selfish genes", may well be provided with a delegated agenda, and a collective strategy, that is governed by a "higher psyche". I am referring to the more recently evolved ego that has been elevated to its current status within our human minds. It alone has the potential to reign supreme within the reconciliatory arena of our conscious decision making. It alone has the potential to undermine, and subvert, the directives that should reflect the valid expression of the nature of mankind.

You will recall the mushroom analogy as representative of the growth and architectural structure of our central nervous systems. Likewise the brain has evolved and grown upwards,(i.e.in a cephalic direction), beginning at the hind brain (brainstem) and progressing towards the midbrain. Some of our most primitive structures have been clustered together within this location. One of the most archaic is the Hypothalamus which dated back over 450 million years ago. Related structures, such as the Septal Nucleus, the Amygdala, and the Cingulate, evolved within this three layered region of the brain, or Allocortex, sometime later. These parts of the limbic system receive most of their input from the lower brainstem. The Hippocampus is unique in so far as almost all of its input is derived from the neocortex, and it resides within this more recent, and more complex five layered region of the brain which is called the Mesocortex.

Within the subsequent phases of evolution this five layered mantle of neocortex arose to enshroud the limbic system and blossom out like the majestically domed mushroom cap. Finally, and as recently as 50 million years ago, the domineering reign of the primitive Limbic system was to slowly grind to a halt. The neocortical hemispheres, and their delegated lobes, would progressively modulate, and temper, the instinctual raw energy that was generated from within this ancient neurological structure. This primitive biological relic had once been constructed in the "garage basement" of the distant past. Safety, efficiency, caution, and more precise control, were the essential features of this newly advancing neocortical design. In the interim the limbic structures also enlarged in size and complexity as they became increasingly responsive to cortical input, external demands, and potential opportunities. Ultimately and more recently, these mental and neurological advancements would culminate within a process that was instigated, and facilitated through the acquisition of human consciousness, intuition, and ensoulment.

Finally, humanity had emerged upon this earth as a unique and spiritual creature. As human beings we could now exercise judgment, control, and careful discernment, prior to the instigation of an action or a deed. We now had the onus of responsibility to contend with in regard to our behavior, our personal welfare, and the welfare of others, within our living environment. The human creature is one who is endowed with intuitive knowledge concerning the nature of self, and the insight to reflect within the content of the mind. This is one who can exercise his objectivity, intellect, moral conscience, and free will. He is the one, and the only one, who has the power to reflect upon the mystery of creation, of life, and the purpose of his existence. He is the only one who can contribute to the realization of that purpose while seeking to facilitate others in the attainment of that goal.

(b) THE AUTONOMIC NERVOUS SYSTEM

The Autonomic Nervous System (ANS) is to a large extent a peripheral reflex system that relays nerve impulses between our organs (viscera) and our brain to control their functional homeostasis. This primitive system operates almost entirely at the level of our subconscious and involuntary control. It regulates our heart rate, respiratory rates, body temperature, pupil size, salivation, swallowing, digestive secretions and the motility of our bowel. In addition it controls our bowel and bladder sphincters, urinary output, erectile responses, and even our level of sexual arousal. While the system functions autonomously, it can also work in association with our conscious (i.e. somatic) nervous system to provide voluntary control within the brain. The ANS is largely situated, and activated, within centres located in the Medulla, and the lower brainstem (particularly at the Hypothalamus). However, there are also a number of autonomic centres located within the cerebral cortex. Furthermore, the Limbic system provides additional input to the Hypothalamus, and consequently to the Hypothalamic Pituitary Adrenal axis (HPA) This hormonal axis provides a means of maintaining systemic homeostasis throughout the entire body, including that of our circadian rhythm (body clock), menstrual cycle, and our mood.

The ANS is primarily subdivided into two major components that include the Sympathetic (SNS) and the Parasympathetic (PSNS) systems. Those elements that control the activities of the gastrointestinal system are now considered as a distinct, yet functionally related, part of the ANS, and are termed the "Enteric Nervous System (ENT). The SNS and PSNS have complementary, or opposing, actions in so far as where one activates a response, the other inhibits it. The SNS tends to act in a rapid response mode, while the PSNS has a more delayed, and dampening, action.

From a functional, and anatomical perspective, the ANS has a Sensory "inflow" (i.e. afferent), and Motor "outflow" (i.e. efferent) pathway. Within each of the circuit pathways there are two major synapses between the interconnecting axons, which are described as "ganglia". These are placed in sequence so that either excitatory or inhibitory impulses may be transmitted onwards to their target destinations. Autonomic Nerve Centres in the brain receive sensory information from their respective afferent nerves which lie peripherally within the body. In turn, these brain centres relay responses back to their target locations (body organs) via their motor -efferent pathways.

FIG. 16   AUTONOMIC BRAIN CENTRES

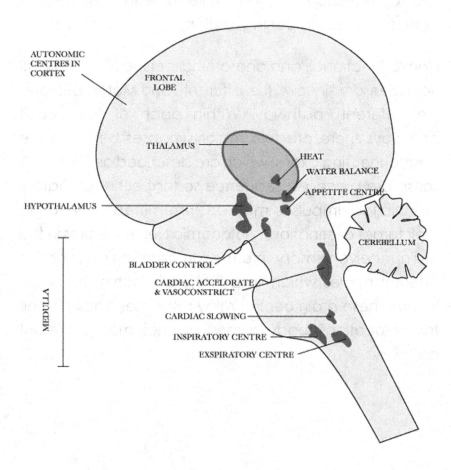

334

The neurons of the SNS begin within the spinal cord from the level of the first thoracic vertebra (T1) to that of the second lumbar vertebra (L2/3). The PSNS neurons have their site of origin within the cranial nerves of the brain. Those that are closely linked to the PSNS include the third, seventh, ninth, and tenth cranial nerves. In addition there are further neurons located at the level of the lower spinal cord (i.e. the "sacral" region) at S2- S4 vertebrae.

A unique feature of the ANS (both SNS and PSNS) is that the efferent-outflow pathways must pass through the sequential set of paired ganglia, (as previously described), before they can connect with their target organs. These special synaptic sites are referred to as the "presynaptic" and the "postsynaptic" ganglia. At the presynaptic ganglia of both the SNS, and the PSNS, the neurotransmitter is a chemical called Acetylcholine (ACH). On the other hand, at the postsynaptic ganglion, the transmitter is Noradrenaline in the instance of the SNS, while that of the PSNS continues to be ACH. For these reasons, the SNS is usually referred to as being Adrenergic in nature, and the PSNS as being Cholinergic in its activity.

FIG 17. SYMPATHETIC NERVOUS SYSTEM

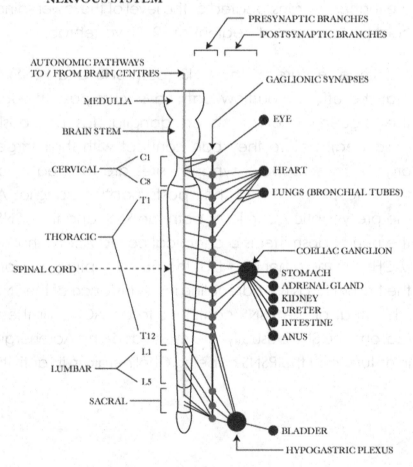

PRESYNAPTIC BRANCHES

POSTSYNAPTIC BRANCHES

AUTONOMIC PATHWAYS TO / FROM BRAIN CENTRES

GAGLIONIC SYNAPSES

MEDULLA

EYE

BRAIN STEM

HEART

CERVICAL — C1 — C8

LUNGS (BRONCHIAL TUBES)

T1

THORACIC

COELIAC GANGLION

SPINAL CORD

STOMACH
ADRENAL GLAND
KIDNEY
URETER
INTESTINE
ANUS

T12

L1

LUMBAR — L5

SACRAL

BLADDER

HYPOGASTRIC PLEXUS

For the greater part a cooperative synergy of effort exists between the needs and demands, of the Limbic system and the reflex spontaneity of our Autonomic Nervous System. It is an entirely different matter as to whether these responses will be in harmonious agreement, or otherwise, with the planned agenda that is fermenting within our conscious mind. This higher system, which reciprocates with the conscious activities of our cerebral cortex, may well be abruptly over-ruled, and hijacked. The mushroom stalk has potent tentacles that can penetrate into the substance of our majestic vault that is our cerebral canopy. The "keeper at the gate" has long since been chosen, empowered, and well-briefed, in the event of such surprise assaults upon our prized citadel. The keeper may be the "Master of the Psyche", or the "Gabriel of the Soul". When the sirens scream within our head or the weir-wolf howls outside your doors, which of these have you instated? To whom do you now beckon, and to whom do you now implore?

This keeper is the one who helps direct and guide our thoughts and deeds. The keeper is your "brother", none other than "Tu Fein" (a Gaelic term that denotes "you yourself") within the social context of other individuals. The keeper is the sacred self who dwells within your soul, and who likewise, dwells in everyone.

CHAPTER EIGHT: CONFABULATION & MEMORY

From the Age of arrogance and of pride,
From the Age of self-delusion and despair,
From the Age of blind folly and of greed,
The Age of Confabulation is now here
Greetings and Welcome
To the pandemic that is unleashed.

From "The Pandemic –
After 1984". by the author.

(a) THE SYNDROME OF CONFABULATION & LEFT HEMISPHERIC SHIFT

The term "confabulation", when used in common everyday language usually implies verbal denial, or simply lying. However, when used in a medical or neuro-scientific context it has a far more specific meaning. In such an instance "confabulation" applies to a variety of neurological syndromes that are the result of some form of disruption within the information transfer system that facilitates the exchange of data between our cerebral hemispheres. This may be the due to either physical trauma, e.g. head injury or surgery, or some form of pathology, e.g. stroke, tumour, multiple sclerosis etc. Invariably the injury involves the right cerebral hemisphere, particularly the Right Frontal lobe, and / or its related interconnections with the language axis of the Left cerebral hemisphere.

The hallmark that is common to these varied syndromes is self- delusion . This delusional state may be related to the nature and extent of the disability that is sustained as a consequence of the neurological insult upon the victim. Alternatively, it may more accurately reflect the precise location of the injury within the region of the Right Frontal lobe and its information transfer network. In any event, the outcome is such that it induces the equivalent of a Left cerebral hemispheric shift, and a related perceptual, and verbal, over expression of the self- defensive ego mind. It is acknowledged that Confabulation is not a unitary neurological syndrome and that there are many different and overlapping variations and degrees of the disorder.

The characteristic feature, and major clinical manifestation, that defines this entity is self-delusion. It is also associated with an absolute inability and subconscious ineptitude to acknowledge the truth, not only to oneself, but to all others. This is despite all the contradictory evidence that supports, and confirms, the glaring reality regarding the true nature and extent of the functional neurological loss.

The term "self- delusion" is used here in order to distinguish it from the terms "denial", "lying", and "self- deception". Denial implies no more than a conscious unwillingness to admit to what is known to be true. The act of lying implies knowledge of the truth while consciously attempting to deceive another. Self- deception implies that the perpetrator partially persuades himself that the lie he is telling is the truth and then behaves as if it were true. It is a simultaneous process of knowing and not knowing, or telling a lie while self- imposing and subscribing to a fundamental belief in it. The person resists admitting what he knows to be true.

In the case of Confabulation, however, the person is not cognizant of the truth and as a consequence is unable to recognize the illogical nature of his analysis and the absurdity of his statement in the context of overt contradictory evidence. Consequently his replies and statements appear to be delusional in the face of reality. In addition, any effort to confront the contradictory evidence may only serve to compound the perplexity of the issue and its explanation. To this extent such efforts can reinforce and augment the self-delusion even further. One may as well be attempting to explain to a severe schizophrenic patient that he is delusional and psychotic in anticipation that such a logical explanation will cure him. There is no conscious attempt on the part of the confabulator to deny, lie, or deceive. While he appears to be suffering from delusion he nevertheless has no generalized thought disorder as in any of the commonly recognized psychotic states.

A typical example of one form of Confabulation, as described here, would be where a patient with a paralyzed limb (e.g. following a stroke) would insist that the only reason that they would not move it on request / command was that they simply did not wish to do so. They might say that they were too tired or stiff, or that the limb belonged to another person. Early neurological studies conducted throughout the nineteen forties, through to the nineteen eighties, demonstrated the general regions of the brain that were involved in the clinical presentation of confabulation. These studies suggested that confabulation could occur when the language centres (especially Broca's area) in the Left cerebral hemisphere are isolated from critical sources of information elsewhere in the right brain. Broca's area is involved in our ability to verbally express ourselves. Injury to this area causes "Expressive Aphasia" i.e. impaired ability to speak. In contrast, Wernicke's area is involved in our ability to comprehend language. Damage to this region of our Left hemisphere causes "Receptive Aphasia" i.e. difficulty understanding what is being said.

When the Right Frontal lobe is damaged there may be excessive verbosity or full- fledged manifestations of confabulation. This appears to be the result of loss of inhibition within the Left hemispheric language axis, difficulty monitoring responses to questions, and resorting to various internal, or environmental, cues to manufacture connections. All of these activities cause the language axis of the Left hemisphere to become flooded with irrelevant associations. The outcome may border on the absurd and ridiculous, as loosely associated ideas become organized around fragments of immediate experience and observation. A hospitalized patient with Right Frontal lobe damage may claim to be a visiting consultant, a member of staff, or an agent who is there to protect their own, or other patients' intellectual property.

Confabulation due to Right Frontal lobe damage may also be due to information retrieval failure. This is a form of memory loss that is associated with inability to retrieve autobiographical and episodic details that are stored as perceptions or in a language format. The resulting information gaps are then inserted by the patient in an effort to construct some kind of plausible answer or logical version of a perceived reality.

We will now consider these facts beyond the limited and confined boundaries that apply to those specific traumatic, or pathological, cerebral disturbances that can result in the syndrome of confabulation. It is suggested that even in the total absence of any specific damage to the Frontal lobes, or any other region of the brain, that confabulation may represent a fundamental compensatory mechanism that is designed to help maintain a felt sense of integrity, autonomy, and ego- based self-esteem. Such a mechanism may be invoked in response to a real, or perceived, conscious or subconscious, personal loss, deficiency, or inadequacy. These compensatory mechanisms are invariably instigated in situations where an individual's sense of unity, autonomy, integrity, and control are felt to be at risk, in question, or under observation. This mental inquisition may be instigated by oneself, or by another inquiring body. A far more dramatic picture, with serious, and widespread, implications for the human race, will slowly start to emerge. We can now begin to consider, and extrapolate, beyond the neurological confines of our current understanding of how our brain functions, of the specific roles of each hemisphere, and the critical functions of the Corpus Callosum and Frontal lobes. In this manner we can begin to comprehend how these neurological activities are instigated within the illusive, and complex, dynamics that apply to our mind. We can now address the issue of Left Hemispheric shift within the context of self- delusion as it is most commonly instigated within the primacy, and the configuration, of our individual mind. In these particular instances confabulation ceases to be a mere medical curiosity that applies to a minority of unfortunate victims of cerebral injury or disease.

Rather, it begins to take on the potentially catastrophic profile of a global pandemic that originates within the matrix of the mind. Rather than addressing the issue of self- delusion within the context of their cerebral correlates, we will consider them as they pertain to the operative dynamics that govern the configuration and expressive content of the human mind. In extreme cases these instances of confabulation are what we often associate with the criminal or sociopathic individual. In other cases it is what we encounter within the media as high profile individuals in various walks of life are eventually exposed following their categorical denial of allegations in respect of professional misconduct, fraud, or corruption. However, far below this glaring radar there is a pervasive confabulatory phenomenon that is threatening to undermine the fundamental fabric of our society on a global basis.

These are the commonplace instances of self- delusion in respect of our attitudes, values, and beliefs, which in turn underpin our expectations within our interpersonal relationships with another individual, or group of individuals. It is what precipitates conflict in the home, at work, and within our institutions at every level of society. In effect it is representative of a phenomenon which we have referred to as a "Left Hemispheric shift". Honor and Integrity, honesty and truth, loyalty and dignity, promise and commitment all are reduced to egocentric opportunism. This is a strategy that is grounded within the rational of a cost-benefit analysis with respect to need fulfilment and self enhancement.

Some basic understanding of how our memory operates is required in order that we can comprehend the nature of this insidious pandemic. This is largely due to the fact that the secondary metaphors, from which we formulate our concepts, are what contribute to our attitudes, values, and beliefs. You will recall how we have considered these issues, and the manner in which we configure our perceptual paradigm, in a previous chapter (see Chap. 3a,"Module of Thought"). These secondary metaphors are derived from our living memory. Consequently memory is a critical factor within the equation when it comes to understanding what influences our mental activities and their cerebral correlates. These are the operative, reciprocal, and self -augmenting factors that apply to our intellectual processes, emotional responses, and our expressed behavior, within the routine of our daily lives.

(b) MEMORY

Once again I must precondition the manner in which language is applied to describe the means and mechanisms, by which memories are formed, stored, and retrieved in relation to our cerebral activities. In this instance, as within a previous context, cerebral functions are referred to only as a personification of a primary mental activity. The brain is the location where these mental activities are functionally expedited and may be applied within the world which we inhabit. It is extremely doubtful that memories are actually stored or retrieved by, and within the substance of the brain. It would appear far more likely that specialized regions within the brain serve as a "key", which can permit access to, and retrieval from, the memories of the mind. In turn, these mental activities can be encrypted, and subsequently decoded, or expressed, within an electrochemical milieu that renders it as a functional and practical modality.

The human mind, and the manner in which it performs and serves mankind, is a universal and shared facility even while it is perceived as individual and personal. It is I alone while it also embodies all humanity within a cosmic context. So it is with consciousness, spirit, memories (lived and unlived), and indeed also as with the universal and primary allegorical substrate of our thoughts as both concepts and beliefs.

Consciousness and memories might be considered as existing in the form of a quantum resonance that diffuses in a bidirectional mode through the cosmos, and may be intercepted by the personal, and individual, "beacon" of our minds. In this manner our minds would function in a receiver –transmitter type of mode. The encoded content contained within these resonating signals would reverberate in an exchange mode between their source and the precincts of our minds. Specific regions within our brains may be genetically designed to hone in to these mentally targeted signals so as to illicit an encrypting form (i.e. enfolded) of neuronal response. These, in turn, may be selectively decoded (i.e. unfolded) in response to our individual prompting and particular requirement. We have addressed some of these issues as they pertain to "consciousness" in the chapter "The Air of Clarity".

We will now consider the type of memory with which we are all most familiar.

LIVING MEMORY

There are two distinct types of what we will loosely refer to as memory "storage and retrieval systems". They are called "Evoked Memory" and "Recalled Memory". Let

THE KEYS TO THE DOORS OF PERCEPTION

us examine how these two encrypting, and decoding, types of systems operate:

EVOKED MEMORY

Evoked memory is the kind that can be retrieved through the direct application of electrode stimulation upon specific sites of the brain. At these sites past events have been individually hardwired into the brain and stored within the subconscious precisely as they were experienced. In this situation, not only are past events recorded in detail, but the visual images are interlinked with what was heard, felt, and understood at that moment in time. The electrode probe will evoke this recorded experience within the individual's consciousness independently of one's will or desire to focus upon it. The specific situation progresses and unfolds just as the original experience had evolved. The event and the feeling are inextricably locked together in the brain so that one cannot be evoked without the other. The process is one of an involuntarily and "relived" experience. The person is momentarily displaced into the past as an "I am there now" response to the electrical stimulus. What is more, since the person is conscious during this electric probing, they are aware of both their current and present location in time and place, and they simultaneously experience and witness a living re-enactment from within their past. Furthermore, when these memories are evoked from the Temporal lobe cortex the experience seems to be in the

347

present and in continuous temporal sequence. The event unfolds in time sequence precisely as it had evolved, and had been recorded, throughout the interval of the original experience.

In effect, the person witnesses and experiences a living bi-location - one within the present tense (and concerning current events), the other within the past (and relating to past events). The relived event is also experienced by the person from the perspective of both active participant and passive onlooker and observer to the scene sequence as it unfolds. Following the evoked memory experience the person may then consciously remember (i.e. recall) what he had witnessed. However, it is only when the electrode probe experiment is over that it becomes recognizable as a vivid memory of the past.

Curiously, a very similar experience has been described within the context of the "near death experience" (NDE) by many individuals. In these instances however, the events are witnessed as they are being recorded in real time. There is a living experience of bi location where the person clearly perceives themselves "out of their body", above, and at a distance from their biological self. This is strikingly akin to the perceptual reality within which the Right cerebral cortex engages. It is objective, inclusive, distant, and discrete. In fact, most of us have had similar, but far less intense and dramatic, encounters of this nature. Most performers, actors and musicians, experience it on a fairly regular basis. It is when you subconsciously "visualize" yourself as the observer (in the audience) even while you are consciously aware, and in command, of your actions and behavior on stage. As long as this is achieved as a passive and non- intrusive experience it may enhance the performance. However, once it is transferred across into the Left brain where focused attention is brought to bear, it is transformed from self -awareness into an experience of self- consciousness. Since this is critical and analytical it impairs fluidity and spontaneity so as to be detrimental to ones efforts.

Many of us also subconsciously and spontaneously engage, at some time or another, and to varying degrees, in this form of passive self- observation. Invariably, for most of us, the magic of the moment is broken by the intrusion of the ego and the emergence of an unsettling self -consciousness.

What is of relevance to us is that all of these evoked memories are directly accessed without the interference of the will and without their being subject to the cognitive meddling of our Left brain and our ego. Unfortunately, this kind of memory is of little practical use to us since we cannot usually gain access to it at will. This is because it lies hidden deep down within the subconscious and beyond the reach of our recall system. Yet, while these memories may lie beyond our willful reach they are constantly integrated and "alive" within the very fabric of our personality makeup. And they frequently explode or intrude, as unannounced, uninvited, and oftentimes, unwelcome guests to impose themselves as the overbearing and dominant character actors upon the present scene. Many of these most irrational and outspoken voices will be those that were hardwired within our childhood memories particularly prior to the age of five, and most specifically before we even reached our second birthday. These memory banks contribute to a very significant degree to "who we are", how we tend to interact and respond for the greater part in a subconscious and reflex mode within the context of our routine lives. Many of these memories are highly charged with emotional energy. This is often an extremely negative, hostile, and defensive form of psychic energy. It may be manifest as the frustrated, naive, inarticulate, and defenseless child who is acting out within an adult tantrum mode.

This concept may be further extended to shed some light on the phenomena of apparitions. The nature and essence of a "miraculous apparition" is that it is a perceptual means by which communication is established with a mortal being within a spiritual or supernatural context. This is precisely what occurs, in varying measure and degree, within the context of what has been mentioned here already. One achieves a level of passive surrender and submission to the intuitive Wisdom of the Spirit via their soul. The Right cerebral hemisphere there upon initiates a process through which the primary metaphorical content of this Unlived Memory becomes consciously apprehended as a perceptually real and lived experience within the context of the material world. The process unfolds in a similar manner as do the events and related feelings within the relived experience of the evoked memory as was previously described.

RECALLED MEMORY

Recalled Memory is the type with which we are all familiar on a normal everyday basis. It is what we retrieve when we try to recollect something. It is prompted by our will, drawn up from storage into our consciousness. In transit it must traverse the Left brain and our ego mind. Therein it may be subject to much tampering and adjustment. We do not store these memories like photographs, hoping that if we store them properly, and in some kind of order, that we can retrieve them in the same condition in which we put them away. In fact, we only extract key elements from our experiences. This is what we store. We then recreate or reconstruct the experience as a memory as opposed to retrieving intact and complete copies of the originals. In the process of reconstruction we may add various pieces of data (knowledge, feelings, and beliefs) that we accumulated since the original experience.

Consequently, the recalled memory is often skewed or rewritten to reflect what we now know, understand, feel, and believe. This is invariably quite different to what had happened back at the first instant of the experience.

Daniel Schacter describes the various malfunctions of memory formation and retrieval extremely well in his book "The Seven Deadly Sins of Memory". It is accepted that these memory malfunctions are exaggerations of traits that can be useful, and perhaps sometimes necessary, for our basic survival i.e. that they are by-products of otherwise desirable and adaptive features of the mind. However, when such traits are magnified, unconstrained, and espoused in the extreme, they have the potential to shift our mind set into an ever spiraling delusional mode that is egocentrically fuelled and directed. In this regard a specific subtype of memory malfunction called Memory Bias is a major contributor to the hidden ego based agenda.

There are three forms of memory bias:

Consistency bias:
Where we rewrite past feelings and beliefs to resemble what we now feel and believe.

Egocentric bias:
Where we remember the past in a self-enhancing manner.

Stereotypical bias:
Where we typecast groups of people to capture their general properties as we perceive them. This can trigger unwarranted and untrue judgments about individuals. It can fuel racial and religious prejudices, conflicts, and war.

The Left Cerebral hemisphere contains what is described as an "Interpreter" which is constantly drawing on general knowledge and past experience to try and bring order to our psychological world. This Interpreter relies on inference, generalization, and rationalization to try and relate past and present. Consequently, in all probability it contributes to Bias modes of memory, including the Egocentric type. It strives to reconcile present attitude with past actions and feelings in order to provide us with that comfortable feeling that we were never fools, were always in control, and always in possession of great stores of wisdom and foresight. We always knew how things would turn out: We indulge in the art of ego enhancement at will.

Egocentric bias explains why people are more likely to attribute successes rather than failures to themselves. It accounts for our tendency to blame and attribute failures to forces outside of ego self. This same feature is commonly seen when people recall what lead to the failure of their business project, to the breakdown of their marriage, or to their being pushed into extreme forms of behavior or lifestyle such as alcoholism, drug addiction, gambling, or criminality.

Egocentric memory bias may reflect several related maneuvers:

Selective recall, including blame, and denial. This involves the exaggeration of past difficulties so that you can infer to self and others that you are a born survivor who can rise to any given occasion despite the great odds against you. Depreciating "past self" to compare with the far greater self that now stands before the world and knows no limits to what it can aspire. All these elements help present self in the comforting glow of positive illusions. This is the realm of the Left brain and the kingdom of the ego mind. Taken a little further what may begin as an innocent exercise in bolstering self- esteem can lead us down the long path of self- delusion.

We burn a synaptic circuit impregnated with the musings of the Left brain until we can no longer see ourselves in a realistic and objective light. We fade out the objectivity of our Frontal lobes, the intuition of our Right brain, and disrupt the cross communication through the Corpus Callosum. We buy the lie. The unchecked Left brain of bias and rationalization descends into the bottomless pit of self-delusion. Fortunately, within the normal functionality of our brain and its psychological counterpart this Interpreter is balanced by systems within the Right brain. These Right brain systems are more attuned to the constraints of the external world so as to help keep the error prone tendencies of the Left brain in check. However, as illustrated, we can choose to alter and adjust this balance in favour of the illusive pursuit of our selfish needs, our greatest personal ambitions, and our heart's desires.

As in Orwell's 1984: *"Who controls the past controls the future; Who controls the present controls the past"*. The "Ministry of Truth", which leads to Totalitarian disaster, equates with a Left brain unfettered and unchecked by the Right hemisphere. Control of the past depends on controlling the memory since the past has no objective existence but merely survives in the records of our memories. If it becomes necessary or desirable to rearrange and reconfigure our memories (i.e. to tamper with the records and files) it is necessary that we forget that we have done so (self-delusion). We rescript our memories to fit with our present agenda, our current view, and our present desires. Memory is the pawn for the Ruling Masters (Big Brother or ego mind) of our cognitive systems (Logic of the Left brain). It can render and reduce our hearts (Right brain intuition) and our souls (authentic self /Spirit) to subservience and to slavery.

(c) UNLIVED MEMORY

Aside and apart from this form of "Evoked and Recalled" living memory, there is an "Unlived" memory that resides deep within our collective unconscious. I am referring to that intuitive and supernatural memory that is enriched with the Wisdom of the Spirit. This is the only form of self-awareness that may be described as genuine, since it reflects only authentic self. This also can only be evoked, not by probing electrodes, but by passive and humble submission as within the realm wherein we have dislocated ourselves from the intrusions of our Left brain so as to dwell in the meditative "Gateway to the Soul". Doubtless, but that an experience of bi location may also be felt and witnessed in the full expression of this transcendental state. By extrapolation, it might be witnessed by another receptive observer who is connected to the collective and shared "spiritual internet". This concept may lead towards a better understanding of a number of such well documented instances of individuals who had this "supernatural gift" of bi -location.

More typical examples wherein the Wisdom of the Spirit may be evoked within the content of our unlived memory include those of spiritually enlightened inspiration which we would most likely attribute to our human intuition or inherent skill and creativity. More extreme examples which few of us have ever experienced include those of ecstasies, profound epiphanies, and celestial apparitions. In these exceptional circumstances the content of our unlived memory may be conceptually configured so that it may be imparted and perceived within the current context of the lived experience. The perception may be rendered and expressed in one or **several sensory modes i.e. visual, auditory, olfactory, or even tactile.** The resolution level and intensity of this sensory imagery is a reflection of the extent to which the individual has been enabled by the gift of grace to experience this phenomenon. Furthermore, in almost every instance of a cited apparition the vision, at least initially, is perceived to be above and at a distance from the observer.

This is very similar to the "out of body" phenomenon witnessed by many in the near death experience. They perceive themselves hovering above, and often in a corner of the room in which their bodies are lying. From that vantage point they passively, and peacefully, observe the near demise of their mortal selves. Most visitations, visions, or transfigurations, described within the Scriptures (Old and New Testaments), and those witnessed in more contemporary times (Lourdes, Fatima, Guataloupe, Knock etc.) have been of this order of felt experience and spatial orientation.

PRACTICAL APPLICATIONS

Should you feel the need or desire to undertake a process of Transformation in your life, to strive to know and understand what may prompt you to respond, or behave, in any particular manner or mode, then some of the answers that are relevant to your personality makeup may reside within the configuration of your "Evoked or Living" Memory bank. One of the most practical means of identifying these "hidden forces" or personality traits that reside deep within the subconscious mind is through the application of Transactional Analysis. We will consider these issues in the following chapter. Additionally, you may wish to refer to the original 1970 publication on the subject: *"I'm O.K., You're O.K."* by Thomas Harris. You might also be prompted to cross check your "Recalled Memory" as recollected within the details of the past with your honest, transparent, and non-defensive self. This may be extended to include your trusted parents, siblings, and / or closest friends. It may well be that either you, or one of them, have been an innocent and misguided victim of Memory Bias! Check the "records" and compare. Invariably it requires that you listen in the silence of your uncertainties and from a distance beyond the boundaries of your subjective truths, your long held beliefs, your self-made illusions, and spurious realities.

All truth is relative, subjective, and sometimes even painful. Ultimately it can lead us towards a personal exaltation, humiliation, and release from a self-imposed captivity. This is the sharp and jagged edge that dispels false pride. It can open the gateway towards a process of Transfiguration and enlightenment and usher in the dawn of a new reality. You may now better appreciate how memory is critical to the configuration of our concepts and beliefs and to the fundamental nature of self-delusion (i.e. Confabulation).

(d) SAVANT SYNDROME & RIGHT HEMISPHERIC SHIFT

Just as a Left cerebral hemispheric shift may be affected within the alignment of our thinking, and our powers of perception, so also may a shift occur towards that of a Right hemispheric disposition. Within a neurological context, when such an event occurs it may become manifest as a neurological disorder that has been termed Savant Syndrome. As with the Syndrome of Confabulation, this relatively uncommon condition may be congenital, or acquired through injury or disease. The congenital form may be seen within the group of medical conditions referred to as Autistic Spectrum disorder (50% of all Savant cases). The acquired form may be most evident among those who sustain injury, or disease, to their left anterior temporal lobe or left prefrontal lobe. The key feature of the individual with Savant Syndrome is the heightened capacity, or ability in one or more specific talents which is far in excess of the norm. In most instances Savantism occurs in individuals who have serious mental disabilities, and below average IQs. Yet they can demonstrate remarkable skills in isolated areas that far exceed their overall IQs. This heightened skill, or brilliance, may be profound and prodigious, and is usually demonstrated within one, or more, of five major areas.

These include:

> Calculation / maths,(esp. calendrical calculation);
> Memory skills;
> Musical ability
> Art
> Spatial skills.

These particular skills are predominantly associated with the cerebral functions of the Right hemisphere. In most instances of savantism, particularly those of the acquired type, there is a related damage, or diminution in the functional activity, of the Left cerebral hemisphere. In some instances there is also impairment in the activity of the corpus callosum. In fact, the individual upon whom the autistic savant character in the film "Rain Man" is based was shown to have substantial brain damage on MRI inclusive of the total absence of his corpus callosum. That deficit alone would have prohibited inter-hemispheric transfer of information between the left and right cerebral hemispheres. Among those who are autistic 10% have some form of savantism. Prodigious savants are extremely rare. Their most common trait is their exceptional memory based skills with many having photographic memories.

We will consider the Savant syndrome briefly so that we can compare, and contrast it to that of Confabulation. However, as well you appreciate; our major concern is in regard to that of our ability to affect a shift within our mental equilibrium as opposed to that of its cerebral correlate. In effect, the entire content of this book is in regard to our understanding of the nature of such a "right sided" mental shift, and the means by which we may endeavor to achieve it. The objective of that exercise, which is fundamentally spiritual in nature, is towards our achieving a firm reinstatement of the soul as the Master of our mind. It is one of seeking to claw back whatever power had been inappropriately relegated to the dictates of the psyche, and to that of the ego- mind.

LATERALIZATION OF BRAIN FUNCTIONS

You may recall that while discussing how the brain functions, and ascribed specific roles to each of the Lobes of the brain, (Chap.2 a), we did not separate any of these functions into those that were preferentially designated to either the Right, or the Left Lobe. In reality, the neuroanatomy of the brain is not only functionally localized, it is also preferentially lateralized, to either the right or left sides to varying degrees. This lateralization applies not only to the lobes of the cerebral hemispheres, (i.e. Neocortex), but also to the more primitive regions of our brain. This particularly applies to the region of the midbrain, and that of the Limbic system. However in chapter 2, section b) and c) we did consider these lateralizing features within the text of the Bipolar brain, and Dual Realities / Dual Agendas. We will briefly recapitulate on some of the more salient details contained within those sectors of chapter 2.

In general terms, as it pertains to the lateralization of cerebral function, the Left hemisphere mediates those functions that are of greater relevance to what is fundamentally instinctual, and self –centred. The nature of its attention is narrow, analytical, and highly focused. These traits include those that are relevant to self-survival, competitiveness, cunning, and manipulative types of activities. All of these abilities are greatly enhanced through the application of intellectual skill, the formulation of conceptual strategies, and the linguistic skill of negotiation within an explicit format.

On the other hand, the Right hemisphere is far more aligned to that of the implicit, the pre-conceptual, and artistic. It is also more aligned with the content of the subconscious, and the collective unconscious. The nature of its attention is far more broad –based, and inclusive, compared to that of the left hemisphere. If you were to sustain damage to the Left Frontal lobe you may lose the ability to talk.(i.e. Expressive aphasia) This is because Broca's area is located in the Left Frontal lobe, and it controls speech. However you would retain the ability to swear, and sing, because these abilities are mediated by the Right Frontal lobe. Incidentally, you would also retain the ability to understand what is being said, (Comprehension aphasia), because that is controlled by Wernicke's area in the Temporal lobe.

In many respects functional damage to the Left frontal lobe may seriously impair the imposition of its mental correlate, the psyche, upon the process of inter-hemispheric synergy. This critical process occurs within the final phase of our cognition, and within the domain of the Right hemisphere. It is what facilitates our ability to reconcile, and express, the content of both hemispheres, and to do so within their relevant contexts. In the absence of the dictates of the psyche, it is inevitable that the agenda will be heavily biased within the context, and the content, of the Right hemisphere, and the primacy of its mental substrate. Memory function is no longer over- preoccupied with the configuration of intellectual concepts from the archives of its Secondary metaphors. Consequently, it will preferentially revert to the content of its original, and Primary metaphors.

If, in addition to injury or impairment of the Left Frontal lobe, one was to sustain some further extension of neurological deficit within the Left hemisphere, inclusive of the Temporal lobe, (and perhaps also injury to the corpus callosum), the outcome would almost certainly be clinically manifest as one similar in nature to that which we describe as full blown Savant Syndrome. This is what we may also describe as a major Right hemispheric Shift.

What is of relevance to us is that we can achieve a selective shift towards the Right within our hemispheric alignment, and do so without compromising any of our intellectual, or cognitive, capacities. We can address this process of alignment within the primacy of our Spiritual mind set, and our mental faculties, rather than within the functionality of any specific neurological location, or any attempt towards reconfiguring our neurological circuitry. The modus operandi of these biological components will be reflected through the process of reciprocity in due course. It is within the appropriate alignment of our spiritual, or soulful, mind and that of our psyche that we can unlock the hidden talents, and the creative genius that lies dormant within all of us. Thus may we be enabled to express, and share, the fullness of our human nature in all its dignity and its sacred glory. It is only within the proper delegation of power, and authority, to the rightful Master of our all that inspires, and guides, us, that we may become fully human. It is in this manner that we may come to discover authentic knowledge, and truth, in respect of the nature of our humanity. Therein resides the pathway that will direct us towards the ultimate realization of the true purpose of our lives.

CHAPTER NINE: TRANSFORMATION AND TRANSACTION

(Or Getting to Know the Ego "I" in You)

Ego Master - Intercept by Stealth

Do you ever stop and wonder who precisely is the "real me"? How valid is the perception which we have constructed, and regard as representative, of our authentic nature? Is the persona, or personas, that we acquire and project, a true reflection of the nature of the real and authentic "self"?

If we are to make any attempt at seeking to relate to the world in a manner that is a genuine reflection of our individual human nature, we must begin by acknowledging a simple basic fact. From a functional or operational standpoint, each one of us is a living expression of a rival and conflictual pair. We have two cerebral hemispheres, and a "bipolar mind", (psyche and soul), each of which present us with two distinctly different agendas, priorities, needs, and values. Consequently, we also have two "personas", or images, that present to us as "self". Sometimes it is self in accord and in harmony, but more often it is self in inner conflict. That conflict is a consequence of the bipolar dispositions of our mental faculties, and of their cerebral correlates, as they are represented within the functional configuration of the left and right cerebral hemispheres.

As we now well know, it is ego within the content of the psyche that poses, masquerades, and presents most forcefully to us, and to others, as the real and genuine self. If we are to avoid living a life within a self- delusional state of mind, and if we are to ever succeed in getting to know this ego "I", or the projected "Me", then we must set about the task of getting to know how to distinguish both aspects of our persona. We must establish an intimate relationship, and mutual understanding, with both ego self and with authentic self.

We will describe the process of attempting to establish such a functionally operative liaison with the psyche and the ego-self as one of "Transformation". The process of acquiring a more intimate and meaningful relationship with the soul is described as one of "Transfiguration". There is a world of difference in the meaning of these terms, and in the nature of the transition, and the personal impact, which they may bring to bear upon our self-perceptions.

Let us focus here upon the ego self. This is the mode to which we all tend to gravitate or revert. It is a primitive, instinctual, self- protective and distinctly human trait. With habit, repetition, reinforcement, and practice, we hone this mode towards a standard and status of commander, dictator, and defender of the perceptual self.

We will adapt the Parent- Adult – Child model of ego states as envisioned by Eric Berne in his theory of personality development as a practical mode of explaining how the psyche is structured. This in turn will assist us in our understanding of the manner in which our personality and behavior is molded from infancy and the extended lived experience throughout our adult lives. This theory, and the manner in which it applies to the practice of Transactional Analysis (T.A.), is well documented in Thomas Harris's book "I'm OK –You're OK". This particular book, which was published in the late sixties, has been a major source of reference for much of the ensuing information.

T.A. is a practical means by which we can reconfigure the modus operandi of our psyche so as to effect adaptive change in how we may seek to relate and respond more constructively within the interactive dynamics of our lives.

All human beings are born with an inherent need for sensory and emotional stimulation. We will refer to this fundamental need as "stimulus hunger. It is simply satisfied by handling or by "stroking". It has well established that even in infancy, if we are deprived of such strokes there are invariably serious physical and psychological consequences. Such infants are more susceptible to disease to the extent that it can even have a fatal outcome. However, after infancy we remain confronted with a life-long dilemma which challenges our very survival and our destiny. Social, psychological, and biological factors obstruct our procurement of strokes as they had been provided in infancy. Yet, we continue to strive to satisfy this hunger for its attainment. Invariably we engage within a process of compromise and transformation where- in we find a range of alternative modes. These are called "recognition –hunger" and "structure –hunger".

All of us are well familiar with "recognition hunger". It may be benignly termed "attention- seeking" or "stroke-seeking" "Structure – hunger" is based upon our need to structure time within a social and stroke- procurement context. The essential feature is the need to avoid boredom which becomes synonymous with sensory and emotional starvation given that sustained boredom can have similar consequences. The function of all social living is to lend mutual assistance to time-structuring.

The operational aspect of time-structuring is referred to as programming. This has three aspects: material, social, and individual

Material programming arises from the unpredictable variations encountered in dealing with external reality. The most common, convenient, and utilitarian means of structuring time is by a project that is designed to deal with the material of external reality. This is what we call "work" or an "activity". Activities are based on cognitive activity or data processing. It is fundamentally a matrix for "stroking", recognition, and other forms of social intercourse.

Social programming results in traditional ritualistic, or semi ritualistic interchanges. Good manners, tact, and diplomacy, are classical examples. The chief criterion upon which it is based is local acceptance within a code of strictures and reinforcements. Usually formal rituals precede semi-ritualistic topical conversations which are referred to as pastimes.

Individual programming starts to emerge as an operative modality as people become better acquainted on a more personal basis. Sequences of interaction and communication spawn "incidents", or circumstances that have a potential to evolve towards a consequence or outcome of some description. Such incidents appear to be fortuitous and unplanned but careful scrutiny reveals that they tend to follow definite patterns which are amenable to sorting and classification. These sequences are also circumscribed by unspoken rules and regulations. These are what constitute what we call "games". The personal modus operandi of our everyday life as it relates to others, be they clustered within organizations, families, or marriage, is through the medium of these games.

With time and experience we personally shape and configure the manner in which we address these substitute modalities to suit our individual needs. It is this individual variation that creates such diversity within the spectrum of our social intercourse. It is also a major determinant of the individual's life experience and their destiny. Specifically it is the Individual programmed ego that engages within the bulk of our social activity and emerges as the Game Master. This aspect of Ego Self can be identified by the characters, and the role moves, which it adopts.

The term "Game" is used in the same context as that which Doctor Eric Berne applied it in relation to Transactional Analysis. Berne defines a Game as a "recurring set of selfish or ulterior transactions, often repetitious, superficially plausible, with a concealed motive or agenda". In effect, it is a series of moves with a specific snare or "gimmick". They are basically dishonest and always have some anticipated personal payoff. They are dishonest since they are opportunistic, having a hidden, concealed, and selfish motive which is to acquire the maximum strokes. The snare need not always is sinister, but directly or indirectly, it is invariably sought at another's expense. Many, if not all, Game motives are related to Greed, Power, or Pride. These are three among the "Seven Deadly Sins".

All of these have their root in fear: Fear of not having enough, of losing one's independence, integrity, dignity, autonomy, or self-esteem. Fear is the core ploy used by Ego to retain control and remain imperative and indispensable.

While the games may be multiple and varied, usually there is a highly prioritized and central "Game Master" with a common theme and objective, a modus operandi that holds centre stage within our personal life drama. As we have seen, the origin and source of Game playing, Recognition-hunger, and the various alternative Structural modes, such as work (data processing), rituals, manners, and pastimes, is based upon our need to find alternative substitutes for the infantile requirement of "stroking".

Stroking implies intimate physical contact and has its analogues in language and social interaction. e.g. "He pulled off that deal with a couple of real master strokes". "He is a cool operator; he knows all the right strokes, makes all the right moves". In the language of transactional analysis, an exchange of strokes constitutes a "transaction". This, in turn, defines the basic unit of social intercourse. What is noteworthy is that in adult life, games and pastimes are no more than substitutes for the real lived experience of genuine intimacy. Intimacy and sexual love, which represents its ultimate prototype, is the only completely satisfying answer to stimulus-hunger or any of its various analogues.

Consequently, our immediate efforts will be directed towards the task of "Game Master" identification. We will focus on the central, or major, set of characters. He is the profiler, the image maker, and the personality shaper. His primary function is in the role of the Director of our game plan and our "Plot" to shape the direction and the course of our lives. He pens the scripts, writes the plots, chooses the cast, and decides on the location and the set design. In addition, the Game Master also designs the wardrobe, controls the lighting, performs the stunts, and executes all of the special effects. For the most part, all of us, to one extent or another, live out our lives within this virtual reality. Both ourselves, and our interactive audience, knowingly or otherwise, submit, contribute to, and participate in, the self- deception and the lie. We all play "The Game".

In practical terms, the varied ego states reflect a system of feelings accompanied by a related set of behavioral patterns. This repertoire of personal ego states is not so much a clutch of roles, as they are actual psychological realities. In transactional analysis we refer to them as Parent, Adult, and Child ego states. We can witness or observe these ego states as they become manifest within varied and often inconsistent, aspects of our behavior. They are reflected within our changes of attitude, posture, body language, viewpoint, voice, and vocabulary. These are frequently associated with significant, and visible, changes in our emotions and our feelings.

The Parent state resembles those of parental figures who protect, advise, criticize, and scorn us. The Adult state is autonomously directed towards objective appraisal of reality. The Child state is representative of archaic relics that have been fixated in early childhood. We can think of these three general categories of ego states as tapes, or circuits that have apparently become hard wired into our personality and our memory banks. In any given situation, particularly within the context of human interaction and social activity, one or more of these recordings or circuits will be activated. Simple transactional analysis is concerned with identifying which ego state implemented the transactional stimulus (from the agent), and which ego state executed the transactional response (from the respondent). The specific situation, circumstance, and content of the proceedings will usually dictate which of the three ego states will first vie to rise to the occasion. In addition, it will often dictate to which ego state the agent will, in turn, direct his message or reaction to the intended respondent.

There are four possible "Life Positions" which can be identified as being held with regard to oneself and others through this form of analysis.

These are:

1. **I'M NOT OK – YOU'RE OK.**
2. **I'M NOT OK – YOU'RE NOT OK.**
3. **I'M OK - YOU'RE NOT OK.**
4. **I'M OK - YOU'RE OK.**

Only the fourth statement is regarded as being healthy, and representative of being in harmony within oneself, and with others.

The fact of the matter is that our personalities have been molded to a very large extent by our primary mentors, particularly those who had such roles within our early childhood. These would include parents or parent figures such as close relatives, older siblings, teachers, friends, and even our real or fictional heroes, and the media. What may be your greatest strengths and vulnerabilities, as you now project and apply them within society, are largely the outcomes of your preconditioning experiences from the past. These are mostly contained within the Parent and Child modes of your personal ego states.

You may consider your Adult mode as being representative of your mature and logical objectivity. It is the adjudicator and mediator who strive to intervene on your behalf in hopes of resolving potential conflicts that may arise in response to the promptings of Parent and / or Child ego states. Sometimes its best efforts are of little or no avail so that we may come to feel trapped or victimized.

What is of critical importance is the extent to which we empower the Game Master in the determination of any specific ego state, and the manner in which that persona is expressed in the thoughts, words, and deeds of our daily lives. There are many and varied pathways towards achieving transformation in the manner in which our psyche operates. The goal is to re-educate our ego states to the extent that a more objective, and better informed, Adult mode holds precedence over the Parent and Child ego states. Transactional Analysis is one means of achieving this goal.

Cognitive Behavioral Therapy (CBT) is another method which is currently more popular among clinical psychologists. CBT assumes that by changing maladaptive thinking, or one's relationship with these forms of cognitive distortions, one can alter their emotional responses and the related patterns of problematic behavior. This technique is used to help people become more aware of their faulty patterns of thinking and replace them with positive and constructive ideas and behavioral strategies. These methods of achieving a greater awareness in regard to the manner in which our psych, and its ego states have been configured provides us with a means of applying active intervention on our own behalf. We can learn to apply leverage so as to alter the inevitability of emotional distress and self- defeating outcomes.

CHAPTER TEN: PERSONALITY DEVELOPMENT AND BEHAVIOUR

Caution: Inner Conflict Wages

We are harmony and conflict, stability and flux,
Forever seeking refuge within turmoil of our mind,
Forever seeking unity within the Spirit of our kind.
Reconciliation is the answer that is so hard to find.

The author.

Our behavior is seen as a reflection of our basic nature and our individual personality. Traditionally it has also been viewed more simplistically as the combined outcome of nature and nurture. In the latter case nature is genetically determined, and nurture is the influence of the pervading environment. However, in either case one could well argue that our behavior is rarely a true reflection of our authentic human nature. Additionally, there is a fundamental problem that is inherent within the use of these descriptive terms of reference. The inference, as commonly understood and defined, is that nature, and nurture, are specific entities that determine the configuration of our personalities. It is now generally accepted that this is not the case. Recent advances in the field of epigenetics have contributed greatly to our reappraisal of these issues.

The nature and personality of an individual are intertwined and share a common root system that is inclusive of both their DNA and the unique configuration of the personal psyche. Then, this is as we ought expect, given that the mind and brain are inexorably bound and are expressed as a collaborative unity within the external world which we inhabit. Furthermore, as we shall come to discover, neither our DNA, nor the freedom of expression which we surrender to the psyche are fixed, stable, and unchangeable entities. It is unrealistic to attempt to consider personality and human nature as separate entities in isolation. Behavioral scientists often refer to the "Big Five" personality features. These are openness, conscientiousness, extroversion, agreeableness, and neuroticism. They believe that these are good predictors of one's capacity to experience happiness and contentment.

As these scientists see it, happiness and contentment are simply figments of our imagination, which in turn are a reflection of our particular personality make up. Perhaps they are, when equated with the pursuit, and acquisition, of perceived needs and desires. Yet, some of us might feel quite differently: that happiness has more to do with one's ability to achieve a sense of genuine meaning and purpose in life. These academics have also informed us that these personality features are about 50% genetic and 50% environmental. But then science, and the language in which it is expressed, have their own specific objectives and agendas. It is one of fragmentation, separation, classification and categorization.

Perhaps what most of us define as happiness is a misrepresentation of the implicit definition of the term. This would seem to be borne out with the recently published World Happiness Report (2015). The estimates of a global happiness rating for individual nations were based on the following criteria: GNP per head, social support, life expectancy, freedom to make life choices, generosity, perception of corruption, and a dystopic factor (i.e. the antithesis of a Utopia). If there is any inherent validity attached to this study it may be concealed within the content of that final criterion. We may experience a sense of happiness as long as the fear of its imminent free-fall into a state of unhappiness through loss of our key criteria is kept safely at bay. Yet well we know how quickly and unpredictably these types of key locks can become unbolted.

Whatever your definition and criteria, enjoy the moment if it makes you feel happy, but do not be too surprised if it proves to be an elusive and transient type of experience!

However, such analytical approaches towards quantifying our perceptions do not always lend themselves to the most accurate description of every concept, thought, feeling, aspiration, or expectation. Within this modern age of intellectual and spiritual growth and transition there are many words that need to be more accurately defined, and many more neologisms generated. This is particularly the case as it applies to the articulation of our concepts regarding the nature of the human condition, and the manner in which we seek to express it within the living world.

The truth concerning our reality, or our paradigm, is only as good and as accurate as is our ability to verbalize or otherwise communicate it to ourselves and to others. Scientific analysis and explicit language have their own in- built limitations even while they are still revered as the gold standards by which we express our truths and realities. Thankfully, we have many alternative modes by which we may express ourselves in terms of our feelings, beliefs, and realities more fully. Metaphor and allegory, music and dance, painting and sculpture, are but some of the examples whereby some of our most important and universal truths are best conveyed.

When I speak of our human nature I am referring to that which constitutes the essential content, and substrate, of our psyche and soul (i.e. the human mind) rather than limiting ourselves to a description that relates only to the genetic determinants that are encoded within our D.N.A. When I am referring to the composition of personality I am doing so within the context of the many factors that shapes the manner in which we strive to relate, and express ourselves, to and within the world in which we live. In addition to the multiple and varied environmental factors, these also include elements of our genetic makeup and the specific configuration of our psyche. Furthermore, we will come to appreciate that the genetic factors are not necessarily fixed and constant. Their individual expression cannot be predictably determined within any given person, nor within any specific time frame or circumstance of an entire lifespan.

The manner and the means by which we seek to address our life's situation is governed by the dictates of our mind, (inclusive of the emotive overlay), and the manner in which these are expressed through the functional and complex circuitry of our brains. Yet, there are a host of factors that may serve to distort or disrupt the expression of our authentic human nature as it is reflected by the variable imposition of the psyche. Likewise, there are a multiplicity of factors that may alter or impinge upon the neurological expression of our dispositions, motives, and intentions as they had been initially established within the silence of our minds. And finally, while we may be endowed with the facility of free will, choice, a rational intellect, and a moral conscience, we may yet remain variably constrained, within certain situations or circumstances, in our ability to effectively engage or consciously control these mutable parameters.

We have already considered the fundamental nature of humanity within the context of his psyche and his soul. We are aware that it is the synergy, and the related conflict of interest and goal, in addition to the proportional representation of these aspects of our mind that mold the command criteria that is encrypted within our neurological circuitry. The outcome of this mental flux will be greatly influenced by the degree to which we have surrendered our will to either psyche or soul through repetition or habit, and by the magnitude of the conflict that arises in any given situation or circumstance. For the greater part it is the influence of our attitudes, values, beliefs, and priorities that underpin these forces. Most of us will freely acknowledge that we rarely achieve expressive perfection as gauged by the standards of our genuine human nature. At best, most of us invariably settle for some form of compromise that satisfies our personal needs within a rather ill-defined and fluid moral context that can be adequately self- justified by the ego.

While the essence of our true nature is reflected through the soul, the individual character of personality is more accurately a reflection of the workings of the psyche. The synergistic interaction of psyche and soul contribute to the formulation of our perceptual reality. The core content of this paradigm pertains to our fundamental set of attitudes, values, and beliefs. The manner in which this personalized reality may be expressed within the context of our lives is, in turn, reflected by the cerebral configurations that have been biologically transcribed from the template of the mind. In addition genetic factors may also predispose us in the precise manner of this transcribing process. When we consider the manner in which the content of the psyche becomes established and evolves from infancy through adulthood we can begin to comprehend the complexities that underpin our human personalities. We have considered these issues in the chapter "Transformation and Transaction". Of particular relevance is the manner in which the three ego states (parent, adult, and child) become established as psychological references within the workings of our mind set and the role of the "game master" in the selective projection of self as representative by our personality.

In effect, there are many aspects within our operative ego states that are beyond our conscious vision and outside of our direct control. From the standpoint of the observer there exists one, or many, projected images of "self" (as personality) and a more valid and hidden aspect that often remains largely out of sight. Moreover, we must also take into account the fallibility of memory, and the propensity towards confabulation, or self –delusion, as factors that can, and do, distort our own objectivity with regard to the kind of person that we really are (or to be precise, the kind that we have become). The only possible means of attempting to clarify the objective validity with regard to oneself is by reverting to the intuitive wisdom that can reveal the authentic self. Most, if not all of us, would find it difficult or near impossible to undertake such a self- revelatory and self- effacing task. Indeed, few of us would be prompted to do so in the absence of some significant measure of emotional distress, or major quandary that demanded an urgent resolution. For most of us, such circumstances present in the guise of personal loss, or bereavement. Some will encounter it within the context of a felt sense of failure, inadequacy, or perhaps even as persistent anxiety and / or depression.

Let us now consider some of the factors that can modify or impinge upon the neurological expression of the contents of our mind and the manner in which these may impact upon our personality and behavior. The frequently quoted case of the infamous Phineas Gage, who had sustained severe frontal lobe damage in a railroad accident in 1848, continues to be misrepresented by many neuro-scientific authorities to this very day. Since Gage underwent a major personality change as a consequence of his injuries the common inference is that it is within the region of the frontal lobes that these attributes have their source of origin. As well you can appreciate, our belief and understanding of the matter is that it is to this area of the brain that the relevant mental determinants are conveyed, encoded, and finally expressed within the world. Disruption of the neuronal circuitry within this region will alter the valid expression of this data. This does not necessarily imply that the origin and source of the factors that determine personality are located within the frontal lobes.

The brain is no more than the biological emissary of the mind. If you were to jiggle or dismantle parts of the circuitry within your television set you might expect that the quality of sound and picture will suffer as a consequence. But it does not indicate that there is a flaw within the studio nor the transmission signal. The human mind, in psyche and soul, is the production unit and transmitter. The brain is the receiver, recorder and display unit .The receiver does not create or produce the program content but in the instance of the brain it does express (i.e. display) its contents to the external world. It may do so in thought, word, deed, emotive display and pageantry. Why is this primacy of mind, specifically of soul, of such interest and concern to anyone? The fate of Phineas Gage (or of anyone who has ever suffered from any form of ill health) is not an isolated and historical curiosity. At any given moment in time thousands of individuals world- wide are the unfortunate victims of cerebral injury or disease. Many of these will sustain varying degrees of alteration in their personalities and personas to the extent that it will impoverish the very basic quality of their lives and impact on their loved ones.. However, such changes do not necessarily imply that the individual has lost or abandoned their intuitive respect, concern, compassion, and morality. Rather, they have lost the ability to consciously apprehend, control, and express these virtues.

It has recently been proposed that it is the activity of a specific type of neuron within the brain that is involved in our ability to experience and express empathy and compassion. This is called the "mirror neuron. They account for approximately 20 % of all our brain cells and are present in far larger numbers within the human brain compared to other primates. These neurons are widely distributed throughout the brain and this suggests that they are intimately connected with our learning processes. They may in fact facilitate the exchange of information between various domains of intelligence and have been implicated in the evolutionary acquisition of cognitive fluidity. The largest concentration is present within the prefrontal area. The frontal lobes account for about a third of our total brain mass while they are absent or minimal in size in other species. These neurons are specialized brain cells that allow us to put ourselves in another's shoes so that we can imagine how they might feel and gauge what they might be thinking or intending. They allow us to reflect upon our own emotions and intents. These facilities provide us with the ability to read facial expressions and another's body language. Mirror neurons function as a "virtual reality network" which allows us to copy, or mimic, (i.e. learn by observation) others actions and behaviors. They can both observe and even imagine actions and so fire off in response to either watching another's performance or imagining any type of activity or skill (e.g. a mother's smile or grimace, playing a musical instrument, mastering a golf swing, or some athletic activity etc.). These neurons can also reinforce and fine tune our actions by a process of rehearsing the act by mirroring the body's own brain responses within the same brain area. Currently it is believed that much of our learning and behavior patterns revolve around the mimicry of other's through the activity of mirror neurons.

The genes that control the functionality of these, and other neurons and their neurotransmitters that are involved in the expression of the persona, can switch on and off. (This newly discovered phenomenon involving a reversible alteration in gene activity is called "epigenetics" and we will deal with that in a few moments). Consequently it has been shown that personality and behavior has more to do with the activity of the individual's genes than with the precise nature and activity of the parent's genes or with the nature of the environment. Recent research also suggests that autism is associated with a lack, or with the deficient activity, of mirror neurons even though there is a strong hereditary factor in this condition. This is ascribed to the transmission of the epigenetically changed gene in the parents sperm or ovum. All of these examples indicate that the expression of personality and behavior is determined to a large extent by the functional integrity of the brain, its various types of neurons and their complex networking. In addition, critical changes can result from any variation with regard to the massive array of neurotransmitters, their individual concentrations, and their corresponding receptor sites within the brain. Once again, it must be said that this is not necessarily indicative of an inherent lack, or deficiency, of any sort or description within the primary mental attributes that define our humanity.

The primacy of soul is of critical importance because it acknowledges that the Spirit has dominion over the totality of the human condition. Acceptance of such a fact, or belief, reinstates the Soul as the true master of our minds and provider of all that is essential to our lives and to our living. It subjugates the psyche, intellect, reason and emotion to their respective status that is subordinate to that which is representative of authentic self. Moreover, recognition of the primacy of Spirit and soul helps to guide and direct our motives, our attitudes and our behavior. It assists us in acquiring a valid and a balanced perspective, a proper sense of values and priorities within our lives. The primacy of the human spirit provides us with the virtues of faith, hope, and love (charity). The spirit is not defined nor constrained by our genes or genome. It is not subject to injury or pathology and there is nothing that is beyond the scope of its remit, be it physical, mental, or spiritual in nature. There is not a single cell within the human body that is outside its sphere of influence just as our cells are in constant communication with our nervous system and its related neuro-endocrine and neurochemical systems. Primacy of Spirit enshrines our human dignity and sets us free from the constraints of the purely material and the biological.

To deny the primacy of spirit is to deny the soul. In so doing we are surrendering ourselves to the power of the ego mind and to the pride and arrogance of our intellect.

We enslave the soul and place our absolute hope and trust in the genius of the scientific and all who serve it as their master. It is my contention that one of the main, if not the only, reason that modern neuroscience has constructed such a flawed and invalid representation of our mind and neurological system is because it is in denial. It is deluded and blinded to the spiritual aspect of our nature. Since the purpose of science is to seek and discern the truth, this demonstration of medical science is no more than pseudo- science since it is inherently false. It accurately reflects pride of intellect, ego mania, and gross disregard for the sanctity of all human life. Indeed there are many well intentioned academics that pay polite and cloaked homage to the Divine and to the spiritual. Yet they fail to express the conviction of their stated beliefs within the realm of their professional work. God and Soul are parked outside the doors of their clinics, research laboratories, and their lecture halls. No doubt they are seen as embarrassing remnants of an ignorant and superstitious past that had once existed before the dawn of their intellectual enlightenment. Perhaps these ancient tokens are still kept at hand, yet beyond the threshold of their scientific persona, for fear that someday the brilliance and intervention of science will fail them. They would be left without hope or trust in the possibility of any spiritual intervention. Intellectual arrogance devours itself as such wisdom is doomed to pass away. Intuitively, we know that the wisdom of the Spirit and the Word will never pass away.

From a more practical, less academic and allegorical standpoint let us consider all of these variables within a different kind of light and from an alternative perspective: Our natures, and personalities, are imprinted upon a human specific and spiritual matrix (soul) over which further layers are encoded within our subconscious. This primary matrix, in its undifferentiated form, contains the basic and characteristic archetypical features that are representative of our authentic spiritual nature. This matrix and our genetic template constitute what in effect we might conceive as a form of "transcendental synaptic gap" This is the location of the functional and interactive interface between the spiritual and biological (Mortal) aspects of our human nature. This, in effect, is the precursor to the "Gateway to the Soul". It is configured in a manner that will subsequently reflect the great range of possibilities and potentials in which our human nature and our genome may be expressed. It will do so not only with regard to our individual personalities, but also in respect of the totality of all that constitutes the expression of our humanity within the living world. This is inclusive of the physical, intellectual, psychological, and spiritual characteristics that uniquely define each one of us. Just as there is a state of continuous flux and volatility within the dynamic of the human mind as evidenced through the conflicts of interest that exist between psyche and soul, so also is there a similar state of dynamic flux within the expression of our genome (D.N.A.). Contrary to traditional scientific beliefs, all of our genes do not provide us with a fixed and predetermined mode of expression. We are not imprisoned and enslaved within a fixed and rigid framework of genetic inheritance.

From the moment of our birth and for the duration of our lives each one of us exist as a living and vibrant being with an indeterminate range of possibilities and potentials within every variable manifestation and expressive stratum of our humanity. While we have a complement of approximately 23 to 25 thousand genes there are a limited number that determine statistically high predispositions to specific traits. Apart from the obvious gender determinant, some of these are related to family attributes with which we are all quite familiar: *appearance, facial expression, speech, likes, and various mannerisms etc.* Others are associated with a number of inherited abnormalities or diseases (some of which may be a consequence of genetic mutation) that may be expressed should such genes be transmitted to the offspring. Yet other genetic factors may provide us with certain desirable traits such as may predispose us towards various skills or talents.

However, most of our genetic material is not fixed within this predictable cause and effect scenario. In fact only 2% of our total DNA is of the genetic encoding type while the other 98% is of the non- coding type that was previously described as "Junk DNA". These regions within our DNA normally exist within a state of balanced homeostasis which may be randomly, or unpredictably, switched "on or off" within the genome with varying consequences. So, most of our genes are not fixed entities, but more like plastic that can vary in shape and expression. These alterations may occur in response to a wide variety of stimuli that can arise from either within the body or from the external environment. The study of these newly discovered genetic phenomena is what we now call "Epigenetics". There are a number of different mechanisms by which any one of these genes may be switched on or off yet a simple chemical reaction called "methylation" appears to be one of the most common. The means by which genes express themselves has to do with their ability to activate the production of specific proteins which are essential messengers or components that are involved at all levels of cellular activity. In most cases methylation stops a gene from working (i.e. inhibits its protein production) while reversing the reaction usually switches the gene back on. For example, there are genes that regulate the production of vitally important neurotransmitters in our brain. When an epigenetic change affects the levels of any of the neurotransmitters, such as Dopamine and serotonin, (which are particularly active within the brain stem- basal ganglia region), there may be marked changes in our level of alertness or in our responses to stress. On the other hand, if the gene that creates an enzyme called Monoamine Oxidase -A is inactivated it may result in the accumulation of certain neurotransmitters that, in excess, lead to aggressive behavior.

Thankfully the overall tendency of the organism is towards the maintenance and preservation of health or harmony.

While a limited number of diseases are a consequence of an inherent flaw within our genes, or a predisposition for such a fault to be expressed, it can also be a feature of disordered epigenetics. Under normal circumstances these changes within gene expression occur as protective responses that are designed to maintain or restore harmony. However, when such efforts are under or over corrective responses disharmony and disease may be the outcome. Unlike the genetic mutations that can occur within our DNA, epigenetic changes are potentially reversible. Consequently, harmony and health can be restored. All of these examples demonstrate to us how even minor chemical changes, such as methylation, can greatly alter our behavior and the expression of our personality. Methylation involves only the addition of a single carbon, and three hydrogen atoms. We are all well aware of how radical a personality change can emerge in response to a few drinks of alcohol or as an adverse reaction to even a small amount of some ingested substance. Yet most of us would accept that such behavior was out of character and was not an accurate reflection of the type of person that individual is in actual reality. We would recognize that they were acting like a different person while acknowledging that they were in fact the same person. We intuitively know that our brain, and the manner in which it functions (or is rendered dysfunctional), does not define who we are. Yet, it quite definitely defines how we present ourselves and the manner in which we may behave.

There are many examples of individuals who recognized that their behavior was seriously out of character with their genuine nature and who on seeking medical attention were found to have a brain tumour or some other neurological pathology. Who we are and how we behave are not one and the same. These examples and the evidence of science itself re-affirm the concept that it is the mind of man, within the context of consciousness that has primacy in defining precisely who we are. The brain is but the material, biologically vulnerable and potentially unreliable, agent of the inspired directives of our authentic self in spirit. Humanity is not defined by the lobes of the brain, by neurotransmitters, amino acids, or microcellular processes. No matter how these elements may be jiggled and made to interact together they will never produce consciousness nor create a human mind. No, we are not out thoughts or feelings, our personalities or behaviors. These are but imperfect, and oftentimes greatly flawed, intermittent, variable, and transient, expressions of whom we are in essence and in actual reality.

It has long been accepted that disease is essentially a form of biological disharmony that is subsequently expressed within the body as a pathological entity. Medical science has identified a great number of causative or triggering agents including infectious, toxic, metabolic, hormonal, neoplastic, congenital, genetic and epigenetic factors. Yet, stress factors were always considered as a contributing factor. Science is slowly getting to understand how stress can predispose us to the adverse influence of these causative agents. However, the precise nature and source of stress, beyond the identification of the specific stressors that pervade our lives, is more elusive.

The manner in which stress is intimately related to a whole range of complex interactions and sequences of events that involve mind - brain - body conflicts are now being identified and better understood. Such conflicts have been traditionally and quite casually referred to in a vague, all inclusive and generic contexts as simply "stress". Indeed it may well be that the nature of these specific stressors is a fundamental expression of the conflicts that reside within the hostile arena of the psyche and the soul rather than to those that exist within our external environment. Perhaps the external stressors simply serve to instigate, or activate, previously unresolved internal conflicts within our mind.

In reality, it now seems certain that, unlike the limited number of inherited diseases that are of the fixed gene type, most common diseases are in fact controlled by hundreds, or even thousands, of genes. This is invariably the case with respect to those diseases in which we did in fact recognize as having some genetic predisposition. These include coronary heart disease, alcoholism, and most forms of cancer, in addition to many other illnesses that we had previously ascribed to a simple unitary "hereditary factor". However, the manner in which the causative factors ascribed to many other diseases can overwhelm our natural "defense mechanisms" so as to initiate the disease process may be closely related to the concurrent, and stress induced, epigenetic changes that predisposed us to the illness in the first instance. As previously stated, one of the mechanisms at work appears to be methylation. This induces an epigenetic deactivation in the genes that control the immune system. We may yet have to better comprehend the mind- brain dynamic if we are to ever fully understand the nature of disease predispositions as opposed to the external "causes" of disease. Few academic scientists are likely to indulge their skills within the domain of the spiritual dimensions of stress and disharmony. Perhaps all of us should be far more attentive, and far less dismissive, with respect to the likely role of the mental-spiritual conflicts and related stress as a major liability to our health in general.

On quite a different note, there is evidence to suggest that there is a genetic factor with regard to intelligence, artistic ability, and athletic performance. It is now acknowledged that these exist more as traits or potentials rather than being the outcome of direct inheritance. The single most critical factor in the emergence of such abilities is the motivation and determination that drives endless practice and effort, particularly from a very early age.

It has been estimated that Work plus Effort x 10, 000 hours = Talent. This, combined with aggressive opportunism seems to be the key to the successful expression of the talent. In other words, actively seek and avail of every genuine opportunity that comes your way. All of us have a great variety of human potentials. Some are strong and some are weak, and some are of the genetic type while others are not. But whether or not such potentials are ever realized may have far more to do with how we direct and orchestrate our lives in harmony with our human spirit and our guiding conscience than with any other single factor. It has to do with our thoughts and feelings and with the effort and the manner in which we apply ourselves to expressing them within the context of our behavior as they pertain to ourselves and to others.

It may be helpful to consider the Gateway Interface between psyche and soul as a modem. This provides us with a means whereby we can interface the biological "hardware and software" which is at our immediate physical and intellectual disposal, with a shared and "spiritual internet". This modem allows us to access this vast Internet which extends far beyond our personal resources, beyond the boundaries of our knowledge, our understanding, and the limits of our human vision. It represents an essential accessory to our operational system and is potentially available to all of us for our personal use and benefit. This is a modem that connects us to a vast collective network that has been programmed by the source of all authentic knowledge and of all authentic wisdom. This internet is what constitutes the common and interactive matrix that defines all souls. This matrix is, in turn, immersed within the infinite substrate of the Holy Spirit that is derived from the source and creator of all. Our common task is to learn how we can come to recognize and use this modem for its intended purpose, for our benefit and that of all mankind. This critical matrix is specific to mankind and defines us as human. It defines what you are and how you are distinctly different from other creatures. The property to which I refer has to do with the why, and how, you should perceive yourself as a member of the human race. It also defines why, and how, we should engage with life in a purposeful manner. The genetic configuration that contributes to our personalities will influence the precise characteristics of the Interface that separates the non-biological from the biological natures of our mind. This is what determines the individual variability in how our authentic nature is uniquely manifest and expressed in all its different forms and to what extent and depth it may have the inherent and latent potential to do so. In effect the precise features of this Gateway Interface, and how you use it, fundamentally determine who you are. In part, this person specific Interface explains the variability that is reflected in the primary strengths and weaknesses of our characters and our personalities. I refer to these in terms of being a primary measure because other facets involved within the process of personality development, and the manner in which we influence this process through our patterns of behavior, can alter these measures. They can be both consciously and subconsciously augmented or suppressed. The final outcome may be considered as the secondary measure. Even so, it exists at a level that is always adjustable through the process of motivation and effort. In the final analysis, as we shall see later on, it is the extent to which we unwittingly empower our ego or wisely empower our soul, that will have the greatest impact upon our personalities and ultimately upon our behavior. Spiritual empowerment is a measure of how familiar and adept we are at utilizing the Gateway Modem which provides direct access to all that is essential. This choice represents the most critical choice in the exercise of our free will. Perhaps it is best described as choosing whether to yield and surrender to the will of our ego, or to the will of our soul. The latter process is a surrender of self to the will and guidance of our creator. *This is what is meant by Divine Providence.*

Personality development is extremely complex and multifaceted. There are genetic factors and childhood phases that are embedded from early on. Then there are further phases of growth and reinforcement by virtue of our learning experiences and repetition of patterns of response to specific triggering factors. Consequently, it would appear that only certain elements within our personality make up would be directly amenable to alteration or realignment while other would not. However, the main focus of our efforts has to do with being motivated to change our behavioral patterns and to strive to identify and comprehend the key factors within our personality make up so as to moderate their influences. This approach has the potential to both modify and reverse the feedback loops that had previously served to augment and maintain the status quo. This can be of great value, particularly where the status quo is problematic and causing stress, pain, and disruption to the general fabric and rhythm of our lives.

The essential point in all of this is that we can rarely conclude that our choices and behavior are necessarily a valid expression or a true representation, of our real and genuine self. It is with this knowledge and level of awareness that we are in a position to re-evaluate the process of our decision making and the patterns of behavior that we feel has come to be a familiar feature of our unique personality and of our type cast disposition. We may discover that we are in fact quite different and far more acceptable to ourselves and even others, than we had previously considered. Moreover, we may feel both enlightened and relieved in the knowledge that we can more accurately fashion a perception of ourselves and of our reality to reflect a vision that is far more acceptable, enjoyable, and self- fulfilling than we had ever imagined. The amazing truth, which remains hidden for many of us, is that each and every one of us can effect a major transformation and ultimately a transfiguration of self. In turn, we can all contribute to a much desired shift in our individual and collective paradigm and a better world in which to live and share between us. We are possibilities and potentials within the constant flux and movement of our daily lives.

CHAPTER ELEVEN: TIME

TIME:

Through all of this,
With all of this,
In all that has transpired;
This, my sojourn through a beam in time,
In union with the Holy Spirit,
I am transfixed.

From sleep I was awoken,
Anointed, gently broken,
As bread at table,
As a loaf at supper time,
Torn, separated, and set aside
Into a small pile of crumbled pieces:

Broken down beyond the fabric and the crust,
Beyond the coarse and grainy husk,
Beyond the cell, and atom,
The tiny fragments of my tissues.

From "Journey of a Soul", by the author.

(a). A DEFINITION OF TIME

We will consider time only within the context of its functional relevance to our lives and not in terms of its scientific nature and properties. The reality of time is acknowledged to be valid within its scientific context. From a perceptual perspective Time may be considered as both a memory and mind projection which we can manipulate backwards and forwards within our brain from a reference point of transient "Now", which is recurrent, and sequential. This occurs within the context of an ever changing, dying, and decaying milieu.

Time then is but a flawed and aberrant variation extracted from the perfection of the constant "Now" that is eternity, and which alone is perceptible by a perfect being - a soul fully redeemed in Christ. Yet, in the light of the Spirit we can grope about and reach out towards this perfection even while we are constrained within this transient now. This transient, dark, and deficient state of our humanity is mirrored within the impermanence of the Now.

(b). ABOUT TIME

It is about seven hundred years ago since Thomas Aquinas made his remarkably insightful remarks regarding Time:

"Nothing exists of Time except Now". Hence time cannot be made except according to some Now. This is not because in the first Now is time, but because from it

time begins. The apprehension of time is caused by the perception of the changing instant and likewise, the apprehension of eternity is caused by that of the enduring instant. The Now of time is not time. The Now of eternity is really the same as eternity. It is simply a constant "Now".

The perfection of eternity is that it is an unchanging and stable constant. It is in perfect equilibrium in every way, manner, and form. Since it is in such a state of constancy there is no change, no past, present, or future, no aging. It is simply, and always, "Now". Any alteration of this perfect equilibrium, any deviation from this perfection would result in loss of stability, loss of the constancy of Now, and the emergence of change.

We could envisage that the error and imperfection brought about by The Fall of man prompted the creation of time through this deviation away from the perfection of eternity. In addition, it was to cause our separation from the perfection of God. Time, then would be created by its removal and extraction from the constant continuum that is eternity. When we also consider that the Fall of man continues as an ongoing and evolving process in history of all humanity, the phenomenon of time, and the universal context within which we experience it, also persists. To this extent it may be said that from both an individual and collective standpoint, we "create" and maintain the experience of our lives, and the human perception which we describe as our worldly reality, within the domain of time.

If we accept that our creator, in His love and forgiveness, has a providential plan to reverse the great error which man inflicted upon himself, and that our ultimate destiny is to be reunited with God in His perfection, then we must accept that time is nothing more than a temporary and transitional zone, dimension, or phenomenon. Time would ultimately be reabsorbed back into the constant Now of eternal perfection when The Kingdom of God is realized within the perceptual content of our concepts, and within our souls, here on Earth. In the context of the privilege which we have been granted to exercise our free will over our ultimate, and individual, destinies, it is apparent that the phenomenon of time provides us with a perceptible means of doing so. We have both the opportunity, and the privilege, to choose to accept, or reject, the will of God in our contributing to the reversal of our separation from our perfection. Since change is an intrinsic element of time, we are afforded a perceptible means, and a record, by which we can gauge and measure our progress as we age and inevitably progress ever closer towards our certain death.

Awareness of change requires that we have the faculty of memory. It subdivisions into short, medium, and long term components provides us with a system by which we can review both rate and progress. Indeed, all of our senses help provide us with a great many prompts, and cues, that serve as constant reminders that every life has a limited span. We are not immortal. Everything changes, everything is in motion; nothing is permanent in this life.

Perhaps the greatest contribution which medical science can make to any of us is that it can help extend the lifespan, and maintain the integrity of the human faculties which are at our disposal in order to best accomplish the true purpose of our living and of our lives.

(c). THE PURPOSE OF TIME

I saw the sun rise and set
Upon the ancestral waters
Of this ancient valley.
I heard the plaintiff call
Of a mother's voice
Fade in the cool damp air

Shadows danced
And twirled upon the sand,
Their footprints now frozen
In this silent moment.
The children have gone home,
Tired, and warm, and gently wrapped
In the shroud of their mother's love.

From "Saint Patrick's Day near
Valleymount", by the author.

Change, as I previously stated, is a perceptual phenomenon that is dependent upon a memory function. Change then is an appreciation that requires sensory input (e.g. visual, tactile, auditory etc.) along with a neuro physiological process within our brain that has to do with memory. Consequently, some people consider time to be simply a perceptual phenomenon, akin to a virtual reality, in that it does not really exist in and of itself. In a similar manner, darkness is no more than our perception of the absence of light. However from our perspective what is of relevance is that time is considered as a means of providing all human kind, with an opportunity to fulfil God's plan for us during our life time. Time provides us with an opportunity to participate, and actively contribute to our personal and our shared redemption in Christ.

Redemption from the fatal imperfection, which is the consequence of our sinfulness, is a prerequisite to our reunification with our creator. That reunification is the meaning of the term "Eternal Salvation". It is only through the process of atonement that redemption is made possible. Atonement means "undoing". It refers to the "undoing of the error of sin", which is the essence of forgiveness. The atonement is the fulfilment of the process which Christ began by His death and resurrection. It is an interlocking chain of forgiveness which requires our cooperation and participation in order that it is fully completed.

The essence of genuine spirituality, within any religious context, is a process of reconciliation, reciprocity, and forgiveness. We seek to reconcile ourselves to our authentic selves, to the universal self of all mankind, and to our creator. Honest and genuine reconciliation is the antithesis of conflict and war. It is also devoid of all judgment and blame. To claim to be spiritually motivated while engaged in conflict of any description is a paradox, nonsense, and a lie. To claim to be a defender of a religious Faith while in active conflict and combat with another is a both a delusion and an act of self-denial. This form of self-delusion is what we refer to as "confabulation". The process of atonement requires that we seek forgiveness for our own imperfections while seeking to extend forgiveness to others in an unconditional manner.

This in effect amounts to Loving God and our neighbor, by accepting God's forgiveness while at the same time passing on this forgiveness to others. It is the privilege, and responsibility, of the forgiven to forgive. That is what all of this, and all of this thing called "time", is all about.

(d). THINKING IN TIME - PONDERING IN THE MOMENT

I have knocked so loudly on your door,
And called your name out loud,
When none answers it's quite clear,
That no one lives there anymore.

I gaze through the windows of your soul,
In hopes that I might find you there,
But you have fled this once warm place,
No spark, no glimmer in the coal.

From "A Winter Soul", by the author.

Despite the common general view that we tend to spend too much time daydreaming, out of touch with reality, our heads in the clouds, it is probably more accurate to say that we in fact spend far too much time thinking. We may indeed also spend excessive time avoiding the basic realities of living by seeking to escape into our private worlds of fantasy. We tend to seek refuge in that space we call the future, lost in the mind-projected illusions of the ego mind. Worse still, many of us seek to evade life by hurling themselves into the abyss of the subconscious, and beyond, by means of alcohol and drugs. But what we are universally failing to do does not belong to any of those domains, but rather to the realm of meditation and reflection. Within the Buddhist tradition meditation is considered as a two phase process, beginning with calming or "calm abiding", and moving onwards to a level known as "insight meditation. We will consider the details concerning these processes when we are discussing stress and the relaxation response later on.

Insight meditation is the realm in which we can connect with our hidden spirit, via our soul. It is the mind-space that is conducive to prayer. Prayer is a means of communicating with our spirit and hence with our creator. It is a process of self-discovery in so far as it concerns our authentic self as opposed to the "I" of the ego. It is a process, by which we seek to see ourselves more clearly and objectively, and to do so with honesty, humility and transparency with regard to self and others. In such a light we can become aware and awake to the extent that we become self-observant with respect to our stream of consciousness, our motives, choices, decisions, and ultimate behavior. In short, meditation is a search to unveil the truth by establishing a line of communication with the Truth. That truth is God!

Pondering and contemplating may be considered as elements that circumscribe the process of insight meditation. I am referring to these activities within the context of a passive activity and not as a consciously guided, and purposely directed, mental itinerary. It is more like floating in water with total confidence and trust that you will not sink. When we so float, we surrender to the properties of the water. We allow the current to take us where it will. We simply lie back, limp and lax, free of thought or concern, while we immerse ourselves within the experience. Unlike swimming, there is neither need nor desire to consciously intrude, to direct or interact in order to exert our influence over the direction, speed, or destination of the process. The essence of the process is meditative, contemplative, or prayerful, is surrender and trust. In other words, it is faith. This is the means by which we approach the Gateway to the soul. Hope is what helps provide us with a means of access through this portal in search of enlightenment. It may be thought of as "grace" since it is not a facility provided by effort of will or technique. Neither is it something we can demand nor to which we can claim an absolute right. All spiritual meditation, or prayer, has a common purpose and destination towards a single source. All prayer is directed to the source to which we are drawn and towards which we constantly yearn to return. This is the source of all love and all forgiveness, since they are one, and He is God.

When we are thinking, we are locked within the realm of time. It is a cerebral function that is primarily conscious, controlled, and directed. Thinking is a process that falls within the domain of the ego mind. As a consequence, it is fundamentally self- centred in terms of the "I" or "me" being the central focus. It is useful to consider time as being in a horizontal plane. We usually visualize time as moving in a linear manner, from left to right (clockwise) along this horizontal plane. This may be considered as the plane that transects the ego mind. On the other hand, when we engage in meditative prayer-fullness, we can envisage that we shift this horizontal axis a full ninety degrees, into a vertical plane. Within this plane time collapses. We are no longer in the axis where there is an awareness of change, nor a perception of the changing instant. This plane is in alignment with our spirit and it transects its axis. It is frozen in time, existing only in the constant Now. This is the eternal domain of the soul. It is where we have aligned ourselves so that we may communicate with that aspect of our spiritual mind.

CHAPTER TWELVE: THE ORIGIN OF STRESS

Life, the pounding pulse, the rhythm
and the beat.
You race in time to melt and merge
With the molten mass on the busy street.
The energy comes pouring in, you are carried
on the tide,
These waves that knock you off your feet,
And get you on a high.

The voices and the music,
The sounds that scrape and grind,
The patterns and the heaving forms
Intoxicate your mind.
A muted voice from deep within,
Cannot be heard above this din.

From "The Rhythm of Life", by the author.

One of the earliest and most primitive mechanisms that all primates, including humans, developed to protect him from injury was a simple reflex system. It is often referred to as the "fright, flight, or fight" response. This primitive system is predominantly under the control of our subconscious, or Autonomic, nervous system. Even today, when injury threatens, this reflex is triggered. Adrenaline is released into our bloodstream causing our pulse to quicken, our hearts to beat faster and harder, and blood is selectively diverted to our muscles, our pupils dilate, our senses sharpen, and bodies tense in a defensive posture. We are prepared to respond in an instant - to fight or to run away. Of course, our response today is far more finely tuned and sophisticated. A highly complex and more recently evolved cognitive system within our brain is activated, prompting us to evaluate and apply reason and judgment to the situation. The imposition of reason to the "flight or fight" reflex serves to modify our response in a manner that is ideally more appropriate to the specific situation.

Today, the occasions that actually require a fight or flight response are somewhat limited. This is primarily because to scream, run, or physically fight would be considered both unnecessary and inappropriate. Instead, we apply logic; generate a plan of action to avert the perceived threat, and thus permitting us to proceed, for the most part unperturbed, with the tasks of our routine activities and our living. However, what really occurs as we attempt to respond to the "threats" of daily life is often quite different. There are many situations and circumstances that trigger our flight or fight reflex. There are also many pressures imposed on us to behave in a manner that is socially acceptable. We place demands on ourselves, and each other, to conform, to succeed, and to excel. Any form of behavior that might be perceived or misconstrued as having the potential to jeopardizing these goals is unthinkable. We are faced with the dilemma of reconciling our need to be socially acceptable with the need to respond to the multiple daily situations that provoke this ancient protective reflex. Sometimes the triggering factor may simply be a disagreement with spouse or children, a critical remark from the boss, or a rise in our taxes. Alternatively, our bodies may feel threatened and our reflexes triggered by factors that we do not even consciously register, such as environmental noise, or the "noise", the information or memory processing, that is buzzing in our heads. Whether we are conscious of the triggering factor or not, the result is the same: adrenaline is released along with a myriad of neuro- hormonal and metabolic reactions that prime us as if to fight or run. Eventually we can become locked into this mode, set in a constant state of readiness to respond to threats and dangers that do not actually exist within our immediate environment. Since today we do not generally attempt to physically injure or kill our spouse, business partner, or social enemies, and in many instances cannot simply flee from every nuance of threat, even if we tried, we are left with the predicament of a physical response seeking "flight or fight", but no physical outlet for this response, since reason has been superimposed upon this primitive reflex. The outcome is a discomforting state of physical and mental frustration that demands resolution. "Stress" is the name for this sequence of events.

Stress is defined as: "A *physical, or physiological, response inappropriate to the situation*". It is inappropriate because it exemplifies our failure to react to the real, or perceived, threats to our wellbeing in a manner that is conducive to the preservation of the wellbeing. Particular forms of "threat" are described as "stressors" since they have the capacity or potential to induce a felt state of stress. Stressors permeate our lives. However, they also provide us with the essential stimulus through which we may grow and mature, physically, emotionally, and intellectually. It is not so much a case of our overcoming our stressors, as it is of our utilizing, and applying, them as motivational agents to excel in our endeavors. In this manner we enhance our self- esteem, and experience a sense of pleasure, and of purpose within our lives.

We also come to understand that when we respond inappropriately to the many and varied stressors in our lives, we are apt to lose more than we gain in terms of our personal health and general sense of wellbeing. The inevitability of stressors is based upon the fact we are constantly, and without exception, faced with challenges and dilemmas that are, for the most part, unpredictable. Unpredictability is an inescapable feature of our world, of nature and its elements. It is also characteristic of human behaviour, both individually and collectively. Stressors have the capacity to induce stress. This capability is based on man's instinctive responses due to his need to survive. The personal goals we set for ourselves in order to succeed and achieve according to some preconceived criteria that we impose upon ourselves, inevitably augments the burden of our stressor load.

Significant and distinct disadvantages are caused by the unpredictability of our circumstances. This is because we are unlikely, on the spur of the moment, to be fully prepared to respond in a manner that is apt to be entirely satisfactory and acceptable to us, both in the immediate, and, more importantly, the delayed and final self- audit of the issue or event. Consequently, we often feel pressured into having to provide some form of instant resolution to a complex problem. On more careful reflection, we may find that our solution was suboptimal or deficient to some extent. It is often the case that we can only clarify the nuances of the more complex issues on further analysis. By careful and less emotionally charged evaluation, we can apply further logic to specific issues, and perceive the longer term implications of our earlier responses.

Since we have both memory and the capacity for reason, we have the opportunity to modify our earlier choices and responses. We can learn from, and improve upon, our flight or fight responses. We are able to correct and make good the imbalance that may exist between our reflex behavior and our greater long term physical and emotional needs. Stress accumulates with our failure to make these emotionally charged and vital corrections. Such failure often results in the persistence of what may well have been, at least in retrospect, somewhat less than the ideal or most appropriate responses. We can readily understand that the greater the imbalance between our initial and desired response in any given situation, and the greater the number of accumulated and "uncorrected reflex" responses, the greater will be the resulting felt sense of stress. It is also apparent that while we can generally tolerate significant degrees of stress that are of short duration, persistent and unresolved stress is only poorly tolerated.

CHAPTER THIRTEEN: MEDITATION AND PRAYER

Waterford Crystal Mandala: The Kingdom of God

Be Now, yet be still
Well within yourself.
Be at peace within the moment,
In the Now that is the always,
Not in the hour that beckons
In some moment that yet cometh.

For Now is always sweet,
Do not ever let it sour.
Be it long sweet, and well
Before the midnight hour.

From "Be Now – Well before the
Midnight hour", by the author.

Motto: *"What is Now – Is. (acceptance of our current reality)*
What is – Now Is" (seeking to address this reality)."

As a brief prelude to this chapter, I will remind you, yet again, of what contributes to the inevitable noise and chatter we hear within our heads.

In Chapter 1 "The Air of Context", it was said that the three keys that would unlock the "Doors of Perception" to the nature of reality were primacy, context, and synergy. These are seen as the keys (together with the unlocking mechanism of "reciprocity") to the acquisition, and the sharing, of authentic knowledge with regard to the nature of our humanity within the lived experience. We have also indicated that what these three "keywords" within the syntax of language, likewise describe the process of thought as it is generated within the mind, and is reciprocated within the neurological circuitry of our right and left cerebral hemispheres. (Chapter3 "Module of Thought" and Chapter 4 "Mind-Brain Reciprocity"). Furthermore, it has been explained that our intellectual concepts are derived from Secondary metaphors, and that these, in turn, are dependent upon the provision of a Primary metaphorical substrate which is derived from the archives of the collective unconscious. The proposition was also advanced that the content of the collective unconscious is derived from the intuitive Wisdom of the Spirit. Finally, the provision of the facility to access, and respond to the Wisdom of the Holy Spirit is what constitutes the essential function of consciousness, and thus renders us as uniquely human.

All of this could be condensed into the statement that the key to knowledge in regard to the nature of reality lays within the critical examination of the process of thought, and its linguistic expression. The conceptual integration of this knowledge determines the nature of our experience. That may be seen to represent the fundamental philosophy of Kant. However, in this instance we are placing far greater emphasis on intuition as a means to knowledge, as it is more explicitly expressed within the philosophy of Ralph Emerson. In this regard we are acknowledging the primacy of the collective unconscious in respect of the original source and substrate of our thoughts. As a consequence, the most valid rendition of reality, as expressed through our human consciousness, is by means of our diligent, and purposeful, efforts to access the intuitive knowledge within the collective unconscious.

The word "prayer" describes such a human form of effort, and type of activity. Meditation, as referred to within this text, is an act of contemplating, or reflecting, in a manner that seeks to provide access to the collective unconscious. However, we are well aware that the term "meditation" is also commonly applied as a means of describing various mental techniques that appear to be unrelated to this specific objective. These include stress and pain reduction, achieving a sense of inner harmony, and improving insight and creative awareness. In any, and all, instances the initial goal is to achieve a state of mental quietness to facilitate the realization of the desired outcome. The imposition of cognitive thought, and the incessant intrusion of sensory stimuli, both pose as formidable obstacles to the performance of this form of meditative activity. As a consequence, any method that can be applied as a means of suppressing cognitive thinking, (inclusive of the spontaneous activities of memory), and the combined sensory input that arises from a rage of external and internal environmental sources, would be conducive to the act of meditation within any context.

External input is conveyed by means of our sensory modalities such as vision, hearing, smell, taste, and touch/ pain /vibration. Internal input refers to the activities of the autonomic nervous system and the related subcortical processes that ascend from the brain stem / midbrain regions (i.e. basal ganglia, and Limbic system). All of this activity is what contributes to the incessant hum and buzz within our heads. Yet, there is also a subdued and barely perceptible chant that echoes in harmony with this clamor. This is the Wisdom of the soul as it continually flows as stream of Primary metaphors from the content of our collective unconscious. However, I will hasten to repeat that the act of inducing such a selective suppression of mental and neurological activity does not in itself constitute the act of seeking to gain access to the collective unconscious, nor to the Wisdom of the soul and of the Spirit.

A mental technique, called the "Relaxation Response", described by Herbert Benson in the early nineteen seventies, was identified as a means of achieving this desired state of interior mental and neurological quietness. Professor Benson, and his Harvard University research team, had undertaken detailed studies in regard to the altered states of consciousness that are associated with the practice of certain techniques of meditation which we usually associate with a number of Eastern religions. The most widely known version of such practice is ascribed to Buddhism. What is commonly, referred to as "Transcendental Meditation" has been trademarked (U.S.A.) by that institution in response to the initiative of the Indian born guru, Maharishi Mahesh. Yogi (1917-2008).

The outcome of the Harvard team's research was to clearly identify what precise neurological and related neurobiological processes were involved in achieving this altered state of awareness and alertness. These included a reduction in sympathetic nervous system activity while increasing parasympathetic activity. These alterations are related to a reduction in adrenergic activity, (reduced arousal), and an increase in cholinergic activity, (increased relaxation).These are reflected in changes in heart rate, respiratory rate, blood pressure, metabolism, blood gases, neurochemistry, and EEG brain wave patterns.(Chap.7b "Autonomic Nervous System"). In effect a variety of spontaneous activities within selective areas of the cortex, particularly the prefrontal region, and the region of the diencephalon, are suppressed. The various neurological components within the diencephalon are involved in the process of transmitting much of the neurological data that arises from the spinal cord, brainstem, and reticular activating system, to higher centres within the cerebral cortex. As a consequence, global cognitive activity that is normally registered within the realm of conscious awareness is radically minimized. A recurrent series of closely knit episodes of cognitive silence is what results. Within this mental and cerebral void one is not actively contemplating upon anything. As we shall discuss, this is distinctly different from that mental status which is related to the act of prayer, or prayerful meditation.

In summary, Benson's research provided scientific evidence to indicate that conscious control can be applied at will to alter and adjust what are otherwise involuntary mind-body relationships. This fact further attests to the primacy of mind over brain. Even those autonomous, and reflex, activities that have been hardwired into our most primitive neurological circuitry can be over-ridden at will by a specifically chosen, and sublimely simple, mental ploy. Find a quiet place, surrender to the moment, relax your muscles, repeat some simple sound or word, or fix your gaze upon a candle flame, and see what you can do!

The practice of the "Relaxation Response" is not in itself a spiritual activity. It may be incorporated as a prelude to some form of spiritual exercise, as it is within the Buddhist religion. Meditation in Buddhism is considered to occur in two phases. The first is a calming down of the mind, and the second is referred to as "insight" meditation. Insight meditation has more to do with one's disposition, (i.e. a spiritual inclination and temperament), than it has with any specific level of intensity, or depth, of neurological, and mental, quiescence. Consequently, what is referred to as the "Relaxation Response", and Spiritual meditation, are not necessarily mutually inclusive, or exclusive. The distinguishing feature fundamentally pertains to attitude, motive, and intent within the context of one's system of beliefs.

The Relaxation Response is simply a mental ploy, or mechanism, that allows us to exit the domain, and unwelcome intrusion, of the psyche. We may consider the psyche as being represented within the original and primitive subcortical regions of the brainstem / midbrain (i.e. as instinctual awareness) and also as residing within its current, and now greatly elevated, "symbiotic" status of mental synergy which it shares with the soul. Within this altered state of awareness we are far less preoccupied with the incessant "chatter" of left hemispheric processing with regard to intellectual concepts and memory recall, and we have damped-down the emotionally laden reflexes, (Limbic and Autonomic Nervous systems), that prompt us to react and respond within our environment. Within the context of "Insight meditation", we can appreciate that this altered state of awareness and alertness has shifted towards that of a predominantly Right hemispheric mode which, in turn, has primacy of affect in regard to the activities of the left cerebral hemisphere. Within such a mode we are more directly aligned to what is implicit and intuitive. We will be referring to this mental state as the mode of access to the "Gateway to the Soul" when it is applied to the process of meditation within a spiritual context.

Regardless of the precise technique, related trappings, or any form of religious Belief, (or none at all), the Harvard researchers defined four basic elements that contribute to the generation of the relaxation response.

These include:

1. A mental device (usually a mantra)
2. A passive attitude
3. Decreased muscle tone (relaxing your muscles)
4. A quiet environment.

PRAYER AND INSIGHT MEDITATION.

We children of the Land of Lir,
Children of the Lord.
Kings and princesses in this swirling pool,
We are the Wild Swans of Coole.

The Prince of love, the chosen One,
Will undo this spell and cast down to Hell
The Demon Dark that dared to claim
The children that were not his own.

From "We the Swans of
Coole", by the author.

Prayer is the ultimate completion by mankind of the circle of reciprocity which was inscribed, and instigated, by the Holy Spirit on, behalf of all humanity. It is the means by which we reply, and respond, to the living Word as the Spirit now speaks to us. The act of prayer is a confirmation of the fact that we have heard, and have listened to, the Wisdom of the Spirit. It affirms the essence of our humanity, and that of the purpose of our existence. Prayer is an act of love and humility. Prayer is an offering, and an expression of gratitude, in praise, and in thanksgiving, to the power and the glory of our creator.

Unlike the practice of the relaxation response exercise, the sole purpose of engaging in prayer is to communicate, and respond to the Wisdom of the Holy Spirit that is the living Word of our creator. It is an act of reciprocity with God. Once a person decides to pray, the process has already begun before its initiation. It begins before the beginning. It does so because implicit within the decision to pray, one has already acknowledged, and communicated, three fundamental facts.

These are:

a) a belief in God
b) in his omnipotence
c) and in his special relationship with us, as it is sealed within his covenant of love, mercy, and forgiveness.

Beyond this, all further dialogue is almost superfluous. It is unnecessary because of the belief in his complete knowledge of us, of our intentions, and our needs. However, to engage in verbalizing the specifics of what it is we may wish to convey may serve as an aid towards our maintaining the central focus of our attention. It also assists us in the act of embellishing our rapport with words of honor, praise, and belief in his love, and powers of intercession on our behalf. To simply contemplate upon these beliefs may be a more appropriate form of prayer than any other specific dialogue. The act of praying requires acute awareness, and a purposeful, willful, and conscious mode of mental activity. It is not an inert mental state within a suspended, anaesthetized, and silent void. Prayer is not an escape, but rather it is an embrace of the most intimate form within which any human being could possibly engage. It is intimate to the extent that it necessitates absolute humility, transparency, and honesty. However, the focus of effort, and attention, may be so intense that any unrelated conscious, or subconscious, mental activity may be suppressed so as not to be registered within the content of the participating mind of the person who is engaged in prayer.

There may be a variety of reasons why one may be motivated to pray. Yet, regardless of the specific purpose, all forms of prayer are of equal merit. This is because they all convey the same thee fundamental facts, and implicit acknowledgments, which we have mentioned above. This is what renders prayer meritorious, sacred, and purposeful. In these particular circumstances we are assured that the human facilities of consciousness, conceptualization, and language, have not been abused, misappropriated, or profaned.

CHAPTER FOURTEEN: THE FINAL WORD

PART ONE: A RECAPITULATION OF THE SUBJECT MATTER

> Once more I am raised up,
> Ferried over a lava sky.
> I sail through burning sunsets,
> Past pale and harvest moons,
> Swim through angry waters,
> Cross deserts and sand dunes.
>
> From "Journey of a Soul", by the author.

The history of our human ancestry dates back to the Spirit of man as first created within a celestial domain. Man was created from the essence of his creator. The individual and collective spirit of this man represents our Last Universal Common Ancestor (LUCA). Consequently, we are the "sons of man". It is in this terminology that Christ alluded to himself. He did so within the context of one who had humbled himself to share in our humanity. The universe, all that is contained therein and all life forms were created within a second creative event and in the aftermath man's fall from the grace of original perfection.

Life evolved within the material milieu of earth in accordance with the Word and its Divine purpose. The evolution of life was to proceed so as to make provision for a biological host that would satisfy the appropriate needs and requirements necessary for the reception and infusion of the spiritual principle, or "spiritual LUCA", that had originally defined the essential nature of man as first created. The term "trans symbiosis" has been coined so as to seek a means in which to convey the process whereby the biological hominid was imbued with this spiritual principle. It was in this manner that a primate creature now existing as an acceptable and appropriate biological temple, was to be utterly transformed and spiritually transfigured. This process is that which defines the emergence of humanity as an entirely new and sanctified species of life upon the earth. As a consequence of this transcendental event, it is proposed that the human species ought to be redefined as is befitting and deserving of our authentic nature. Human kind is both a wise and a spiritual creature. Furthermore, it is only because of our spiritual nature that we have become truly wise in intuitive wisdom and in conceptual knowledge.

Our perception of reality as a phenomenal experience is derived from an interpretative composite of our intellectual concepts and of our intuitive beliefs. In this respect what we ascertain as representative of our perceptual validity is grounded within a binocular type of mode that may be expressed within the terminology of "seeing is believing" (intellectually explicit) and "believing is seeing" (intuitively implicit). In this instance the question that arises is in regard to which, if either, of these modes might we ascribe Primacy of Affect.

Since our intellectual concepts are based upon Secondary metaphorical constructs, the fundamental essence of which originated within the content of their antecedent Primary metaphors, it is evident that intuitive belief has primacy in regard to that which we conceptually construct. As expressed within a neurological context, this is to state that the Right cerebral hemisphere has Primacy of Affect as it applies to the cognitive activities of the Left cerebral hemisphere. Consequently, the authenticity of our paradigm of reality is a measure of the extent to which it is a valid representation of the content of our Primary metaphors. The human potential towards the realization of perceptual authenticity is only achievable within the context of "believing is seeing". The biblical account of the doubting disciple Thomas is a testimony to this fact. Thomas could only see, and comprehend, the reality of the resurrected Christ having relegated perceptual primacy to the wisdom of the soul.

We have described the process by which we acquire these Primary metaphors (i.e. archetypes) as neurologically configured compositions that have been constructed from an elementary substrate that originated within the content of our collective unconscious. The content of our collective unconscious, as "first principles", is derived from the Wisdom of the Soul through the agency of our human consciousness. The Wisdom of the Soul is representative of the wisdom, and the power, that is imbued within the Spiritual essence of man as first created. As such, this Wisdom is a reflection of the content of the "unlived memory" to which all humanity has been afforded a means of access.

While the term "Wisdom of the Soul" refers to the substrate of all human knowledge, the term "Wisdom of the Spirit" may be considered within the broader context as being derived from Spirit of Wisdom. The Wisdom of the Spirit is the means by which the Will of the Holy Spirit is expressed and is made manifest within the content, and the context, of all creation. It is within this broader context that we refer to "first principles" as being representative of "true substances" or metaphysical units that are perfect and real (i.e. "monads").

It is only through the vision of the first principles of the Wisdom of the Soul that we are enabled to perceive the authentic reality of self, life, and the universe, as they exist within the holistic composite and transcendental format, of the first principles of the Wisdom of the Spirit. Our ability to "Open the Doors of Perception" is dependent upon our acquisition of the four essential "Keys" that unlock the content to this reality. It is only through the application of the metaphysical content of our Primary metaphors that such an authentic rendition of reality is revealed and made manifest within the mind of our humanity as a phenomenal experience. As a consequence, we may have every good reason to question the individual, and collective, validity of our existing paradigm as it is scientifically acknowledged and philosophically accepted within the Western Hemisphere. We can only hope to catch a glimpse of the metaphysical units, or monads, that constitute our authentic reality in the light of our first principles (i.e. primary metaphors). In effect, that hope is dependent upon faith.

It has been proposed that the acquisition of consciousness and that of ensoulment were the primary events which contributed to the instigation of the explosive evolutionary changes that characterize the modern human brain. These biological variations were precipitated in response to the introduction of an interior, (i.e. endogenous), spiritual environment as compared to that of an adaptive response to the prevailing conditions within the external, (i.e. exogenous), and material environment.

The neurological changes within the brain were instigated primarily as a means by which every individual could address and contribute to the spiritual survival and eternal salvation of the human species, as opposed to the exclusive preservation of its biological integrity. The primary instigating event was that of a spiritual enlightenment within the mind of man in regard to the true nature of his humanity. This transcendent event has been described as one of "ensoulment". It was to be mankind's first epiphany and the keystone of all that would be revealed to him throughout the entire history of our species.

Spiritual enlightenment was conveyed through the provision of a means of access to the content of the

Wisdom of the Spirit. The animation of the mind of man through the process of "ensoulment" was to awaken an intuitive awareness within the collective unconscious of man in regard to the authentic nature of his humanity. This was conveyed to man through the medium of "Primary (archetypical) metaphors".

The massive influx of Primary metaphors from the collective unconscious initiated the process whereby the construction of a vast repository of Secondary metaphorical concepts was made possible. It is upon these mental constructs that we depend in order that we may independently formulate our concepts, and our thoughts. This would have rapidly led to a situation wherein our living memories would have been inundated with a massive cohort of retrievable metaphors. This great pool of source material would provide us with an ever expanding range of reference options from which we could choose within the formulation of our concepts as thoughts and their subsequent linguistic expression. The collective integration of these mental concepts and those of our intuitive beliefs is what shapes our perception of reality.

The cognitive brain was now working on the enormous task of defining and verbalizing mental concepts from the ever growing content of this extensive data base. The neurological circuitry, its related content of interconnecting synapses, and its limited supply of neurotransmitters were driven to respond within a supercharged or over-drive mode. The configuration and complexity of the neuroanatomy of the human brain would be mirrored within the magnitude and the nature of its biological response to this great influx of cognitive needs and demands. It is precisely in this manner that a state of "cognitive fluidity" became established within the mind of man. It was the work of the Holy Spirit within the "cathedral" of the human mind (Chap.6). Let there be no doubt about that as you reflect upon these awesome events within the sacred sanctuary of your own mind. Reflect upon them within the silent sanctuary of your very soul.

We are fundamentally human in our nature only because we have acquired the facility of consciousness. Thus have we also been ensouled. These unique qualities enable us to be in receipt (i.e.to hear) of the Word through the medium of the Holy Spirit. They also provide the means by which we may listen and respond to the Spirit of the Word. The Word is written in your heart; it is written and encoded within your Primary metaphors. Yet, it is within the measure of our response to the Spirit of the Word that we also have the potential to become more fully human. The essence of our humanity is embodied within the content and the context of this form of reciprocity. This is what defines the authentic nature of our humanity:

The Word has spoken,
Now the Spirit speaks,
And it is heard,
Therefore "I am".

So hasten for to listen,
Respond with all your being,
That you may be on earth,
As our Spirits are in heaven.

Consequently, it is suggested that our human species be redefined and reclassified within its proper and appropriate terminology. This is adequately expressed within the following description:

"Homo sapiens-Spiritus Sapiens".

The process of "ensoulment" describes the manner in which humanity was provided with a means wherein he was enabled to become consciously aware of the spiritual nature of his authentic self. The precursor of humankind as represented by the primate hominid was constrained within the biological confinement of an instinctive awareness. This is because he was devoid of the facility of consciousness.

Consciousness describes the means by which this unique and purely human form, of conscious awareness was endowed to humanity. Consciousness is the means by which the Wisdom of the Holy Spirit is conveyed to humanity. It also provides us with a means by which we may communicate this Wisdom as authentic knowledge to others. In addition, consciousness enables us to respond and to reciprocate this gift of knowledge with the Holy Spirit. We do this through the agency of our thoughts, words, and deeds, and as these are expressed within the routine context of our lives. These offerings become what we describe as our prayers. Within the Catholic rite, these humble offerings are made worthy of their acceptance to our creator by virtue of the sacrificial offering of Christ within the liturgy of the Eucharist. It is in this manner that the human race contributes, in union with the Holy Spirit, to our spiritual salvation and redemption. This is the ultimate manner in which we can give glory and honour to God. The celebration of the Eucharist is the ultimate, and most perfect, act of reciprocity:

Love begets love.
Love is reciprocity.
Reciprocity is love.

The precise means by which the Wisdom of the Spirit is conveyed and imbued within the mind of our humanity is through the agency of our collective unconscious. Therein it is archived within a metaphysical format which is conceptually and linguistically reclassified as the "Wisdom of the Soul" as it exists within this domain of our subconscious mind. This specific form of preconceived knowledge is neurologically encoded and reconfigured within a symbolic or metaphorical format to which the term "archetype" is applicable. The term "Primary metaphors" refers to the content of these archetypes as they are expressed and apprehended within the realm of our conscious and cognitive awareness. These Primary metaphors are what constitute the fundamental

THE KEYS TO THE DOORS OF PERCEPTION

essence of that which we more commonly describe as "intuitive knowledge", "human intuition", or simply "faith". As it exists within our collective unconscious,(and the related correlate of the Right cerebral hemisphere), this spiritual wisdom has yet to be presented to our analytical and rationalizing Left hemisphere . In other words, within the content of the human mind and right brain it is cognitively pre-conceptual in its nature and its presentation. Consequently, the pre-conceptual substrate of knowledge is by definition allegorical or metaphorical in its very nature. Without concepts there can be no thoughts, and in the absence of analogy/ metaphor there can be no concepts.

Humanity has been endowed with the facility of free will so that we retain the onus of responsibility in the manner in which we subsequently choose to formulate and apply our concepts to, and within, the world. This explains why the Wisdom of the Soul presents itself within a metaphorical or symbolic, format. However, since symbols are representations of something else, their construction is dependent upon the pre-existence of some form of associated meaning or notion as what that something else is, or may be. The Holy Spirit has no doubt as to the implicit meaning contained within the content of our archetypes. In this sense, we may describe archetypes as being "preconceived" by the Holy Spirit.

It has also been proposed that apart from intuitive knowledge the archetypical content of our collective unconscious is imbued with a living and animating property. This is a unique quality that becomes manifest within the content of our perceptions and their expression within the context of our lives. While the archetypical symbolism conveys the interpretative meaning that is implicit within their content it is also imbued with the spiritual content of the Word of God. We have described the "event character" that is implicit within the proclamation of the Word as it is conveyed to us through the medium of our archetypes. It is in this manner that the human expression of the Word within the content of our thoughts, words, and deeds, (inclusive of spiritual rites and rituals), becomes a living and phenomenal experience. As a consequence we can acquire a more authentic perceptual construct in regard to the nature of our reality and the purpose of our existence within the lived experience. In this manner the fruit of our concepts become animated and imbued, with a spiritual form of life that is an authentic expression of our human nature. We have also chosen to illustrate the ultimate manner in which this form of actualization of the Wisdom of the Spirit, within its most perfect expression, was to be made manifest in the event of the Incarnation. In this instance the Word was made flesh in the person of Christ, and conceived through the power of the Holy Spirit.

Since these archetypes have been instigated by the Holy Spirit and retrieved from the Spiritual essence of man as first created they are identified as that which is derived from our "unlived memory". The term "Primary metaphor" has been coined so as to clearly identify the content of these archetypes as that which is contained within our collective unconscious.

These observations also support the contention that human works that have been inspired and created through the faithful conceptual configuration of the content of our Primary metaphors are highly imbued with the quality of authenticity and universality These are works whose intuitive content has not been subjected to the dishonesty, manipulation, or self-deceptive reconstruction of the psyche and the human intellect. Neither have they been subjected to, nor debased, within the related facility of their linguistic expression. The measure of their integrity is the degree to which they remain firmly loyal and true to the content of their Primary metaphors and do so within the implicit context of their original primacy. The value that is inherent within our work is a reflection of our dedication, commitment, and the extent to which it is imbued with this form of integrity. This provides us with a firm foundation in regard to our work ethic in all that we do and in every walk of life.

Examples of human works that most closely approximate and authentically reflect the content of these Primary metaphors include those of Holy Scriptures and Revelation, "primitive" art, (including children's artwork), and ancient mythology. You will recall that it is within this form of authentic context, as it relates to Scriptures and Revelation, (which fully reflect the authenticity of their source) that we identified this observation as being one of the two most important statements contained within the content of this entire work. We have applied the term "Secondary metaphors" to identify and distinguish these from metaphors of the Primary types.

Secondary metaphorical concepts reside within our human memories (i.e. living memory). They were first "seeded" within that domain through the acquisition of Primary metaphors. That is to say that the initial Secondary metaphorical concepts that were to subsequently give rise to additional ones which we ourselves constructed were derived from the preconceived content of our Primary metaphors. Since those early days of cerebral immaturity, and paucity of conceptual analogy, we have acquired an enormous facility to efficiently construct vast quantities of Secondary metaphors through our powers of observation and experience. Secondary metaphors are what are retrieved from memory in order that we can formulate concepts as thoughts. We can then express these thoughts in language and within the mode of our behavior. Even so, additional Primary metaphors continue to be integrated within our memories so as to augment the total complement of our available human resources. The facility to do so is further magnified in a spiritual format that is unique to each individual through the reception of the seven gifts (virtues) of the Holy Spirit within the sacramental rite of Confirmation within the Catholic Church. However, all of us retain the freedom of choice in regard to our willingness to acknowledge and accept the content of our Primary metaphors within the construct of our concepts and their expression within the world.

The linguistic expression of our thoughts, whether within the spoken or the written word constitutes our Tertiary metaphors. What is spoken are the verbalization of sounds (vowels and consonants) which symbolize something specific to which we wish to refer. What is written is a series of symbolic characters, (an alphabet of letters), within a sequence of units. As with sounds, these inscribed units represent something specific to which we are referring. This enables us to convey our thoughts to others. These symbolic representations are what constitute our Tertiary metaphors.

You can now appreciate that the formation and expression of our thoughts proceeds through a hierarchical series of three symbolic metaphorical phases. The foundation and the root of what is expressed reside within the content of our Primary metaphors. In their absence we would be unable to conceptualize. In the absence of this critical substrate, ("Wisdom of the Soul") provided through the medium of our consciousness, we would not be human beings.

The process of Primary metaphorical augmentation also serves to facilitate the configuration of entirely new and innovative concepts. In other words, it is a means towards assisting in our further human enlightenment. Such a form of enlightenment is what enables authentic human progress to be realized within the historical context of our humanity. Such a form of progress is that which facilitates our advancement towards our ultimate objective. That objective concerns the fundamental purpose of our human existence.

The purpose of our lives is to identify and acknowledge the authentic spiritual nature of self; to give honor and glory to god through our willingness to unconditionally reciprocate our love with each other and with our creator; and in so doing to contribute towards our ultimate redemption in Christ. It is in this manner that we may reunite with the spiritual essence of our humanity and with the body of Christ within whose essence we are contained forever and for all eternity. Ultimately, fully redeemed within the perfect purity of our spiritual essence, we become united with the body of Christ within the unity of the Holy Trinity. This incomprehensible and extraordinary event occurs in a manner that is impossible to apprehend, or to explicitly and comprehensively express. It raises the question once posed by Owen Francis Dudley, (and which inspired the title to his book), some eighty years ago: "*Will men be like Gods?*" Alas, it has not entered into the heart of man what god has prepared for those who love him.

PART TWO: A JOURNEY OF THE SOUL

He pours me out as water,
Changed mystically to wine,
A lowly draft of human blood
Drawn from a human well.
Released it flows as ought it should,
From this hardened heart of mine.

From "Journey of a Soul", by the author.

Perhaps you are among the multitude of those of us who have become accustomed to an ever increasing dependency, and reliance, upon our conceptual powers of deduction in order to derive, and experience, a genuine sense of self as an individual within the world.

Many of us feel the need, and desire, to apply our intellectual skills towards comprehending who we are, and what precisely it is that constitutes our humanity. In addition we may continually strive to find some means to identify the manner in which we formulate our perceptions in regards to the reality of life, and our lived experience. This form of quest is an inherent part of our human nature.

Yet, there are many others, who regardless of their level of intelligence, or human interest, do not share this need as a prerequisite to self-acceptance, or to peace of mind. Their needs in these particular regards are well satisfied through their faith, their core beliefs, and their human intuition. For these, conceptual knowledge is a garnish that provides an additional means by which such enlightenment may be expressed, and applied, within the context of their lives. It is seen as another unearned gift to that which they most value, and most cherish. From our particular perspective as rational human beings, there is a need to examine the manner in which we perceive the realities of life, and of ourselves as sentient beings within that paradigm. The unexplored life is an unfulfilled life. Furthermore, most of us have a need to try to reconcile our intellectual concepts with those of our faith (if any), or intuitive beliefs. In fact, within the Christian religion, it is acknowledged that as rational human beings we are obligated to apply our intellect in such a manner, and in so far as we are capable of doing so. All of us are well aware of the invariable polarities that exist between our conceptual knowledge and the intuitive knowledge which we describe as faith. For many of us one of the most vexing issues, as we have seen, is in regard to which, if any, of these bipolar positions should we ascribe primacy of affect, and primacy of context.

Perhaps the majority of us do have a need to see, to touch, and feel, with outstretched and, that which we wish to validate as true. We have conditioned ourselves to doubt our human intuition. We have lost the knack for faith, and have learned to delegate our unconditional trust to the dictates of our intellect. Invariably, and inevitably, many of us discover that such a level of trust is misappropriated to the extent that the reassurances, and certainties, that we seek are not forthcoming. Therein resides the inner conflict such that a clear vision of self, and self in harmony with life, remains elusive. As stated in the lyrics of a very popular song performed by a renowned Irish band "Still, I cannot find what I am looking for".

The language of intellect and of science can contribute greatly towards our further enlightenment. Regrettably, and all too frequently, the manner in which scientific knowledge is interpreted, and expressed within the context of life and the world in which we exist, deprives us of these valuable insights and benefits. Such a loss and deprivation is inevitable when scientific knowledge is extrapolated beyond the parameters of its intellectual, and contextual boundaries, and misappropriated within the context of the living world and of our humanity. Authenticity and clarity of communication can only be achieved through the correct appropriation of terminology and its expression within the world, and to its people, within their related and their proper context. A prerequisite towards achieving this level of clarity and authenticity of content is that we have the capacity to identify this specific and appropriate form of context. We must have a means and a way of discerning these specific qualities as they apply to the world, and to the nature of our humanity. We must be motivated, and inspired, to seek and unveil these illusive and authentic properties. This is the only means by which we can hope to further our knowledge and our understanding. The only means by which this is humanly possible is in the listening, and the acquired appreciation of the content and the context of the substrate contained within the Wisdom of our Primary metaphors. It is by this means alone that we can ever hope to make genuine progress along the path of our shared, and universal, quest of self-discovery. Within our Western Hemisphere has this quest been logistically reduced to one of a materialistic philosophy towards the achievement of global economic growth, the creation of wealth, and its control in respect of its generation and distribution. Who precisely is the infidel, who the militant dissident?

Even among those who have been baptized into the Christian church, there are many who have begun to have serious doubts in regard to its religious doctrines and have ceased to either adhere to, or actively practice that faith. Amongst those who may have so lapsed, some continue to profess these fundamental beliefs but are unsure and uncertain as to their unqualified validity. They entertain doubts and apprehensions in respect of their interpretation, authorization, and proclamation by the institutional church. They have serious misgivings in regard to the application and relevance of these doctrines as perceived within the constraints of our current paradigm. Similar types of reservations have also emerged within other faiths or individual systems of spiritual beliefs. Might many of these doubts and apprehensions arise from the fundamental misconfiguration of our perceptions in regard to the true nature of our shared reality. There are many who feel that they cannot sustain, nor be sustained, by a faith for which they have but a threadbare intellectual understanding. The oft repeated phrases contained within the wording of their Baptismal rite, or those of the Creed, fail to resurrect or bring to life these fundamental tenets of faith. They remain dormant within the shadows of their minds and the fabric of their daily lives.

For those among you who may be Christian, be it in name only, or by virtue of your birth right and upbringing, this book may enable you to better comprehend and communicate some of the fundamentals in regard to these rather complex doctrines and beliefs. It will provide you with a more explicit vocabulary in which these concepts and your corresponding beliefs may be shared with others. There are many who are anxious to hear and better understand this good news. There are some who will not want to listen and who will refute your every word. Some may ridicule and scorn you. They may call you a "Clown of God" or "Jongleur de Dieu", and laugh at you. Yet, he who laughs last laughs everlastingly. These skeptical provocateurs are often among the intellectually gifted who cannot or do not want to relate to these human intuitions and revelations. They fail to acknowledge or accept the primacy and authenticity, of the intuitive knowledge that is available and accessible to all of us. For many of these individuals their sense of worth, purpose, and self-esteem are dependent upon the retention of this intellectual stance. Likewise, for others their sense of value, worth, purpose, and self-esteem are founded upon the adherence and the sharing of these spiritual beliefs. For these very reasons neither group are likely to capitulate too easily. This invariably leads to conflict, ill-feeling, intolerance, and verbal abuse, or even physical violence.

Spiritual beliefs can be easily undermined when placed within the context of material fundamentalism and intellectual pre-eminence. One of the greatest sources of conflict and confusion arises as a consequence of the interpretations that are frequently applied to modern scientific discovery as they pertain to creation, evolution, our human nature, and our universe. If one cannot relate to the authentic nature of self, life, and the universe within a meaningful context, then it is highly unlikely that they will be able to do so with others whom they wish to communicate, or advise. This form of personal mental deficit or "blind vision" has fast become a global malady. It is a malady that has become all too prevalent amongst the intellectually gifted within society. These are usually the agents of our new enlightenment. They are the ones who most contribute to the configuration of our paradigm through the application of their intellectual endeavors and their verbal skills. There is a disproportionately high incidence of this form of aberrant and extrapolative thinking within the scientific community. It is also strongly evident within the artistic community, in literature, art, the film and music industry. As with any earthly pandemic, it does not discriminate and it knows no boundaries. I invite those among you, who consider yourselves to be rational, intelligent, and well informed people that having read this work to dwell at length upon its contents with an open mind. Only then may these words become etched upon the pages of your mind and memory. The book is specifically addressed to those of such a cognitive disposition.

Unfortunately there is a growing trend within our modern culture in regard to our reservations and reluctance to express genuine love, to love, and be loved unconditionally and unreservedly. Something vital and elementary gets lost in the translation. We are creature of caution and restraint. We are becoming increasingly distrustful in our covenants, in our judgments and discernments. We now need proof of entitlement, evidence of motive and intent and guarantees of satisfaction. In many respects allegiance and loyalty may be inadvertently perceived as acts of submission, subservience, and dependence. Some individuals may even view these virtues as medieval relics that should be consigned to the era of feudalism within the distant past. Yet, might we have simply transferred, and reassigned these allegiances to a centralized bureaucracy in the name of "Democratic Freedom"? Has control of the "Global Mind", and its cerebral correlate, been delegated to an autonomous and centralized authority? What if an ever expanding majority of our well intentioned citizens are the unwitting and contagious carriers of the Confabulatory mind-set? Political propaganda predisposes most of us to "buy into the lie".

Our modern culture is more defined as one of independent self-reliance, competitiveness, freedom of choice, self-expression, self-proclaimed rights and civil liberties, and self-enhancement. We have fast learned how to manipulate our world through the application of our intellect and deployment of human cunning. Human love is being progressively reduced to a mutual contract of self-gratification and the satisfaction of individual needs and desires. In the event that these expectations fail to be delivered upon the contract is terminated. The vow that once sealed this covenant is broken. We are steadily abandoning the virtue of reciprocity, the expression of gratitude in the receiving, and the open generosity of the giving. It is these that define the true essence of love. The greatest challenge posed by this work has been one of striving to identify a form of language that might convey some of the answers, or provide some further insights, in relation to these complex issues.

The most central of these issues pertains to our human nature, and what it is that constitutes the essence of self as a unique individual within the world. We are also concerned with the issue of self in accord, and in command of self. These are the areas on which we have focused our significant attention My expressed hope is that I have succeeded, at least in part, in my efforts to identify such an insightful "language of enlightenment" and that it will speak to you in a manner to which you can relate and adequately comprehend. Each of us can contribute in our own small way towards the configuration and the construction of the conceptual bridge that provides safe passage to our shared enlightenment. The keystone to this "Bridge over Troubled Waters" is the intuitive Wisdom of the Spirit. Endeavour to traverse this bridge so that you may lay thee down where there is green pasture, and still waters. To entertain some doubts concerning one's spiritual beliefs may be the most powerful stimulus towards our seeking a greater understanding in regard to the nature and the source of those beliefs. The "Gateway to the Soul" is open to every one of us. It is there that we must place ourselves and seek the grace that is required to enter through its hidden doors. These are the "Doors of Perception" to our authentic reality. Therein resides the Wisdom for which we intuitively all yearn so that it may be well placed within the context of our lives. This submission is not presented as a book of evidence and proof. Neither is it intended to apportion judgment, blame, or guilt upon any sector within our society. It is an affirmation of your human dignity, a confirmation of your ancestral lineage and of your rightful inheritance. May it ring true for you as a symphony to the Spirit of our humanity. Perhaps then it may be reciprocated, and returned to you upon the wings of silence. Listen out and take heed and then it will surely speak to you as an Anthology of Love.

As with consciousness and cognition you are more fluid than fixed. You are more flexible and plastic than you are rigid and unyielding. Yet, neither are you a reed that is blown in the wind or carried on the tide of human blindness. You may choose to drink from the "Water of Life" or from the Primordial Pools from which our hollow carcass had arisen at the dawn of time. So, with a firm heart and the grace of the Holy Spirit, may you be guided onwards into the Light of Christ.

Finally, you may stand up filled with confidence and a firm belief in the dignity of your humanity. Step forth beyond the shadows of the ancestral primate and the inherent imperfections of your ego self. Stand firm in the light of your Spirit. You need only girth yourself in what is essential in order to pursue the object of your mission in this life. You are free to discard the heavy mantle of all your fears and anxieties. Regardless of the past you own this "Now". It is only within this current moment that you can seek to pursue the true purpose of your life. Fix your gaze firmly on what can be and know that it is achievable. Share all that you have learned and all that has yet to be discovered and revealed with those who you meet along the way. Now, you have no good reason to ignore or forget precisely who you are. You are Homo sapiens Spiritus Sapiens. Thus have you been chosen and highly honored. What was lost has now been found, rediscovered, and redeemed. Recall, reinstate, and listen to your Spirit. Use intellect and reason with integrity and compassion as befitting their source. Remember always exactly who you are. Know that as you have been greatly blessed so also are you deeply loved:

Verbum quod locutus est,

Spiritu audem locquitur,

Et auditum est. Ergo, "Ego sum".

This song will make your heart take flight,
The air that surely is the
Music of the Night,
As is the music of this draft
That I have written here alone,
While I gaze through these foggy windows,
On this dark night of the soul.

From "Journey of a Soul", by the author.

Amen.

The Christ of Blessington Lakes

THE KEYS TO THE DOORS OF PERCEPTION BIBLIOGRAPHY:

A) Scientific Sources:

1. Brain Mind Lecture Series . Professor Rhawn Joseph. Academic Press,New York. 2000.

2. The Journal of Clinical Psychology. 42,845-860,1986. Rhawn Joseph.

3. The Master & his Emissary, Iain Mc Gilchrist. Yale University Press. 2009.

4. The Prehistory of the Mind. Steven Mithen.

5. The Undiscovered Self. The Problem of the Individual in Modern Society. Carl Jung. New American Library. 2006.

6. The Relaxation Response. Herbert Benson.

7. I'm OK – You're OK. Thomas Harris. Pan Books Ltd., 1967.

8. Games People Play. Eric Berne, M.D. Penguin Books. 1968.

9. Metaphors we Live By. George Lakoff & Mark Johnson. University of Chicago press. 2003.

10. Oneself as Another. Paul Ricoeur. University of Chicago press.1992.

11. Identically Different. Tim Spector. Weidenfeld & Nicolson. 2012.
12. The Seven Deadly Sins of Memory. Daniel Schacter.
13. Ancestor's Tale. Richard Dawkins. 2004
14. Surfaces & Essences. Douglas Hofstadter & Emmanuel Sander.

Basic Books. N.Y. 2013.

15. Biology. fifth Ed. Solomon. Berg. Martin.

Saunders College Publishing 1999.

16. Medical Neurology. John Giroy & John Sterling Meyer.

Macmillan Publishing Co. Inc. 1975.

17. Consciousness . Orch OR study. Roger Penrose. Hameroff. 2011.
18. The Quantum Universe. Brian Cox & Jeff Forshaw. Allen Lane. 2011.
19. The Blank Slate. Steven Pinker. Penguin Books 2002.
20. Lectures on Analysis of the Mind. Bertrand Russell.
21. Aping Mankind. Raymond Tallis. Acumen.U.K.2011.
22. The Tell Tale Brain. V.S. Ramachandran.

William Heinemann. London.2011.

23. Creation. Adam Rutherford. Penguin / Viking. 2013.
24. The Power of Now. Eckhart Tolle. Penguin.
25. Thrive. Richard Layard . David Clark. Allen lane. 2014
26. Descartes Error. Antonio Damasio. Vintage Books, London.2006.

27. The Science Delusion. Rupert Sheldrake. Coronet U.K. 2012.
28. Happiness by Design. Paul Dolan. Allen Lane. 2014.
29. The Doors to Perception: Heaven and Hell. Aldoux Huxley.
30. Drawing the Map of Life. Victor Mc Elheny . Basic Books. 2010.
31. Cosmic Consciousness. Richard Maurice Bucke. N.Y. Dutton.1969.
32. The Lives of a Cell. Lewis Thomas. Penguin Books. 1975.

Recommended further reading:

a) Out of Eden. Stephen Oppenheimer. Pub. Constable & Robinson.2004.
b) The Origin of Our Species. Chris Stringer.Pub. Penguin Books. 2012.
c) The Collected Works of C.G. Jung. Pub. Princeton University Press. Bollingen Series.
d) The Singular Universe & The Reality of Time. Roberto M. Unger and Lee Smolin. Pub. Cambridge University press.2015.

B) Spiritual sources:

1. The Holy Bible N.R.S.V. Catholic Ed. Darton Longman & Todd Ltd. 2005. The Scripture quotations contained herein are from the New Revised Standard Version Bible, copyright©1989 by the Division of Christian

Education of the National Council of the Churches of Christ in the U.S.A., and are used by permission. All rights reserved.

2. The New American Bible. Thomas Nelson Inc. 1970.
3. The Latin Vulgate. Saint Jerome.
4. Catechism of the Catholic Church. Veritas. 1994.
5. The Catholic Catechism. John A. Hardon. Doubleday. 1974.
6. Thomas Aquinas. Summa Theologica.
7. The Phenomenon of Man. Pierre Teilhard de Chardin. Harper Perennial Modern Thought.(First pub. 1955).
8. Letter & Spirit. Scott Hahn. Darton Longman Todd. 2006.
9. Will Men Be Like Gods? Owen Francis Dudley. Longmans. 1935.
10. Agenda for the Third Millennium. Pope John Paul II. Harper Collins 1996.
11. The Case for God. Karen Armstrong. Bodley Head.
12. The Evolution of God. Robert Wright. Little Brown.2009.
13. Thomas Merton-Prophet of Renewal. John E. Bambiger.
Cistercian Publications. 2005.
14. Mind & Spirit. Pat Collins. Columba Press. 2006.
15. Psalm-Prayers for Every Mood. Kevin Lyon. Columba Press.1996.
16. The Case for Religion. Keith Ward. Oneworld Publications 2004.
17. The Purpose Driven Life. Rick Warren. Zondervan. 2002.

18. Soul Medicine. Helen Graham. Newleaf Pub. 2001.

19. The Message of Matthew. Michael Green. Inter-Varsity Press.1988.

20. A Rumi Anthology. Reymond A. Nicholson. Oneworld. Oxford.

INDEX

The Apostles Creed.

I believe in God,

The Father almighty,

Creator of heaven and earth,

And in Jesus Christ, his only begotten Son, our Lord, who
was conceived by the Holy Spirit,

born of the Virgin Mary, suffered under Pontius Pilate,

was crucified, died, and was buried;

he descended into hell;

on the third day he rose again from the dead;

he ascended into heaven,

and is seated at the right hand of God the Father almighty;

from there he will come to judge the living and the dead. I
believe in the Holy Spirit,

The holy Catholic Church,

The communion of saints, The forgiveness of sins,

The resurrection of the body, And life everlasting. **Amen.**

Printed in the United States
By Bookmasters